# Language, Image, Media

Edited by
HOWARD DAVIS
and PAUL WALTON

ST. MARTIN'S PRESS · NEW YORK

© Basil Blackwell Publisher Limited 1983
© Editorial organization and introduction
Howard Davis and Paul Walton 1983

All rights reserved. For information, write:
St Martin's Press, Inc.,
175 Fifth Avenue, New York, NY 10010
Printed in Great Britain
First published in the United States of America in 1983

ISBN 0-312-46747-8

**Library of Congress Cataloging in Publication Data**

Main entry under title:

Language, image, media.

Includes bibliographical references and index.
1. Mass media and language—Addresses, essays,
lectures. 2. Visual communication—Addresses, essays,
lectures. I. Davis, Howard H. II. Walton, Paul.
P96.L34L36 1983   302.2'34   83-3124
ISBN 0-312-46747-8

# Contents

*Acknowledgements*                                                      vi

*Editors' introduction*                                                 1

### Part I Radio and Television

1 Death of a premier: consensus and closure in
  international news
  H. DAVIS AND P. WALTON                                                8

2 The social background of the language of radio
  G. LEITNER                                                            50

3 Dominant discourse: the Institutional Voice and
  control of topic
  C. L. LERMAN                                                          75

4 Cultural transformations: the politics of resistance
  D. MORLEY                                                             104

### Part II Printing and the Press

5 Linguistic and ideological transformations in
  news reporting
  G. KRESS                                                              120

6 'The economy': its emergence in media discourse
  M. EMMISON                                                            139

7 'Reality' East and West
  W. PISAREK                                                            156

## Part III Advertisements

8   Myth in cigarette advertising and health promotion
    S. CHAPMAN AND G. EGGER                                    166

9   How is understanding an advertisement possible?
    T. PATEMAN                                                 187

10  Understanding advertisers
    K. MYERS                                                   205

## Part IV Photography

11  Seeing sense
    V. BURGIN                                                  226

12  Marketing mass photography
    D. SLATER                                                  245

## Part V Problems of Evidence and Methodology

13  Textuality, communication and media power
    J. CORNER                                                  266

14  Some constructs for analysing news
    P. L. JALBERT                                              282

References                                                     300

List of contributors                                           312

Index                                                          314

# Acknowledgements

We wish to thank our colleagues in the Glasgow Media Group, the University of Kent and Goldsmiths' College, University of London, for their interest and encouragement. We owe a special debt to Jill Matthews, Policy Officer of NACRO, for her assistance with the research described in the first chapter. Paul Taylor, who teaches photography and holography in the Visual Communications Department at Goldsmiths' College, contributed to the design of the book and prepared the illustrations for publication.

We also wish to thank the following for permission to reproduce copyright materials: NBC News for the transcript of the NBC Nightly News broadcast on 9 May 1978; *The News*, Adelaide, for the editorial page on 6 August 1980; Larry Pickering for the cartoon appearing in *The Australian*; Rothmans of Pall Mall (Australia) Limited for the Winfield cigarette advertisement; W. D. & H. O. Wills (Australia) Limited for the Hallmark cigarette advertisement; Philip Morris Limited for the Marlboro, Chesterfield and Du Maurier 25s cigarette advertisements; British Telecom for the Buzby poster; *Cosmopolitan* for material from the magazine; D. C. Thomson & Co. Ltd. for material from *Jackie* magazine; Collett, Dickenson, Pearce and Partners Limited for the Benson & Hedges Special Filter 'circuitry' advertisement; Lee Friedlander for the photograph 'Madison, Wisconsin, 1966'; and Gary Winogrand for the photographs 'couple with chimpanzees' and 'women in street'.

Chapter 1 is a substantially revised and extended version of an article which appears in the *International Journal of the Sociology of Language* 40, 1983. Chapter 12 is an extended verison of an article which first appeared in *Camerawork*, no. 18, March 1980.

Finally we thank the SSRC, whose grant in 1978-9 enabled us to undertake much of the research and editorial work for this collection of papers.

# Editors' Introduction

We came to collect and edit these papers as a result of our research and teaching experience in the area of media studies and socio-linguistics. This includes our involvement in establishing the Media Group in the Department of Sociology at Glasgow University and co-authoring the Group's major study of television news output. It also includes contributions to new and existing courses at Goldsmiths' College and the University of Kent.[1]

We have come to feel that there is a strong and growing interest in media 'languages' (visual as well as verbal) which is not fully satisfied by the present range of publications in media studies and in the sociology of language. As teachers, we feel that there is a need for a book which assembles contributions from a variety of contemporary writers and seeks to provide a cross-section of innovative work in the several disciplines concerned with language and the media. The present collection aims to do this. It also has a definite international flavour, with contributions from the United States, Australia, Germany and Poland as well as the United Kingdom. In addition, we have deliberately included work which shows how the themes of language, image and the media can be analysed histori-cally (cf. Leitner on radio language, Slater on photography). There is little wish in any of the papers here to provide some general theory of cultural production, even if this were possible at the present time. Rather, there is a sensitive concentration on the communications and cultural questions involved in analysing contemporary cultural practices, whether small-scale or large-scale.

If one were to isolate a discipline or term for this collection, it would most readily fit into a slot called 'communications'. Communications is probably best defined as the conveying or exchanging of information and ideas. As Lerman puts it, the central questions are: 'Who are the speakers?' and 'What are they really talking about?' One of the pioneers of communications studies in the UK, Raymond Williams (1976), notes that the term 'communication' entered the language around the fifteenth century, but that it was not until the development of rapid means of passing information in the twentieth century that communications came predominantly to refer to such media as the press and broadcasting. The communications industry, as Williams and others have called it, is now recognized as very distinct from the transport industry (canals, railroads), which dominated the nineteenth-century conception of communications.

The birth of a new discipline or area of academic study is always difficult to chart, especially if, like communications studies, the area is essentially interdisciplinary. Communications studies draws from areas such as sociology, psychology and linguistics, and from more practical subjects such as photography and art and design. However, it took time for the technical and economic aspects of the communications industries to be regarded as an integral part of the analysis of communications.

The technical changes in communications brought about in the nineteenth and twentieth centuries remained little studied in the UK until the early 1960s. Prior to this and the appearance of a mass audience habitually locked into television and cinema, literary analysis of modern works had concentrated almost exclusively on great traditions. Even when communications studies emerged, a 'high culture' conception dominated English literary and cultural criticism. Indeed in the 1950s and early 1960s one of the objections to commercial television was that by providing popular programmes it would cause a decline in cultural values.

Against this backdrop two pioneering works appeared, Richard Hoggart's (1957) *The uses of literacy* and Raymond Williams's (1961) *The long revolution.* These works and their authors were highly influential in directing attention towards the study of the present and the recent past. Both books analysed the relationship between popular beliefs, values and the range of cultural forms available (e.g. magazines, newspapers). In short they focused upon the nature of the modern communications industry and its effects upon popular ideas and beliefs, and so helped to widen literary criticism into cultural analysis.

In the USA, in contrast to the UK, communications studies kept pace with the rapid development of technology. The subject was based initially on work by sociologists and psychologists on the 'mass media' and their ability to persuade consumers through advertising and influence voters through political propaganda.

Since these early days in both Europe and America, communications studies have benefited from the ideas and techniques of a succession of special disciplines, so that, for instance, workers who use 'content analysis' are more likely to take account of linguistics and semantics in making their assumptions about written or spoken language. The present collection illustrates some of the results of this cross-referencing and examines the relationship between signs and symbols, the visual and the verbal, the senders and receivers, in a whole variety of areas. It focuses initially on empirical studies of particular media and attempts to span the whole gamut of communications experience from large structures to individual perceptions, though not in any attempt to be fully representative. This would be impossible in a single volume, and in any case there is currently an imbalance between the methods and techniques available for the analysis of verbal languages and those for visual languages, which are still at an early stage of development.

At their best, these articles provide both a practical and theoretical grasp of some of our most important cultural filters and prisms. They allow an understanding of much that is taken for granted in the modern environment (Freud first taught us that to pay attention to slips of the tongue may pay dividends for self-understanding) and promote critical and positive pressures for cultural development.

In compiling this collection we have interpreted 'language' broadly to mean visual as well as verbal messages and have sought material which examines the whole problem of image—text relationships in media like television, advertising and the press. This view of language draws on a number of established and emergent disciplines and methodologies, including sociolinguistics, stylistics, pragmatics, discourse analysis, semiotics, the sociology of communications and cultural criticism. In one way or another they all study language as a means of establishing, maintaining and mediating social relationships. They also seek to develop categories which go beyond those of existing grammars. Two sets of problems thus converge. First, there are problems of ideology, distorted communication and cultural hegemony which higherto have been the province of social and political theorists. Second, there are problems of message encoding and analysis which have led to a search for models of performance that include the social assumptions, conventions and codes which govern the production and reception of messages.

We have chosen and assembled a range of articles which recognize and exemplify this development. The collection therefore includes theoretical, analytical and empirical studies. Whilst many of the contributors have earned reputations in the fields of linguistics or sociology, many have also been active in the cross-disciplinary work which the 'language and media' theme requires. We therefore expect that the contents of the volume will interest a wider readership in higher education and the media professions than is normally the case with academic collections rooted in a single discipline.

In one sense the collection can be regarded as a contribution from contemporary practitioners to the emergent discipline of communications. There is an important unifying factor across the range of media and approaches. What a great many of the contributions have in common is that when they are dealing with apparently macro- or large-scale questions (e.g. the bias of the news media, the properties of political discourse, long-term shifts in social categories and definitions, the processes of marketing) they turn out to be using assumptions and developing hypotheses which can be tested, verified and made evidentially sound using both established and novel techniques from other areas. Typically, their propositions are expressed in forms which are amenable to the agreed methodological procedures of special disciplines and subdisciplines such as sociolinguistics, textual criticism, semiotics and ethnomethodology.

It is a pity, therefore, that some of the representatives of this latter field (Anderson & Sharrock 1979) have so far apparently failed to appreciate the powerful new combinations of analytical and empirically testable methods which have begun to form the hallmark of the best of the work in communications and cultural studies. Their recent debate with Murdock (1980) and McKeganey & Smith (1980) has highlighted a central issue, the solution to which is sought by the majority of contributors to this volume. The issue is: how can one move from what C. Wright Mills called the 'grand social problems' to small-scale empirical questions without losing sight of the propositions and assumptions which inform the larger problems?

In this respect, the areas covered here — the nature of advertising, the construction of fact by radio and television, reading photographs, in short the emergence of dominant, conventionalized ways of producing and consuming cultural phenomena — are part of the 'grand social problem' of the state of our culture and its institutions. With the exception of part V, which gives two examples of current work on methodology, we have arranged the contributions according to the simple logic of media technologies. It is in the nature of such a collection that we have had to leave out more subjects (e.g. musical languages, design or film) than we would wish. However, we anticipate that the methods and approaches represented here will be improved upon and give rise to further work and that we will have an opportunity to remedy any serious omissions in a future publication.

## Notes

1 Our previous joint publications in this area include the work listed in the References to this book, and contributions to Glasgow University Media Group 1976, 1980. See also Philo *et al.* 1982.

# Part I

# Radio and Television

# 1

# Death of a premier: consensus and closure in international news

## HOWARD DAVIES AND PAUL WALTON

One of the publicly and politically important objectives of research into the 'language' of the contemporary broadcast media has been to document bias or systematic distortion in news reporting. This is often done with the intention of testing how far television news deviates from its requirement to be impartial. One research strategy is to undertake systematic analysis of events which are obviously matters of controversy or events which could attract a range of competing interpretations, and then to examine whether a variety of viewpoints is present in the reporting of such events. Conflicts between employers and employees, between political parties, between blacks and whites, between deviants and law enforcers, have all received some attention in communications research.

The findings tend to reveal that where there is very close public scrutiny and where the criteria of balance or impartiality are clearly defined (as in the legislation governing party political coverage), broadcasters often make scrupulous efforts to be 'fair' regarding these matters. For example, in a study of the 1979 British general election based on 217 broadcast election programmes, both the Conservative and Labour party leaders were shown to have had access to an identical number of programmes (Clarke *et al.* 1981). Where the point of 'balance' is less obvious (as in the coverage of an unofficial dispute between trade union members and an employer) journalists typically resort to 'news sense' and 'news values' which are normally systematically skewed against the interests of labour.[1]

However, there are many topics of news reporting in the Western industrial democracies which are not governed by the criteria of symmetry between competing viewpoints. Northern Ireland is one important example. Subjects like political violence, criminal deviance, international sporting competitions or the royal family are not approached from a neutral stance but rather from an assumed moral consensus. In such cases, the problem of analysing media content, including language, assumes a different form. For example, in covering such issues the broadcasters may encounter the problem of maintaining 'closure' against certain points of view instead of ensuring balance or openness to a range of perspectives. Alternatively, broadcasters may have to find appropriate ways of condemning acts of criminal violence in such a manner that legitimate violence (e.g. state violence by the police or security forces) is somehow placed in a different category. This can lead to incongruous relationships between the sound and visual 'tracks' of a broadcast. An instance of this in our own research is a shot in the story of the search for Aldo Moro's kidnappers (illustration 1). The voice-over commentary

The terrorists were demonstrating only too well that the state was powerless against them.

*Illustration 1    ITN News at Ten, 9 May 1978, armed police in Italy*

accompanies a shot depicting a heavily armed member of the state security forces engaged in a search. This preference for reporting from within the framework of the state is of course openly acknowledged by the broadcasters. Recently, the Controller of BBC2 has written:

If...I am operating in a parliamentary democracy, where it is a primary assumption that broadcast journalism will take its cue from the workings of the parliamentary democracy, then I for one am not surprised to find the political language settling somewhere around the broad middle of that democracy. How could it do otherwise, without taking unto itself agenda-setting roles which are not its proper province? (Wenham 1981, p. 491)

These examples indicate that even in the West the range of broadcast information and views seeks its legitimacy and security within a middle-of-the-road state set agenda.

The research reported here assumes that the broadcasting systems of the Western democratic countries are the appropriate place for examining these issues of consensus, consistency and closure not only because broadcasting occupies a central place in terms of audiences and perceptions but also because its reporting is generally obliged to be non-partisan, whether the broadcasting organizations are 'commercial' or 'public' service'. The dominant values and purposes of broadcasting in Britain, Western Europe and North America are similar enough to be regarded as examples of the same genre, distinct from the values and purposes of the networks of, say, the East European countries. In each country, however, certain basic problems of information gathering, editorial control and consensus formation are solved in alternative ways. Some of the differences in output can be traced to variations in the historical development of broadcasting organizations, supervisory bodies and professional practices. Not all are equally significant.

We had three main research objectives. First, we set out to develop techniques for comparing the output of news from the broadcasting systems of three countries — Britain, Germany and the USA — in the period 8-19 May 1978.[2] These techniques were a modified version of those used previously in studies of industrial news coverage on British television (Glasgow University Media Group 1976, 1980). Secondly, we sought to establish as far as possible within the limits of a two-week sample the parts played by cultural, organizational and professional processes in the coding of the news. Thirdly, by studying cross-cultural variations in news language and visuals, we aimed to reveal some of the dynamics of the encoding process. This chapter is mainly concerned with the third aspect, and the lexicon — verbal and visual — of one lead story in particular. Initially a number of general observations can be made about the content profiles in the sample period and the structuring of the bulletins in which the story appears.

The most notable finding to emerge was the absence of any clear contrasts between the channels apart from the obvious one of language, accent and to some extent geographical emphasis. It appears that the rules by which newsworthy *events* are identified, selected and routinely transformed into items of *news* are even more similar across countries than one would have anticipated. At least one earlier study (Golding & Elliott 1980) has found significant differences. In our sample all six channels were closely alike in their selection of political and economic news (both home and foreign) as being of high priority and their tendency to choose 'light' categories (sport, human interest, etc.) to round off the bulletins. Moreover, there were close parallels even in matters of presentation. Apart from the introduction of the 'Kommentar' by ZDF (a carefully signalled opportunity for a personal statement or reaction from a journalist), all six channels used a similar 'mix' of presentation forms. There were even close resemblances between the finer details. For example, the twin hemispheres in the BBC's title shot are matched by the ARD's world map. Only the projection is different.

Although cross-national variations do not generally override the basic rules of selection and presentation which stem from shared or closely similar professional assumptions and practices, the analysis did reveal a few possibly significant differences. One of these is the relatively large percentage of American news which could be described as 'foreign' or 'home and foreign' (i.e. relating to American interests in other countries). This appears to reflect the United States' position as a leading world power and/or the resources of its news organizations. In view of the pattern of international news exchange this may have serious practical consequences for those countries which are net importers of television news. The German networks' relatively fuller coverage of terrorist incidents — including those outside its frontiers — appears to be related to that country's recent preoccupation with internal security. ITN's increasingly 'popular' format over the past two or three years is expressed in the relatively high percentage of sport, disaster, crime and human interest stories.

These are some of the cross-national variations which occur in routine network news coverage. However, it is clear that they are generally small and cannot be traced directly back to simple causes like the public service tradition of the BBC, the commercial context of the American networks, organizational differences, or the 'establishment' orientation of the German networks. Of far greater significance is the fact that major foreign reports are often the product of international cooperation. They are rarely just the work of a single network news team. In short, the strong regularities across the different countries show that these are systems of the same type. Variations which do occur in styles of presentation, language and visuals are variations on a single theme, solutions to similar basic problems. Some variation can be attributed to what might be called 'network chauvinism' or national cultural influences in the encoding of news. In order to assess the importance of these influences we made a detailed examination of a major international story which was reported on all six channels at similar length. It was the account

of the murder of Aldo Moro, the former Italian prime minister, by
the Red Brigades on 9 May 1978. On that day each channel carried
extended reports of the discovery of Moro's body in Rome, followed
by obituaries and reports and comment on the terrorist phenomenon
in Italy and other Western European countries. In each case the item
was based on film from an Italian source — RAI — and material from
networks' own sources.

### The Moro story: social context

Before turning to the detailed linguistic issues contained in these
materials it is appropriate to examine the publicly available facts
about terrorism in Italy and to assess the significance of Aldo Moro
as a target for the Red Brigades.

A permanent feature of extra-parliamentary Italian politics since
the 1960s has been the existence and activities of armed groups of
the left and right, the 'red' and the 'black'. While this is not unique
to Italy, the scale of the activities in the late 1970s was unusual.[3]
The Red Brigades, who are believed to have been responsible for
about 40 shootings of prominent people in 1977, had established a
pattern of attacking senior officials of government or private companies and prominent figures in law enforcement and the media. The
clandestine nature of the Red Brigades makes detailed description
difficult but a decade of operations has brought to light certain
information about their membership, activities and ideas as well as
the wider political and social context within which they operate.

Their origins in 1969-70 coincide with the ending of Italy's postwar 'economic miracle' — two decades of continuous, rapid economic
growth, urbanization and relative political stability. In contrast with
other countries in Europe and North America, radical opposition to
the education system in the late 1960s immediately met with sharp
resistance, with the result that some activists went 'underground',
deliberately increasing the distance between themselves and the
'orthodox' Communists and Socialists who were choosing to affirm
their commitment to conventional parliamentary strategies. At the
same time, neo-Fascist organizations became active and were later
recognized as being responsible for 'anarchist' bombings and for
infiltrating leftist groups as provocateurs. In spite of this, however,
the media both then and later perceived the main threat to be from
the left.

The first large-scale news coverage of the Red Brigades came in

1974 with the kidnapping of the deputy public prosecutor in Genoa. He was later released without the demand for the release of Red Brigades prisoners being met. In the years which followed, the activities of the Red Brigades (and numerous other groups of the right and left) escalated to a frequency and level of coordination which is unparalleled in European societies in 'peacetime'. The preferred tactics of the Red Brigades ('kneecapping', kidnapping and murder of carefully selected 'exemplary' targets) met with only temporary setbacks, including the capture in 1974 of their then leader Renato Curcio, the killing of his wife in 1975, and the imprisonment of numerous members and alleged members.

The scale of the Red Brigades' support is a matter for informed guesswork, but in July 1977 there were 263 leftists and 343 Fascists under detention in Italy in connection with offences related to terrorism (Bowyer-Bell 1978, pp. 254-5). According to Alberto Ronchey, estimates of membership of terrorist groups run from 800 underground with 10,000 semi-clandestine sympathizers to as many as 3,000 'combatants', a figure similar to the number of partisans active in the Italian cities of 1944.[4] Whatever the precise details are, the activities of the armed groups are one expression of quite general opposition to unresolved social issues including the resistance of political institutions to changes, the endemic problems of inequality and unemployment and, perhaps most significantly, the chronic difficulties of a university system which can guarantee neither education nor future careers for its students.

The immovability of the central social institutions is most clearly represented by the stalemate between the major political parties and the parallel inertia of the 'Catholic world' and the 'Communist world' in Italian society. However, instead of remaining entrenched in mutual opposition, a new source of stability was emerging in the late 1970s — the 'historic compromise' between the ruling Christian Democratic party and the Italian Communist party. The significance of this development was that it confirmed the pragmatic turn of the Communist party and its full incorporation into the parliamentary scene. Aldo Moro, as the chief architect of the historic compromise and president of the Christian Democratic party was therefore the perfect symbol of the triumph of liberal democracy (for the Red Brigades, betrayal of the revolution) and a prime target for attack. He was 'the heart of the state' as the Red Brigades were later to claim.

The 'Moro story' began for the news media on 16 March 1978 when the Red Brigades ambushed his car, killed his bodyguards and abducted Moro, the first nationally prominent politician to be the victim of a terrorist kidnapping. It was to have been the day of a debate in parliament on a confidence motion that would have confirmed the government of Premier Giulio Andreotti. It was also the time at which 14 alleged members of the Red Brigades were under trial for terrorist offences in Turin and a demand for their release was quick to follow. The government made no reply, and in the weeks which followed it consistently refused to negotiate for Moro's release. News coverage was framed in terms of the pros and cons of the government's position and was fed by a succession of 'developments' which included the police operations, the release of a photo of Moro by the Red Brigades, speeches and pleas in parliament and elsewhere, hoaxes, and letters from Moro.

Moro's ordeal in captivity ended on 8 May, when he was shot by his captors. His body was found in a parked car in the centre of Rome on the following day. With characteristic attention to detail, the Red Brigades parked the car almost exactly midway between the headquarters of the Communist party and the headquarters of the Christian Democrat Party. It was at this stage that the reporting of the Moro story took on the form of 'moral closure'. The issue of negotiation or non-negotiation was finally closed, allowing the abductors to be condemned without reservation, without the need to keep open the loophole of a possible bargain. Network news broadcasts on 9 May 1978 illustrate how the central media ensured moral closure and the isolation of the Red Brigades from 'everyday' explanations, the normal run of events and social processes.

### Analysis of news vocabulary

Working from video-recordings and transcripts of the main network news broadcasts in Britain, Germany and the USA, we analysed the macrostructure of the text of the Moro story (headlines, boundary markers, paragraphing, sequencing, quotations, etc.), listed the descriptive terms (nouns, qualifiers) applied to the protagonists and made comparisons with the language and style of a sample of press reports.

We found close similarities between countries and channels in the encoding of the story and in the interpretative frameworks used in the reporting. For example on 9 May, each channel led with this story and constructed the item according to the following pattern, usually with the same simple headline 'Aldo Moro is dead' (BBC, CBS, NBC, ARD, ZDF):

1 the details of the discovery of Moro's body (including voice over film):
2 situation report (with reporter in vision and voice-over film) including details of public and family reactions;
3 obituary section detailing Moro's life story and achievements;
4 comment from world leaders.

The two examples, shown in parallel in figure 1, provide particularly clear illustrations of the shared routines of news manufacture in two unrelated networks. While there are some rather obvious differences between the styles and content of press reporting in the three countries, these do not appear to affect broadcasting to anything like the same extent. In other words, in major international stories, the cross-cultural differences are too small to require any major amendment to our hypothesis that the patterns of television news reporting can be explained as a function of shared professional norms and practices.

In part, this is explained by the generally higher level of redundancy of television reports compared with press reports — the fact that although press and broadcasting make use of a similar vocabulary, the latter uses a smaller range of terms with greater frequency (Glasgow University Media Group 1980, pp. 128-9).

There is more to the problem of description than the frequent use of the term 'terrorist', however. Where this term is used — and it is by far the most frequent — the significance of news reports turns on the wide range of possible meanings the term can have, its ambiguities and connotations. It is not self-explanatory, and it attracts a variety of glosses in the majority of reports. This is partly because its use as a descriptive term in the mass media is a relatively recent phenomena — for example, there is no entry under 'terrorism' in the *New York Times Index* until 1970, its use being historical prior to that (see Bowyer-Bell 1978, ch. 2). And it is partly because the term 'terrorist' is applied to a range of activities which have independently-derived systems of labelling (criminal, political, military, etc.).

The 'need for closure' which overrides the 'need for balance' in the case of reporting the Red Brigades means that reports will be structured and presented to demonstrate their divergence from the core values of society and the self-exclusion of terrorist groups from normal life. In practice this is achieved in a number of ways.

*Figure 1   The Moro Story,*

*Introduction*
(Newscaster in vision and voice-over film)

Good evening. Italy tonight is mourning the death of Aldo Moro, murdered 55 days after terrorists kidnapped him in a Rome street. His bullet-ridden body was found in a car a short distance away from the head-quarters of the ruling Christian Democrat party which had repeatedly refused to meet his captors' demands for the release of imprisoned terrorists.

Police found the body after an anonymous telephone call said a time-bomb had been planted in a car nearby.

Signor Moro, five times prime minister and expected to be Italy's next president, was told he was going to be executed last Friday. He wrote a farewell message to his wife which reached the family at the weekend. It was the last in a series of letters he wrote while a prisoner

of the Red Brigades. Many were emotional appeals to his party colleagues pleading with them to come to terms with his captors. But the cabinet refused to give in. From Rome

*Handover*

David Willey has just sent this report.

*Introduction*
(Newscaster in vision)

Good evening. Aldo Moro's body was found in downtown Rome today. The Italian political leader, one of the most respected men in the country, had been brutally murdered by his Red Brigades kidnappers. When word of his death spread across the city, thousands of grieving Romans left their homes and offices in what may have been the largest spontaneous demonstration there since the Second World War.

*Handover*
Fred Briggs has the grim details:

**BBC**

The Red Brigades terrorists played their latest macabre trick on the Italian government by dumping Aldo Moro's body right

in the centre of Rome, under the very noses of the police who'd been vainly searching for him for almost two months. Only a few hours ago, political leaders were still discussing

how the kidnapped politician's life might be saved. His body told the tale of how he met his death. Five bullets had been

pumped into his back perhaps 24 hours ago. A post-mortem on Wednesday will determine exactly when he was killed. The terrorists tipped off the police with an anonymous phone call.

*Situation report*
(reporter in vision and voice-over film)

It was an anonymous call shortly after noon that

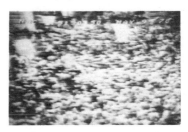

brought police to the old Renault station wagon parked just one block from Italian Communist party headquarters.

The caller said there was a bomb planted in the car, but another anonymous call to Moro's wife, a call monitored by police, said

it was Moro's body. Police could see through the car windows what appeared to be a body under a red blanket, but demolition experts were called in

They'd dodged all the road blocks around Rome and deposited Signor Moro's body almost next door to the Communist party headquarters. Italians were stunned at the news of Signor Moro's murder. A general strike was called and the country mobilized itself for some extremely difficult days that inevitably lie ahead. Signor Moro's widow and children paid a brief visit

to the morgue where Aldo Moro's body was taken for examination. His family issued a statement asking that Aldo Moro's will,

expressed in a farewell letter, that there should be no state funeral, no national mourning and no speeches, should be respected. 'The family demands silence,' they said; 'history will pass judgement on the life and death of Aldo Moro.'

The finding of Signor Moro's body took everybody by surprise, although the Red Brigades had sentenced him to death

to check the tail gate before it was opened.

When it was and the blanket was removed, there was no doubt now that, after 54 days of propaganda, messages, playing on the nerves of the government and people by giving out false leads, no doubt now that the Red Brigades

had carried out Aldo Moro's death sentence.

He had been shot in the back. Police believe that he had been shot where he lay. A great deal of blood and some shell casings were found on the floor of the car, and there

**BBC**

(shot held)

and announced his execution. I think most Italians thought there was still a faint shred of hope

was a quantity of sand found in Moro's shoes and trousers cuffs, indicating that he had been made to walk along the beach somewhere. The time of death was believed to be Saturday, the day after the Brigades announced they would execute their captive.

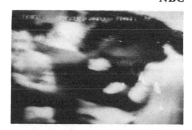

The body was taken to the Rome University Hospital morgue,

while police tried to keep the crowds back, sometimes rather violently. The Italian police have been on the spot during the entire Moro affair, and

having the body found right under their noses in an area under constant surveillance because of its closeness to a political headquarters was a further embarrassment.

**BBC**

(shot held)

that he would be reprieved. But now the worst has happened, and he has been murdered. The question is,

Mrs Eleonora Moro was escorted to the morgue from her penthouse apartment in Northern Rome. She said he wanted no public demonstrations. As for the funeral,

one of her husband's last letters said he wanted no government officials,

no members of his Christian Democrat party in attendance.

Despite Mrs Moro's wishes, some demonstrations for her husband have already occurred, one at the Coloseum, another in Milan.

**BBC**

what's going to happen next? Nobody really knows. The Christian Democrats who rule Italy, their party headquarters is here,

(shot held)

The Italian trade unions announced an eight-hour general strike this afternoon.

The country is obviously shaken,

even though Moro's murder was not unexpected.

Already there were calls for stronger police measures, and much bitterness over what many feel to be police incompetence.

**BBC**

have to decide exactly how they're going to combat this new threat. It's basically a war of nerves, psychological warfare, something new in Western European democracy.

(shot held)

*Handover*
(newsreader in vision)

There is also fear of what the Red Brigades might do next. Police have had little success penetrating

the terrorist ranks in the past. Most people expect the Brigades will continue

being one step ahead of the authorities.

It's the political parties that don't know what to expect. This coming Sunday there will be municipal elections all over Italy. About four million voters are involved in these, and the Communist party and the Christian Democrats are wondering if the Moro incident will affect their fortunes in any way. That'll be the real barometer.
Fred Briggs, NBC News, Rome.

*Handover*
(newsreader in vision)

Signor Moro's death has brought messages of sympathy from the Queen, President Carter and many other heads of state. All spoke of their shock at the death of Italy's most influential politician. His kidnapping 55 days ago set off the biggest manhunt in Italian history and it left the country in the grip of the Red Brigade terrorists. Mike McKay reports.

*Obituary*
(voice-over film and stills)

At the height of his career Aldo Moro was seen as one of the few men who stood between stable government and total anarchy.

Amid fierce political rivalries he was a man who knitted together a coalition

that kept in power the scandal-ridden Christian Democrats. Moro pioneered the historic compromise between the Catholic ruling party and the Communists.

Moro was a man of quiet, conservative habits, who liked tending his rose garden, smoking five cigarettes a day and no more. During the Johnson administration, he came to Washington as premier and there was a White House dinner for him. Afterwards Johnson wanted to dance half the night, but Moro left early and went to bed. Here's more from John Poma:

*Obituary*
(voice-over film and stills)

Aldo Moro was a fixture in Italian governments for more than 20 years. Five times he served as premier. The thin, stooped law professor had a gift for compromise that helped guide Italy through the numerous political upheavals that followed World War II.

Moro was a distant figure to most Italians. He was often pictured in political cartoons as a Sphinx,

a man who had the patience to sit through ten-hour meetings without getting up or even asking for a cup of coffee.

**BBC**

The Moro kidnapping

and the murder of his five bodyguards occurred in March as he was driving to Parliament.

A new cabinet was being formed, old rivalries forgotten, but not by the Red Brigades.

It was their most horrific attack,

He won many of his compromises by simply

outlasting his adversaries. In his personal dealings, Moro was cautious. He never learned to drive, limited

himself to five cigarettes a day and preferred trains to airplanes.

He was a personal friend of Pope Paul and attended Mass every day. But, to the ultra-left Red Brigades, who kidnapped and murdered him, Moro, as leader of the Christian Democrat party, was a political 'godfather', who they said was responsible for all that is wrong with Italy.

an outrage which police now believe had been festering for more than two years. Troops and police

were completely baffled by the Moro disappearance.

The humiliation of the Italian security forces was one of the prime objectives

of the Red Brigades. As investigations continued, the terrorists issued a flood

Moro's last and most important compromise came earlier this spring, when he averted yet another political crisis by allowing the Communist party

a voice in the government without actually bringing it into the cabinet.

He was expected to assume the largely ceremonial post

of communiqués, often simultaneously in different cities.

In Turin today, the extremist prisoners whose freedom

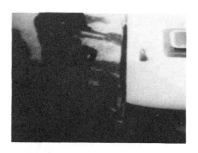

had been demanded by the Red Brigades appeared

once more in the beleaguered court. Throughout the Moro affair,

of president of Italy later this year, a chance that never came.

John Poma. NBC News.

**BBC**

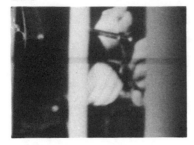

they've taunted the authorities, saying that their comrades outside were fighting a political war against the Italian state. The captors of Aldo Moro have shown a new mercilessness.

But those men were still in prison; the government had stood firm.

The European parliament in Strasbourg was one of the many legislatures on the Continent which suspended business on hearing of Signor Moro's death. And here at home, the prime minister Mr Callaghan sent a message to Rome to say the British government shared Italy's grief over the tragic end to Signor Moro's long ordeal.

*Report on reactions*
(Newscaster in vision)

When Pope Paul heard the bad news, he went to his private chapel to pray. Messages denouncing the assassination were sent by leaders all over the world, President Carter, Tito of Yugoslavia, all the Europeans. The Italian cabinet met in emergency session. The French parliament suspended its session. The Canadian parliament adjourned in tribute to a foreign leader — the first time that's happened in Ottawa since the death of John F. Kennedy.

First, there are simple linguistic markers and qualifiers which have the effect of reducing status or removing legitimacy from the object of the description. In the German press, for instance, but not regularly elsewhere, the term 'Red Brigades' was nearly always surrounded by inverted commas. The term 'self-styled' occurred several times in the English-language press. The broadcast equivalent used several times was the prefix 'so-called'. It was a premise of almost all this reporting that the Red Brigades were a very small group without political status which commanded little support from the Italian people.

The second linguistic technique of exclusion is one which places the Red Brigades outside 'normal' society by the application of heavily value-laden labels and stereotypes. 'Criminal' was one such label used, together with kindred terms like 'killers', 'gunmen' and 'murderers'. A number of newspapers used the word 'gang' (*Sunday Times, New York Times, Washington Post, Miami Herald, Los Angeles Times, Daily Express, Daily Mirror, Guardian*). A full list would contain examples from the entire range of the 'popular' and 'quality' press, and would include 'professional killers' (*Washington Post*), 'a hit team (*Miami Herald*), 'common murderers' (*Daily Express*), 'a handful of violent criminals and psychopaths' (London *Times*), 'a small band of criminals' (*Guardian*) and 'base criminals' (*Chicago Tribune*). The broadcasting organizations were more sparing in their use of the 'crime' vocabulary, but in terms of frequency it is the second most important category of descriptions after the expressions 'Red Brigades' and 'terrorists'.

Another group of terms is derived from *military* and *political* vocabularies and they are frequently used in combination. There were references to 'guerrillas' or 'urban guerrillas' (*Chicago Tribune, Daily Telegraph, Miami Herald, Times, Guardian, Washington Post, New York Times, Los Angeles Times, Daily Mirror*); 'commandos' (*Miami Herald, Guardian, Chicago Tribune, Die Welt*); 'a guerrilla squad' and 'a highly organized guerrilla army' (*Times*). The political descriptions most frequently invoke the left/right continuum, extremism and revolution, with references to 'left-wing', 'extremist', or both. The *Miami Herald* called them 'Marxist revolutionaries' and the *Washington Post* 'Marxist urban guerrillas' and 'Marxist terrorists'.[5] The *Daily Mirror* said that they were 'violent anarchists' and the *Daily Express* called them 'political killers'. Once again, the networks employ a more restricted vocabulary but it derives from the same stock.

A third interpretive category is used more widely in the press than in broadcast news. It assumes the *psychopathological* nature of the Red Brigades' activities and adopts the viewpoint that the Red Brigades were mindlessly vicious monsters who had committed a senseless sadistic act that could only be interpreted as insane. Newspapers employed such terms as 'fanatics' (*New York Times, Daily Express, Los Angeles Times*), 'crazies' (*Chicago Tribune*), 'evil-minded children' (*Daily Express*), 'moral morons' and 'sick addled characters' (*Daily News*), 'willing sadists' (*Guardian*) and 'inhuman political savages' (*Chicago Tribune*). The broadcasters appeared to avoid specific use of a psychopathological model but were working with similar assumptions when they referred to the Red Brigades' 'latest macabre trick (BBC) and 'sadistic torments' (ZDF). As if to emphasize the alien and peripheral character of the Red Brigades, there were references to 'a handful' (*Times*) and 'a small band' (*Guardian*). On occasion, the varieties of labelling were used in combination with each other to give expressions like 'left-wing urban guerrillas' (BBC) and 'links extremistischen Überfallkommandos' (*Die Welt*) or 'linken Verbrecherorganisation' (*Die Welt*).

Each of the models of interpretation described here (the criminal, military, political and psychopathological) can of course be applied to other quite distinct groups and activities. The significance of their conjunction in the Moro story is to provide multiple guarantees of the Red Brigades' exclusion from the membership categories of the audience — 'the overwhelming majority', 'the people', 'ordinary citizens'. These inclusive categories are widely used in descriptions of the public shock, outrage and sorrow which followed the news of Moro's death. Linguistically, they express the consensus from which the Red Brigades are excluded by the means described above.

Only a few reports acknowledge that this consensus is incomplete, but, typically, they repair the possible damage which this can inflict on the consensual framework by making reference to 'other terrorist networks' (*New York Times*), 'underground networks' (*Financial Times*) and 'sympathizers' (*Times, Weilburger Tageblatt*). The implication that the activities of the Red Brigades might be part of a phenomenon called 'international terrorism' (for example, ARD) appears to have a similar function, so that the possibility of the existence of widespread disaffection or large numbers of people who might be susceptible to the ideology of armed revolutionary struggle is generally ignored. The *Financial Times* did admit to the existence of 'unknown sympathizers in factories, ministries, the means of communication and probably in the security forces' but it was the *Guardian* which came closest to acknowledging the precariousness of the consensus when it referred to 'the vast number of young people, unemployed, attached to the extra-Parliamentary Left, and disillusioned with the achievements of the traditional parties'.

This raises a question which can only be answered by analysis of a third aspect of linguistic structure. We have considered what might be called 'distancing devices' and the varieties of reference in descriptions of the Red Brigades. The third aspect is the interrelationship between the categories of description and the key figures involved in the Moro story (Moro himself, his family, the Church, the state, the police, the Red Brigades and the Italian people). The potentially wide range of categories finds actual expression in a limited number of permutations which include or exclude individuals or groups from the sphere of 'social normality', rather than order or differentiate within the social sphere. In practice, social descriptions are polarized and tend to operate with simple binary distinctions, for example: workers/non-workers, dropouts; peaceful/violent; organized/unorganized; moderate/extreme; democracy/civil war, anarchy. We therefore encounter contiguous and overlapping use of descriptions for all the protagonists in the story except for the Red Brigades. It is not unusual to read of the 'Italian' government, people, parties and public opinion but rare to find the Red Brigades qualified in the same way, although the expression 'Italy's Red Brigades' does occur. They are described as 'professional' and 'organized', but these terms are not used to qualify the activities of, say, the police or state. The opposition between workers and non-workers and between peace and violence is neatly captured in two press descriptions of the Red Brigades — 'people who've never worked' and 'enemies of peaceful life'. In similar vein, the *Daily Mirror* described Renato Curcio, the imprisoned leader of the Red Brigades, as a 'university drop-out'.

This tendency to reduce complex system of social relationships to simple opposites is a feature we noted in an earlier analysis of the language of industrial reporting on British television news (Glasgow University Media Group 1980). In that case it was the reduction to 'the two sides of industry' and simple causal explanations based on the assumption that labour is the active partner in disputes and management the passive partner. This, we argued, cannot be defended as a necessary loss of detail in the interests of brevity and clarity but it is a significant form of 'ideological reduction' or simplification which goes beyond factual description to weigh in favour of one side rather than another.

In cases like industrial reporting in broadcast news, where impartiality must be upheld, this amounts to consistent though not necessarily intentional bias. In the present case, where impartiality is not sought, the real significance of the patterns of language which we have noted appears to lie in the 'ideological work' which is routinely performed at the boundaries of *inclusion* and *exclusion*. As far as Italy is concerned, these linguistic patterns may have contributed to what one commentator described as many people's simple reaction 'of associating, directly or indirectly, the Red Brigades with left-wing parties as a whole, and mainly the Communists'.[6]

## Analysing the visuals

Elsewhere we have shown that the verbal element of television news reporting has a lexical and semantic character which amounts to a 'restricted code'.[7] Whether televisual images share the characteristics of verbal language — either directly or by analogy — is a debatable and unresolved issue. At its simplest, the problem is that there is no general science of visual language, like linguistics, which delivers agreed methods of description and analysis.

Semiotics attempts to hint at ways in which an analysis might be done but, with the significant exception of Peirce's categories of 'index', 'icon' and 'symbol', it suffers from an underdeveloped system of descriptive and analytical categories. Our approach has been to work with this limited descriptive apparatus and to identify the appropriate units of television news film which can be used for generating empirical data and findings. It may then be possible to generalize from these. We have described in *More bad news* a basic technique for constructing data from a moving visual medium (live television, film and video-recordings). Units of analysis (shots) are defined by cuts in the film or tape, so that the object of analysis in the first instance is the direct expression of the practices of shooting and editing, not the image *per se*. For most purposes, each shot can be captured as a photographic still and any camera movement within the shot can be described according to a finite range of moves (pan, zoom, crab, etc.). When the stills are mounted alongside a transcript of the news script, the initial task of visual transcription is complete (see figure 1) and it becomes possible to analyse relationships between the constituent elements. Without this preparatory work, analysis is bound to be inhibited in the same way that linguistics would be if there were no general agreement on the boundaries of the lexeme. As often happens, adequate methods for analysing visual media are being developed only long after the invention of film and television. By analogy with linguistics, the comparative method is particularly useful in beginning to examine the patterns and relationships in moving pictures.

In analysing television news as a visual medium we have to recognize the variety of possible reading or viewings. One can imagine a shot representing a soldier in a particular stance. This shot can be read as telling someone how they should stand, how they should not hold themselves or how a particular person did stand in such and such a place, and so on. Then any reading or viewing of such a shot can contain a cultural assumption or proposition. Wittgenstein points out that we might call the shot a 'proposition radical', for there are a number of propositions which could be read off. However, words and things, pictures and propositions, still images and shots are normally situated in such a manner that there is usually a 'preferred' reading or viewing. It is because words and things, pictures and propositions, take on meaning by virtue of being 'keyed' by such preferences that we can use the analysis of sets of given shots or 'visual phrases' to decode the ideological preferences of the broadcasters.

Roland Barthes (1977) has argued, somewhat differently, that photographic images tend to be 'polysemic' or indeterminate in meaning. Whilst this might be so with any individual shot or mechanically reproduced picture, we would argue that it is not the case with television news film because of its 'seriality'. Each image *can* be considered as if separate but this is not a likely reading under normal reception conditions. Moreover, as is clear from the reproduction of the text and images in figure 1, images rarely appear without accompanying verbal statements.

Contrary to the professional myth that televisual images dictate the story, we would argue from both the earlier and the present study that the dominant element for encoding and decoding (production and reception) of television news is the verbal story line. However, there is some apparent structure to the visuals which is shared by both BBC and NBC in the above example. The BBC story opens with a Moro portrait, as does NBC, and both portraits have similar framing and expression. Again, the BBC closes with the newscaster, after a shot of prisoners behind bars, whilst the NBC closes with newscaster/Moro portrait as at the opening. This 'return to the newscaster' is really the visual equivalent of the textual devices which allow the text to be edited (closed off) at a number of possible points. The general structure has the following logic:

| a | where a is the newscaster |
|---|---|
| a.b. | b is voice-over film |
| (a).b.c. | c reporter in vision |
| a.b.c.d. | d is voice-over library film. |
| ....etc. | |

This 'hierarchical recursive structure' comes from the editorial need to allow for the possibility of closure at any point, for reasons of time or style of presentation. It could, incidentally, be one reason for the high level of lexical or visual redundancy. This is an editorially imposed grammatical structure, it is not a structure determined by extrinsic events or a 'natural' logic of narrative.

A central finding of the previously reported work (based on all the shots in one week's news output on BBC1, BBC2 and ITN in May 1975) was a low degree of iconicity in television news visuals (Glasgow University Media Group 1980). An icon is an image which is a direct representation of that to which it refers, so that a photograph of a wire-haired fox terrier is an icon of that animal. (An example of an indexical image of the same animal could be a line drawing of a dog; a symbol of the same could be any representation, although in our culture symbols of 'dog' commonly include kennels, leads, bowls and other items which are associated with dogs as domestic pets.)

In television news, in fact, a relatively small proportion of the total number of shots is iconic or *directly* representative of the people, places and events which are the subjects of the news text. A far greater proportion of shots has an oblique relationship to the text; they 'stand for' the subject matter indexically or symbolically. If iconicity is to be measured by the number of shots in voice over film which have a simultaneous direct verbal reference to the shot itself (e.g. 'his body was found in a car...' over a shot of the car in question), excluding shots of the newscaster, then:

> *in the BBC item* (total 33 shots, including 4 of caster to camera) 48% (14/29 shots could be considered iconic;

> *in the NBC item* (total 37 shots, including 3 of caster to camera) 41% (14/34) shots can be said to be iconic.

Even this measure tends to *over*estimate the degree of iconicity because a single concrete object or person is often used to connote abstractions as well. For example, the BBC has a shot of Aldo Moro seated at a desk and the accompanying text reads: '[he] was seen as one of the few men who stood between stable government and total anarchy.' 'Aldo Moro' is the direct verbal reference to the shot, but the symbolism which accrues by virtue of the text is arguably more significant.

Of course, any threefold categorization system is open to ambiguities, and the nature of this particular story means that there is a greater probability of iconic shots than in most. For part of it is an obituary, and as television news stories go, it is lengthy and detailed, implying a commitment in resources and production which works to raise the level of iconicity. Yet despite this, more than half the shots are predominantly indexical or symbolic and do not bear a direct relationship to the news text. We must therefore conclude, as our previous studies have done, that to make semantic or cognitive sense of the visuals, the average viewer would have his or her viewing guided by the preferences of the verbal track — which is telling the audience to read it this way rather than that. One clear example of this is the NBC shot of the demonstrators' placard I GIOVANI CONTRO IL TERRORISMO (Youth against terrorism) and the accompanying voice over, 'the country is obviously shaken'. Elsewhere, there are some examples where the text appears to offer a hint of an alternative viewpoint. For example, the BBC quotes the Red Brigades prisoners' statement that 'their comrades outside were fighting a political war', but closure is achieved by the shot of a prisoner handcuffed and behind bars. It is this use of the relationship between image and text which suggests some clear possibilities for the preferred reading and viewing of this story.

Our findings suggest that the relationship between image and text is more than purely illustrative. They reveal that there is often no direct or even indirect correspondence between the content of voice-overs and the shots which appear. It would seem that the relationship is more of an imperfect parallel. The extent to which the parallel elements contradict one another may depend on the ideological sensitivity of the subject matter. Thus, the closest correspondence in the above examples occurs in the sections which relate the events of the finding of Aldo Moro's body in a Rome street. There is less correspondence where the text refers to such issues as the possibility of a 'bargain' with the Red Brigades for Moro's life, the aims of the Red Brigades, and the ineffectiveness of the security forces.

This could be expressed as a hypothesis that in areas of moral sensitivity efforts are made to close off the possibly ambiguous meanings of the visual track or efforts are made to reduce the ambiguity of the verbal track by using the connotations of the visuals.

But this may imply a level of attention which is not present. Another way of expressing this might be to say that the correspondence between the two tracks will tend to be closest when the need to reduce ideological uncertainty in the message is greatest.

This is not to suggest that television news is merely propaganda. Indeed its function as ideology would be considerably undermined if it lacked credibility. Nor is it to suggest that in the practice of reporting the visual and verbal languages are always used in such a fashion as to allow only one reading of a situation (although this sometimes happens, e.g. NBC: 'our reporter has the grim details'). Rather, television news language, visual and verbal, is open to a number of interpretations, yet routinely there emerges a reading of actions and events which restricts the range of legitimate views and interpretations. The broadcasting of talk or messages is not a simple, unidirectional process in which the government's viewpoint is always given preference over others. But there is a set of routine practices whose use often effectively reduces the plurality of meanings inherent in any social conflict to a set of simple formulae or frames of reference which are at base an ideological defence of the legitimacy of a given status quo. The examples given of the relationship between verbal and visual elements in television news show that the values of international news broadcasters are brought into play in such a manner that the ambiguities and divergences between the two tracks can often be used to present a set of meanings which amounts to ideological as well as moral closure.

In the three countries represented in our sample, the reaction to the news of Moro's death and the part which the media played in reporting it is at present a matter for speculation. However, the comparison does reveal a certain amount of cross-cultural variation in the drawing of boundaries of inclusion and exclusion, and it suggests that the function of these reports may relate quite closely to internal conditions within each of the countries. For example, there is a propensity in the German media to draw the boundary of exclusion around a wider range of (left-wing) political activity than is the case in the British and American media, there are more frequent references to 'international terrorism', and many reports contain explicit comparative mention of terrorism within Germany. The American media are more inclined to see an underground network of terrorist organizations without any sympathy or support from the Italian people. The media in Britain occupy an intermediate position when they imply that substantial numbers may be 'susceptible' to revolutionary thinking even if they do not identify themselves with the Red Brigades.

## Conclusion

Without further research it is not possible to determine the precise contribution which the verbal and visual language of reporting terrorism in another country makes to the interpretation of indigenous terrorist phenomena and to the maintenance of social consensus. However, the evidence so far is at least compatible with the thesis that the activities of relatively small armed revolutionary groups (including those abroad because they are implicated in 'international networks') are 'a welcome pretext for sealing off a whole society against any possibility of the growth of a political extra-parliamentary opposition' (Cobler 1978, p. 12). The language and content of the media in Germany (the word 'sympathizer' has special significance here) lend most support to this thesis. In the United States, where politically motivated violence is less apparent, the preferred vocabulary and framework of interpretation is that of 'criminal violence'. If each country to some extent reports external events in its own image, then the media in Britain carry echoes of their own troubled consensus.

By way of general conclusion we can say that the evidence from the reporting of the Moro story in the press and the television networks points to a universally assumed consensus (in Western media) within which, with some cross-cultural variation, the complex causes and impact of armed opposition and revolutionary violence are reduced by the inferential frameworks of 'law and (dis)order', the 'violent society', the threat to democracy, and international terror, to a simple picture of a temporary and unprovoked outbreak of irrational violence in an otherwise ordered and peaceful society. The moral imperative to condemn the Red Brigades leads to routine practices of moral closure at the level of language and, we would maintain, at the level of the visual track where attempts are also made to close off possibly ambiguous meanings. One byproduct of this appears to be a pattern of description which is not simply biased in favour of parliamentary democracy as one would expect, but which strongly prefers certain parties, positions and ideologies over others which legitimately inhabit the legislative sphere both in and outside parliament. Consensus and closure, two distinct structural phenomena, are thus merged. The visual and verbal content of the Moro news story tells more about the maintenance of an ideologically safe version of consensus by media demarcation than it does about the 'events' which constitute the news.

## *Notes*

1 This is acknowledged in Annan Report 1977.
2 We collected the main evening news on two television channels in each country: United Kingdom (BBC, ITN); United States (CBS, NBC); German Federal Republic (ARD, ZDF). For comparison, we also collected a range of 'popular' and 'quality' newspapers in each country. The research was supported by the Social Science Research Council (Grant HR 5383). We warmly thank Jill Matthews for assisting with the work described here.
3 According to Alberto Ronchey (1978), there were 702 terrorist episodes in Italy in 1975, 1,353 episodes in 1976 and 2,081 in 1977. The number of terrorist incidents remained at this high level for at least the next two years.
4 Ronchey, quoted in Sheehan 1979, p. 22. In addition, an unknown number think of the Red Brigades as 'mistaken comrades'.
5 It is interesting to note that the East German television network described the Red Brigades as 'pro-fascist terrorists' (*Aktuelle Kamera*, 9 May 1978). This underlines the fact that the present analysis applies only to the media of the advanced liberal democracies.
6 *Times*, 10 May 1978.
7 Glasgow University Media Group 1980. especially pp. 126-30, 173-5.

# 2

# The social background of the language of radio

GERHARD LEITNER

Words are one of radio's raw materials, and people are very
properly interested in how we use them.

*A. Singer, Director of BBC Radio*
*(quoted in Burchfield et al. 1979)*

Radio is dominated by words or, to be more precise, by spoken
language. This does not merely pose questions of language use.
There is ample evidence that the language of radio, as of any mass
medium, is deliberate and often planned linguistic behaviour — a
fact that raises issues of sociolinguistic and social importance. Like
the media institutions themselves, their language must be seen within
the context — and as a result of the intereaction — of the wider
sociopolitical climate, the technical and economic circumstances,
and the sociolinguistic structure of the speech community.

I shall explore these questions by taking the BBC as an example.
The analysis will focus on three phrases in which relatively homogeneous, but contrasting, pictures emerge: the period 1926-54,
excluding the Second World War; the period from around 1959 till
today; and the present, with its debates about the future of broadcasting. Historically, these phases are marked by the transition from
a national and public corporational pattern to a national vs. local
dichotomy in radio (and a regional pattern in television), and a public corporational vs. commercial organization on TV. The future may
further accentuate the present structures, but reassign the BBC a
more centralized role.

The BBC lends itself to this kind of investigation as one of the oldest and most prestigious broadcasting corporations in the world and because its early history is relatively well documented.[1] The results of this analysis should not only provide insights into the relation between language, media and society in Britian, but serve as a basis for similar investigations on other media in other countries.

## The specification of radio language

If the language of radio is assumed to be deliberate or even planned, there remains the question of which aspects of language output or language behaviour are most relevant at any given time. Answers to this question have led to two kinds of interest in media language, one closely related to the projects of the Glasgow University Media Group (1976, 1980), Kress and Trew (1978) and Schumann (1975), the other being pursued here and elsewhere (Leitner 1979, 1980). There are four aspects to the linguistic specification of the language of radio (LOR):

the *selection* of one or more than one variety for LOR;
the *codification* of the(se) variety(ies);
the *scope* of their use, i.e. the determination of who is expected to use them, and in what programmes;
the relationship between *LOR-use and reality.*

The first, second and fourth have to do with the control of the language code or codes, while the third specification refers to their implementation. We will examine that first.

There is a broad consensus across media that not all of the output and all speakers appearing in it can or should be expected to conform to the general standards applied to selection, codification and language use. Generally, only speakers who are media personnel, professional journalists employed by the institution and acting in this capacity, are required to do so.[2] It is also felt that programmes like the news, current affairs, magazines, and announcements are more central to the maintenance of such standards than others. Radio drama and comedy are normally excluded because they are governed by different aesthetic norms. A more precise delimitation is possible if one looks at specific media institutions and countries. For instance, the scope of LOR was defined as extremely wide in prewar Germany, even including drama, and as fairly narrow in Britain.[3]

Selection, codification, and the relationship between language use and reality are best introduced with some examples from radio and television programmes:

**1 BBC Radio 4, March 1975. Consumer Advice Programme with Jimmy Young and David Tench.**

JY:     ...takes us on to...the reappearance of Mr David Tench after his long-running commercial for the National Consumer Congress. Now Sir, the first of today's listeners' queries, questions or whatever. Are you prepared to proceed?
DT:     Ready, willing and able.
JY:     Right [in Cockney accent] ...

[second half of the programme]

JY:     Now then. Meanwhile back with legal eagle David Tench, erm a lady is taking issue with you, master...

**2 BBC Radio 4, 20 April 1977. 'The Future of Broadcasting', Analysis Special with Michael Charlton, Lord Annan and others.**

MC:     Well, therefore, Lord Annan, erm what significance should be attached to one of the principal findings as I take it to be of your report that the...that you have confirmed the independence of the broadcasters?
LA:     We have, but we have balanced this against greater public accountancy...

**3 BBC Radio News, 22 September 1934, read by Stuart Hibberd, on the Gresford Colliery mine disaster.**

...ən  ðə  'reskju wə:k  iz  biiŋ  'vigərəsli  kən'tinju:d...
...and  the  rescue  work  is  being  vigorously  continued...

'bʌt  ðə  'wə:k  iz  'trædʒikəli  'difikəlt
But  the  work  is  tragically  difficult.

**4 BBC Radio News, 7 March 1936, read by Frederick Grisewood, on the German reoccupation of the Rhineland.**

i'vents  əv  'meidʒərim'pɔ:tṇs  'hæpṇd  in  'jɔərɔp  tə'dei
Events  of  major importance  happened  in  Europe  today.

ðis  'mɔ:niŋ  'dʒɜ:mən'tru:ps  'meid  ə 'fɔ:ml  'entri intə ðə  di'militəraizd
This  morning,  German troops  made  a  formal  entry into  the  demilitarized

'zoun ɔn ðə 'left 'beŋk əv ðə 'rain    hi    'vigərəsli ə'tẹkt
zone on the left bank of the Rhine...He [Hitler] vigorously attacked

'bɔlʃəvizm ænd ðə 'fɹæŋkou'rʌʃṇ 'pẹkt
Bolshevism and the Franco-Russian pact.

5 BBC 1 TV, Nine O'Clock News, 2 September 1977, read by K. Kendall.

KK: The crucial TUC debate on pay will be next Wednesday. But tonight, the Prime Minister carefully reemphasized that the government's pay guidelines must be adhered to...

6 Independent Television News, News at Ten, 2 September 1977.

Newscaster: The Prime Minister has warned that excessive wage claims above the government's ten per cent limit will lead to what he called the 'cancer of unemployment'...

Trade Unions who oppose the ten per cent say that the motion (against the limit at the TUC) will be overwhelmingly carried. Our Industrial Editor says that even if the 12-month rule (for the duration of wage settlements) was endorsed by Congress, the cash limits motion will introduce an element of doubt on whether support for the rule really exists.

These examples illustrate clearly that the language of radio and television is extremely varied, and that Quirk (1980, p. 1) is right in saying that if any single set of standards is applicable to this diversity at all it can only be at the most general level.

In (1), there is the question of the co-occurrence of address forms of varying degrees of formality, e.g. 'Sir' and 'master', or the co-occurrence of formal items like 'proceed', 'take issue with', and the informal 'legal eagle', as well as the switch from Standard English into Cockney. The second example illustrates the 'proper' use of formal, even stilted, language, witness 'attach significance to', 'principal findings', and the defensive hedge 'as I take it'. Examples (3) and (4) raise similar questions from the angle of pronunciation. Should unaccented vowels be retained, as in 'tragically' /'trædʒikəli/, or deleted, as in 'formal'/'fɔ:ml/ instead of /'fɔ:məl/, 'importance' /im'pɔ:tns/? The pronunciation of 'pact, 'bank' and 'attacked' with the lower-mid front vowel / ẹ / instead of with the low front vowel / æ / not only raises stylistic issues but social ones: /ẹ/ is socially marked as upper-class or as typical of the 'Oxford accent'.

Example (6) brings up questions of grammar: according to 'ordinary' grammatical rules, there is to be tense concord between reporting and reported clause and between conditional and main clause. In other words the third sentence should be either:

'Our Industrial Editor *says* that even if the 12-month rule is endorsed, the cash limits motion *will* introduce...'

or:

'Our Industrial Editor *says* that even if the 12-month rule *is* endorsed, the cash limits motion *would* introduce...'

The application of several words like 'pay guidelines'(5), 'ten per cent limit' (6) 'cash limits' and 'rule'(6) to what is fundamentally the same thing, a central aspect of the industrial policy of the then Labour government, brings up the relationship between language and reality. There is a wide semantic gap between *pay guidelines* and *cash limits*.

An interpretation of these examples in terms of the intentions underlying the encoding process is relatively straightforward. Note the would-be humorous effect through code switching in (1), the linguistic expression of the 'weight' of the problems and events in (2) and (3), or the desire to remain uncommitted and objective in (6).

Cases like these illustrate problems of selection (1), codification (1-6) and the relationship between language and reality (6). With regard to the latter problem of language use, one can discuss the choice of particular lexical items (Glasgow University Media Group 1980), the use of syntactic structures like the passive (Kress & Trew 1978), or the sequencing of information and its linguistic correlates (Glasgow University Media Group 1980). With regard to the first two issues, there are problems of appropriateness, correctness and style (Kress & Trew 1978; Leitner 1979; Quirk 1980). On a deeper level the use of language must be responsive to the media-political requirements of impartiality and balance, while the role of the media in language standardization and language planning will be expressed through selection and codification.

Obviously, there will not always be a neat boundary. Referring to one and the same event with the words *slaughter, murder, killing* or *assassination*, or to the same group of persons as *terrorists* or *freedom fighters*, may raise questions both of style (appropriateness) and fact. Note the difference between *murder* and *slaughter* and *murder* and *assassination*; or between the more descriptive (*freedom*) *fighter* and *terrorist*. The distinction is also difficult to draw between a 'personal' approach to the audience, which allegedly brings in a note of subjectivism, and the 'impersonal' one, which is said to be objective (cf. below pp. 65ff). In general, however, it is a useful and valid one.

The present analysis is most concerned with the selection, codification and implementation of the language of radio. It will be shown how these aspects were related to the wider sociolinguistic and social context in the historical development of British broadcasting. Some comparisons with prewar Germany will help put the British case into relief and bring out some more general hypotheses.

## The domain of radio

It is a widely accepted view in sociolinguistic research that the language of radio (or mass media in general) constitutes a domain. Domains are, according to Fishman (1974), associated with widespread sociocultural norms and expectations and lead to congruent social and linguistic behaviour. Although this is true in principle, it needs to be made clear which areas of the media are decisive.

I will first describe them briefly and in general and then show their evolution and change in the BBC. Figure 1 sums up the major aspects so that the subsequent outline can concentrate on particular points.[4]

1 *Wider media context.* This refers to the overall media pattern in a country. It is this or, rather the uses that audiences make of the different media, that determines the role of radio.
2 *Radio goals.* The overall objectives that radio is to fulfil, i.e. to inform, to entertain and to educate, and their particular interpretation at any given time.
3 *Radio structure.* This refers to (1) its legal basis (public corporation, commercial or a mixture of both), (b) its reach (national, regional or local) and (c) the number of channels there are.
4 *Programming policy.* The structuring of programme output. There are two accepted policies: mixed programming, i.e. the provision of any kind of programme on all channels; or streamed, generic programming, i.e. the provision of predominantly one type of programme, for instance music or sports, on each channel.
5 *Technical and economic circumstances.* These include the number of wavelengths, the power of the transmitters etc. They indirectly influence (1-3).

*Figure 1   History of BBC Radio*

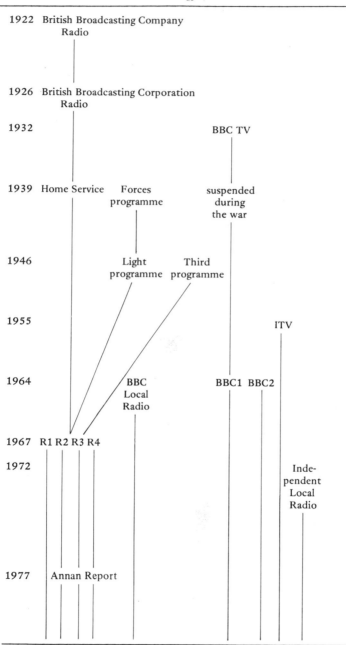

| Phase | Status and structure | Goals | Programme policy | Media context |
|---|---|---|---|---|
| I | Commercial enterprise with regional and local networks | as in II | unclear for lack of evidence | press and film |
| II | Public corporation with national network and five regions | 'education information and entertainment' (an instrument of high culture) | mixed programming on one channel | as in I (TV irrelevant) |
| III | " | de-emphasis on education | beginning of streamed programming on Forces programme | as in I (TV interrupted by war) |
| | | | streamed programming reinforced after the war | growing role of TV |
| IV | " | as in III, but widespread insecurity because of TV competition | streamed programming but widespread insecurity | ITV (and BBC TV) as major competitors |
| V | enhanced role for regions, introduction of local radio | radio as an instrument of entertainment and information for varying consumer needs | streamed programming as an accepted policy to fulfil diverse audience needs | Radio and TV are used at different times: radio has morning and lunchtime peaks. Growing importance of local radio |
| VI | proposal for separate local radio authority | proposals for re-emphasis of national role | proposals for re-emphasis of mixed programming | restructuring of media context |

These factors constitute the external frame of LOR. They are not merely additive but interact with each other. Thus, if a medium sees its prime function as educative, it will find it easier to succeed in a monopolistic position and with a mixed programming policy. Competition generally gives greater weight to entertainment. Mixed programming can, but need not, lead to a diversified form of LOR, streamed programming definitely leads to a more homogeneous LOR (within each channel).

By phase II of its development (see Figure 1), the BBC was a basically national medium. It had become an extremely homogeneous institution and was under the strong influence of the upper and upper middle classes.

The transformation of the British Broadcasting Company Ltd into the Corporation in 1926 followed the proposals of the Crawford Committee, which had been appointed by the government to make recommendations for the future structure of broadcasting. This body had felt it necessary that radio should 'be conducted by a public corporation acting as the Trustee for the national interest', and it suggested that it be founded by Act of Parliament. The fact that it was established by an extremely liberal worded Royal Charter is indicative of its high social status and, to some extent, of upper-class influence.

Although Reith, who had been director-general of the Company and became the Corporation's first director-general, had already introduced a certain amount of educational programming into the Company, the decisive step to make radio an instrument of education in the widest sense came in 1926. The BBC's overall goals were education, information and (a certain amount of) entertainment. This meant the propagation of 'high', i.e. elitist, upper-middle-class culture. Its cultural role was further reinforced by the fact that initially it was not allowed to provide its own news bulletins and that restrictions were imposed on the amount of (controversial) political broadcasting. However, strong pressures, especially from commercial continental radio stations, led to a rapid increase in more popular entertainment programmes, so that by 1938, according to Black (1972, p. 62), the BBC had become the biggest source of light entertainment. But in most areas the BBC still acted as an educator, and the underlying philosophy was, in Reith's own words, 'to give the public a little more than it wants'.

Reith also dissolved most of the local stations of the Company, a move made possible by a very powerful transmitter in London, and retained only five regional stations, in Scotland, Wales, the

Southwest, South and North. Their programme output was limited and mainly restricted to 'optouts' in their own areas.[5] The Corporation thus quickly became a very homogeneous institution imbued with a firm commitment to the Corporation's goals, later to be termed the 'Reithean ethos'. This guaranteed that particular attitudes, as on LOR, could be translated into practice.

The 1950s and 1960s brought radical technical, economic and political changes which affected the wider media structure (see Figure 1), and which account for the decline in centrality of radio and its present role as largely a daytime entertainment and information medium (cf. Emmett 1972).

In the fourth phase of development after 1955, the BBC had to compete with commercial television, which provided mass entertainment, and later with 'pirate' commercial radio stations which broadcast from outside the British territory and addressed themselves to the young. The BBC was in danger of losing large proportions of the middle and lower classes, as well as the younger generation, to commercial media. Radio was at an added disadvantage in that it had to stand up against television as a new medium.

The BBC responded slowly. But under Hugh Greene, who was director-general for much of phase V (1960-9), some decisive steps were taken. First, the number of national channels was increased to four and they were geared to serve specific audience tastes. Radio 1 was to be the main pop music channel providing some information for younger listeners, Radio 3 was geared to minority tastes, e.g. jazz and classical music. Generic programming, which had been practised as early as 1940 on the so-called Forces Programme, was now an accepted policy. Second, local radio was introduced in 1967 to cater for local needs, thus abolishing regional broadcasting. Third, the BBC redefined its goals, de-stressing education and making quality entertainment its first priority. Lastly, the BBC widened the scope of its output and attempted a more pluralistic approach to its audiences, in an effort to free itself from the old Reithean ethos and assume a more popular role.[6]

Phases II and V therefore stand in marked contrast in terms of both the BBC's internal complexity and the underlying philosophy. In the most recent phase, substantive criticisms of the present media structure and performance have been voiced which may eventually have far-reaching implications for the BBC and for LOR.

The Annan Report (1977, pp. 79ff) assesses the claim that media competition has led the BBC to overemphasize professionalism and audience numbers and diagnoses a definite shift from 'public service broadcasting'. The adoption of streamed programming is criticized because it led the audience to confine itself to particular channels and programmes instead of making use of the diversity available. Although programmes on each channel 'trailed' themselves, they insufficiently trailed each other. The Report also concludes that local radio would be better off in the hands of its own institution instead of being an 'appendix' to the commercial broadcasting authority and the BBC.

As far as the BBC is concerned, these criticisms, and the recommendations derived from them, amount to assigning it a more national role. It would be deprived of local radio, regional television would be given to commercial television, and the BBC would be expected to 're-endorse' public service broadcasting as its ideal. There is no room to assess the validity and usefulness of the proposals, and the 1980 Broadcasting Act does not in any case directly implement the recommendations of the Annan Report. However, the Act does legislate for changes which are likely to alter the frame of LOR. These changes will have to be considered in subsequent analyses.

Having mapped the areas of the changing domain of radio which are relevant for LOR, I can now consider (1) selection and codification, (2) their implementation or scope and (3) the sociolinguistic and social assumptions underlying both. It will be seen that while LOR has always been closely connected with (upper-) middle-class attitudes, neither LOR as speech practice nor LOR as a set of normative ideas has ever been homogeneous. Codification occurs within the standard or prestige variety.

### One best way

In phases I and II there was a strong tendency towards conformity in programme presentation, including LOR, and the exclusive use of Received Pronunciation (RP).

Conformity was the undisputed goal as early as 1924, when Captain Eckersley, Director of Programmes, wrote to all station managers of the Company: 'I think a standard form of announcing should be adopted...There should be a best way, and while one does not want to be dogmatic, I think uniformity would be a good idea.' By 1926, concrete steps were taken to achieve this even within the accepted range of variation of RP. The formation of the so-called Advisory Committee on Spoken English (ACSE), which included amongst others R. Bridges, G. B. Shaw and L. Pearsall Smith representing the Society for Pure English, and the phoneticians Lloyd James (Honorary Secretary and later also Linguistic Adviser to the BBC), D. Jones, H. Wyld and H. Orton, must be seen in this light. The decisive motivation for it is clearly formulated by John Reith in the preface to *Broadcast English* (BBC 1928): 'There has been no attempt to establish a uniform spoken language, but it seemed desirable to adopt uniformity of principle and uniformity of pronunciation to be observed by Announcers with respect of doubtful words.'[7] But codification within RP and its selection are separate aspects of conformity.

Selection was never widely discussed. RP became established because the BBC was run by members of the upper middle and upper classes who were either RP speakers themselves or speakers of one of the so-called national accents, i.e. Scottish, Welsh and Irish. The BBC also only employed speakers of RP as announcers. Most of them had attended one of the public schools, the universities of Oxford or Cambridge, or had followed an army career. RP thus became the 'natural' way to communicate, helping to conceal the unspoken assumptions.

RP was a non-regional prestige accent with an exclusive social basis in the above-mentioned social classes. It was used in practically all public domains, including education, law and the Church, and it was the natural accent for reading texts written in Standard English. As radio was a means by which many could be addressed by few simultaneously, and announcing was defined as a public function[8] — which, in the early days, consisted in reading Standard English texts — it was not surprising that RP was to extend its functions to this new form of communication. The fact that, from 1926, the BBC was a national medium strengthened its position further. It was widely accepted, although never proven empirically, that RP was better understood in Britain than any other accent and that it was the only socially appropriate accent for radio. Lloyd James had expressed this view in a talk to announcers as early as 1925: 'taken over the whole of the British Isles, there are many dialects, and usually one that causes less offence to the majority than others.'[9] It would seem then that from a sociolinguistic point of view RP was an adequate choice. However, there were other important reasons for it.

It was believed that the overall objectives of the BBC, and the educational intent in particular, required the choice of RP. There is no clear-cut evidence to this effect, but it may safely be assumed that the attitudes about codification within RP carried over to radio.

The Director of Programmes commented on one of Lloyd James's talks in 1924: 'We are daily establishing in the minds of the public the ideas of what correct speech should be. This is such an important responsibility.' Pointing in a similar direction are the recommendations of the Crawford Committee:

That the claims of those listeners who desire a larger proportion of educational matter, though relatively few in number, should, if possible, be met.

That every effort should be made to raise the standard of style and performance in every phase of broadcasting and particularly in music.

One can infer that RP was considered an appropriate vehicle for the BBC's objectives. Its position was further reinforced by a quite different view held by sections of the middle class who were aware of social inequality and felt that accent was one of the prime factors which stabilized and perpetuated class barriers and put the lower classes at a disadvantage. The proposed remedy was to 'unteach' the younger generation particularly stigmatized features, like the dropping of /l/ in preconsonantal position, as in 'field', the hypercorrect use of /h/ in for example 'Oxford', or the use of the intrusive /r/, as in 'Shah of Persia'. It was hoped that the socially and regionally marked accents would ultimately come closer to RP. This was the prime motivation for a language course, entitled *King's English*, that Lloyd James produced in collaboration with the firm Linguaphone and which was broadcast by the BBC to over 130 schools throughout England but not in Scotland. Lloyd James's final evaluation is summed up in the *Manchester Guardian* of 15 December 1932 as follows:

The case for such attempts to level up pronunciation, as put by Mr. Lloyd James, is that it is the business of the State education to remove improper, or at any rate socially unpopular, forms of speech behaviour, because this is in practice an obstacle to getting on in the world. 'You cannot raise social standards without raising speech standards', he says...

It is clear that the BBC was considered an important medium for propagating the 'desirable' forms of speech. This sociopolitical attitude is not only in latent conflict with the above-mentioned one, but also with the proclaimed descriptive orientation of Lloyd James's phonetic research. There is no indication that this conflict was felt at all.

A third reason for the choice of RP, and for a particular style within it, emanates from the BBC's goals and the requirement to be impartial. Announcing was to be done in an impersonal manner to ensure that the announcer did not intrude between the word and the audience. Lloyd James expressed this policy clearly in a discussion reprinted in the *Listener* of 2 March 1939:

For better or for worse this Corporation's policy is to remove the man [i.e. the announcer] as much as possible, in spite of the fact that other broadcasting corporations throughout the world have decided that personality is the great factor in broadcasting. These are two great conflicting policies in the use of speech for broadcasting in the world today, either sober recital or emotional reaction. It is my conviction that the British Broadcasting Corporation is right in its policy.

Speech was intended to convey the Corporation's authority, it was to translate the demand for impartiality, and there is ample evidence that standard or prestige varieties do serve this purpose better than regional accents (Leitner 1980).

As a side-effect, but entirely in line with upper-middle-class attitudes about interpersonal communication, the resultant normative idea of spoken style defined social distance as extremely wide. There was to be no possibility for the audience to identify with the speakers – who, at the time, were not known by their names.[10]

Very little further need be said about codification, as it was guided by closely similar attitudes. The brief of the ACSE was to make recommendations for uniformity within RP. The most important aspects of their work can be summed up as follows:

1   Codification was confined to aspects of word phonology. Sentence phonology, for example the pronunciation of strong and weak forms, was never discussed. At the same time, its principles and decisions had effects on style, and supported the emergence of a slow, formal reading style.

Speech style was, however, discussed by the Artistic Director and Lloyd James as Linguistic Adviser. Both repeatedly emphasized the need for a personal or private approach to the audience, which would have led to a more informal style.[11]

The latent conflict between the ACSE's recommendations and those of the 'practitioners' was never raised, and an investigation of LOR as speech praxis (Leitner 1979, pp. 93ff) demonstrates that it contained aspects of both.

2   Codification with respect to grammar, lexis and usage, i.e. within

Standard English was not deemed necessary, although there are some signs that it was suggested on occasion.

Pearsall Smith, who represented the Society for Pure English, repeatedly demanded that the ACSE look into questions of word formation for 'new' concepts: for instance viewers should be called 'onlookers' or 'televiewers'. However, a subcommittee of the ACSE, which was eventually formed in 1936, was soon disbanded because of its too overtly normative tendencies.

Lloyd James had written a memo to the Controller on 12 March 1936 suggesting that the ACSE discuss questions of lexis etc. He concluded that: 'they transcend pronunciation, but in the end resolve themselves *into* [emphasis his] questions of pronunciation, i.e. spoken style.' There is no evidence that his proposal was pursued.[12]

3   The ACSE was strongly attached to the British orthoepic tradition that focused on the prestige variety. Their insistence on the pronunciation of unstressed vowels, on the avoidance of homophones, and the close relationship of speech and writing are clear indications of this.

The scope of LOR was limited to announcers and to 'all people whom you [station managers] employ in the Children's Hour and in station features of this order. As I said before, nothing is to be done with regard to regular speakers in lecture series etc.'[13] Although most of them will have spoken RP, they did not need to conform to the ACSE's advice, and used a more colloquial and informal form of RP.

To sum up. The exclusive use of RP corresponded to, and extended, the then dominant functions of RP. It was associated with the overall objectives of the BBC and class-specific attitudes. In this sense, it was not merely a reflection of the sociolinguistic structure, but a means to various goals, which, although in some conflict with each other, combined to strengthen its position.

Codification was officially limited to a small area of speech behaviour, but this did have important effects on speech style. Again, there were latent conflicts among personnel within the BBC, and the results can be traced in LOR as actual speech behaviour.

The scope of LOR was limited in terms of the BBC's output as a whole, but by virtue of its public prominence it easily overshadowed the remaining areas of the medium.

## Variety within limits

The response to the radically changing media structure in the 1950s and 1960s took shape towards the end of the earlier decade and was gradually implemented under Hugh Greene. It amounted to limited variation and little explicit codification. It led not only to a loosening of the prewar situation but to a number of qualitative changes as well. The new policy on selection, codification and scope can be summarized as follows:

1   The status of RP diminished, although its use was confirmed in several important functions, especially the news. Other modified standard and regional accents became acceptable.
2   Codification in word phonology was restricted to place and proper names and to the anglicization of foreign words. In grammar, lexis and usage, as well as in sentence phonology (speech style), there was a moderate amount of codification.
3   The scope of LOR widened so as to cover a greater amount of the — now more varied — programme output. Non-BBC speakers were, as before, not expected to conform to any of the regulations.

Language behaviour on radio (and, by now, television) was more subject to the factors which govern interpersonal communication, including topic, (intended) relation to the addressee in interviews, setting, time and audience. Above all, the broadcaster's personality became more salient.[14] The following two quotations characterize the situation extremely well:

No attempt has since been made [i.e. since the Second World War] to resuscitate the former policy of strict conformity, as it would be out of keeping with educated usage. (BBC 1974, p. 3)[15]

In the early 1960s, the BBC felt that it would be more realistic to throw the stage open to the men behind the scenes, so news men participated personally in news broadcasts, meteorologists gave the weather forecast, policemen enlisted our aid direct from Scotland Yard...This created a greater sense of immediacy between the listener and those at the heart of the event. Naturally, there was no longer insistence on purely southern usage, as these experts are likely to be drawn from all parts of the country. Their prime advantage is that they are informed and articulate on their own subject...At the same time, a more colloquial element has been introduced which has disposed even further of a sense of formality. (BBC 1971a, p. v)

Many of these changes can be understood as BBC broadcasting's gradual adaptation to the rapidly developing media context. The increasing complexity of the BBC itself, the new role of radio as a daytime entertainment and information medium, the growing size and stratification of audiences, competition and interdependence between the media called for a new approach. The changes were, however, also based on a new philosophy of the relationship between broadcasters and the audience. According to Hugh Greene, there can be no proper relationship 'if the language in which they are talking, and the assumptions they are making, seem too remote from the language and assumptions of the audience and the times in which they are communicating' (quoted in Burns 1977, p. 152). In other words, it was not only a question of the adoption of the 'personal policy', but of creating a closer and more symmetrical relationship with the audience. There is significant evidence that this aim met with only partial success (Elliott 1972, p. 18), and it is difficult to see precisely what its translation into language behaviour would have meant.

The quotation about 'throwing the stage open' is interesting in that it sheds some light on how selection, the widening of the accent spectrum, was achieved. It says in fact that much of what had been done by the announcer or newsreader alone in former times could now be split up between various persons, including the newsreader, reporters, the 'weatherman', interviewees and industrial editors. Part of the limited variation of accents was thus obtained through a new policy on scope, the diversification and professionalization of tasks, an increase in the number of speakers and the 'intake' of more outside speakers. They were now selected on the basis of their communicative competence, their ability to express a subject and to broadcast to an audience. As this meant in practice that they spoke predominantly (colloquial and informal) RP or some other educated regional standard, selection was still controlled very tightly.

The widening of the accent spectrum did not imply any substantial change in the social class influence on LOR. The previous quotation indicated that changing attitudes to codification were related to the belief that 'educated usage' no longer required strict conformity. This impression is supported if one takes into account the present social status of RP and its dominant form in BBC broadcasting.

In the prewar period, RP was closely associated with public school education, the term 'public school English' (Wyld 1936, p. 3) being symptomatic of this. However, it has since considerably broadened its social base so that it 'can no longer be said to be the exclusive property of a particular social stratum' (Gimson 1970, p. 85). Recently, it has been suggested that it may even have split into two distinguishable varieties, the older one related to the upper class (and presumably, to the older generation), the other associated with those sections of the middle class that have had some form of tertiary education (Munby 1978, p. 87) and the middle generation (Gimson 1977). It follows that despite the widening of the social spectrum, there is still an identifiable link with the middle and upper social classes.

RP has changed in the course of this process. The older form or 'conservative RP' gave way to the now prevalent 'general RP', which may even show slight regional features.[16] It is the form in general use on the BBC of today.

These two pieces of sociolinguistic evidence show that LOR is still largely influenced by (some sections of) the middle class. Both the widening of the accent spectrum and the restriction of codification to names and foreign words, as well as the shift to lexis, grammar and usage, are perfectly compatible with this. A new form of LOR was found that more accurately reflected the prevailing sociolinguistic structure.

Codification was generally left to the institution and the broad casters themselves. It is particularly interesting to note that a limited amount of codification and the continuing attempts to translate the 'new' philosophy into linguistic practice produced two rather conflicting styles of speech. The dissatisfaction with this result is undoubtedly one cause for the present debates about LOR discussed below.

The adoption of the personal approach, the attempt to create a more symmetric relationship with the audience and the new policy on scope combined to favour the emergence of more informal and colloquial, even personal, styles of RP. They were not only to narrow the social distance between broadcaster and audience — according to the type of programme and channel — but also to allow a certain amount of empathy between them. They were, so to speak, 'audience-related'. However, the interaction of these with certain other factors, especially competition between the institutions for audiences and the tendency to translate the assumed importance of events, decisions and the like into stress in speech, produced a more dramatic '(speaker-)topic-related' style.

Both styles show similar phonetic qualities: a great number of elisions, assimilations, weak forms. Although there is too little research on styles, it appears that they differ markedly in some para-linguistic and prosodic properties, for example in voice quality and speech rhythm. These features regularly occur in different contexts. Thus, the 'topic-related' style is common among reporters, the 'audience-related' one among newsreaders.[17]

To sum up. Despite significant changes with regard to selection, codification and scope, the dominant social influence has remained unchanged. LOR has changed with it and adapted to it.

LOR has, however, also adapted to the more complex media context and the new demands made of radio. New forms of LOR have emerged, including the use of styles deemed appropriate for the younger generation and the deliberate variation of style between different channels. As in phase II, the heterogeneity of LOR con-tinued to mirror contradictory interpretations of a single philosophy within a complex and changing context.

### The search for standards

The background to the recent inquiry into the BBC's use of English (Burchfield *et al.* 1979) and the concomitant debates consists of two converging developments: first, the discussions of the future of British broadcasting which followed on the report of Lord Annan's committee (1977) and, second, the growing interest in, and criticisms of, media language and its 'ideological use'. Even the Annan Report found it necessary to go into aspects of language and reality (1977, pp. 276ff).[18]

The criticisms of the retired BBC announcer, Alvar Liddell, helped to provoke the inquiry. He claimed in the *Listener* of 5 April 1979 that the BBC's news reading on radio and television was charac-terized by 'widespread distortion, an endemic disease arising from insinuation and implication', and he criticized the BBC for neglecting to ensure proper training and continuous monitoring of its staff. He called for a 'specialized unit of staff training, concerned with seman-tics' and continued: 'readers should be taught to discern and stick to the *facts* [emphasis his], and to avoid shaded, argumentative or opinionated inflexions, unless the need for them is present in the writing'.[19]

What is new in comparison with the work of the ACSE, and what may explain the extremely sensitive reaction of the BBC, is the fact that Liddell phrases his criticisms in terms of 'semantics'. This might suggest that the root problems have to do with language, its relation to reality and ideology, but it is not entirely clear whether this was really meant. Most of his arguments fit perfectly the old orthoepic tradition, and this is the aspect which was taken up immediately by the public. Typical responses were:

If the BBC is not to set standards, who is? (*Listener*, 3 May 1979)

It seems to me that the BBC has a clear duty to uphold the standards of spoken English...(Timothy in Burchfield *et al*. 1979)

The continuing discussion is ill-structured and rather confusing. I will attempt to highlight the most important lines of argument and set them against the background of likely developments in the BBC's role within the context of the media generally.

The question of selection is hardly touched upon and left 'to those who are informed on the subject' (Burchfield *et al*. 1979, p. 18). If accents are referred to at all, it is terms of aesthetic judgements. The quality and naturalness of the accents used may be a source of disagreement, but they are generally accepted in some contexts, including regional programmes and weather forecasts.

However, one line of reasoning goes far beyond this. It rejects all or some of the styles of RP on the BBC as unnatural, and derives from this a claim for regional accents, and northern ones in particular, because they are 'more vigorous' or 'closer to the soil'.[20] This kind of regional orthoepism, probably linked to sections of the educated middle class in some regions, had already made itself heard before the Second World War. Thompson, who is described as a 'champion of regional culture from Lancashire' in the *Listener* of 2 March 1939, had argued against the BBC's Oxford English: 'To my thinking, there is a suggestion of class standard about modern pronunciation that the announcers use. The Oxford accent is the hallmark of a class.' He saw class associations not only in pronunciation but also in lexis and style, and concluded that northern accents would be much more genuine. The re-emergence of this regional, dialect-based orthoepism is interesting, but its influence will, in view of the generally accepted national/local dichotomy in broadcasting, be minimal.

With regard to codification, the BBC continues to be blamed for errors in pronunciation, lexis and grammar, but these are insignificant compared with the problems of speech style, which now covers all areas of language structure. The BBC inquiry rates the overall performance as good, but singles out three kinds of style for criticism: the 'over-refined' style heard on occasion on Radio 3;

the dramatic, 'topic-related' one common with reporters, but not exclusively used by them; and the style of disc jockeys in programmes intended for the younger generation, mainly on Radio 1 and Radio 2. There are numerous reasons why these are considered unsatisfactory but there is repeated mention of the 'intrusion of personality':

The abuse of speech...mainly arises from the intrusions of 'personality', verbal gestures designed to render the speaker memorable.

...what mars this service [Radio 3] is a kind of strangulated utterance that creeps in from time to time...I have not often heard an announcer on Radio 3 who sounded happy or cheerful...(Burchfield *et al.* 1979, pp. 18, 22)

Competition between channels or between broadcasters and the objectives of particular channels are said to help account for these stylistic features. They are symptomatic of the increasing difficulty broadcasters have in defining their role in relation to topics and audiences.

The stylistic criticisms and the arguments which are used continue to be based on social assumptions linked with traditional middle-class and middle-generation attitudes. Criticism of the 'over-refined' style deliberately rejects the 'highbrow', elitist tradition. The criticisms of reporting and disc jockey styles can, although they need not necessarily, be interpreted as criticism of the personal approach and of Hugh Greene's attempt to close the distance between the medium and the audience.[21]

If one considers the social basis for the unquestioned acceptance of RP, strong associations with traditional, conservative, middle-class values become apparent. Although variety in speech style is considered important — and broadcasters generally accept the implications of streamed programming for LOR — this variety is measured from the baseline of southern educated usage. The language of radio should avoid 'the fashion of the day' and 'slow down linguistic change' (Burchfield *et al.* 1979, p. 18).

It is by no means clear what these recommendations would mean in speech practice, but the attitudes correlate well with those expressed by Lloyd James and John Reith. Lloyd James had condemned 'affectation and pedantry' in whichever class it was found and advocated 'the current usage of educated speakers'. (BBC 1928, pp. 7, 10). Reith called for a speech that 'would raise the least amount of relevant adverse criticism' (letter to R. Bridges, 9 December 1929).

There is an alternative approach to questions of LOR which deserves to be mentioned. It accepts the need for broadcasting to uphold standards but seeks to ground these standards on functional criteria. It is well put by Quirk (1980, p. 1):

Self-evidently, it is the BBC's first responsibility to ensure that it 'be known what is said', and it is only to this end (and not, for instance, for the sake of language standards *per se*) that the duty to uphold standards of 'Spoken English' arises.

This approach would lead the controversies away from questions of 'appropriateness' as such and relate them to the ease with which the messages can be understood by the audience.[22] It would thus anchor the discussion of language, and its relation to reality and ideology, in the concrete circumstances of listening and viewing.

## Conclusion

It would be premature to estimate the impact of these debates in the longer term. It will be interesting to see which attitudes prevail and which models for LOR will be adopted in view of the likely development of the BBC into a more nationally orientated medium.

This analysis of LOR in the BBC has demonstrated that the selection, codification and scope of radio language is influenced by institutional developments in the domain of radio and by a specific range of sociolinguistic and social attitudes. It is particularly striking to see how the scope of discussion about LOR has widened. In the prewar period it was restricted to aspects of word phonology, style being left to the Artistic Director, whereas today it encompasses practically all levels of language behaviour. The broadening of interest can also be seen in the fact that the problems of language use and ideology are now being aired. In routine decisions about programme presentation on the one hand and lexis and grammar on the other, the tasks of selection and codification are being related to the wider question of broadcasting's role in reflecting, stabilizing and even changing sociolinguistic — and therefore social — structures.

## Notes

1    I am grateful to the BBC's Written and Sound Archives for their continued

help. I am indebted in particular to Miss Cox, Mrs Kavanagh, Miss Jones and Mr Wallach (all BBC).

2   Media differ in the extent to which they can enforce regulations. Quirk (1980, pp. 2ff) draws attention to the fact that the press have the means, if not always the desire, to impose a 'house style' by editing, which is practically impossible for broadcasting media. An important factor is undoubtedly the degree of (in)dependence of the journalist from the institution. Freelance journalists, who work for different media, and prominent figures, are probably more difficult to control than announcers.

3   The German case is related to the fact that the prestige variety in question, the 'deutsche Hochlautung' or 'Bühnenaussprache', was developed out of the language of the stage, cf. Kohler 1970; Leitner 1980.

4   This list differs somewhat from a previous list (Leitner 1980) due to the different orientations. For example, in a prewar context, there was no need for (3c) or (4), whereas it was desirable to separate the additional goals assigned to radio. They were in fact the most important features for the evolution of LOR in Germany and Britain. For detailed studies of the history and development of British broadcasting, see Briggs 1961, 1965; Black 1972; Burns 1977.

5   This policy differs sharply from the one adopted in Germany. Despite powerful transmitters, radio was regionally structured, but subregional and local output always contributed to the regional (cf. Schütte 1971). Obviously this favoured regional accents.

6   Obviously, these structural and philosophical changes were only the frame for a different programme output. The 'response' is another matter (cf. Black 1972). The importance of these responses for LOR, although essential, cannot be investigated here.

7   This group included words of scientific origin and those which permitted alternative pronunciations, e.g. 'towards', 'often', 'zoological', The ACSE had suggested that any tendency towards homophones should be resisted, that weak vowels should be pronounced, etc. See also Leitner 1979, 1980.

8   Lloyd James had expressed this view in an interview in *The Times* of 16 Jan. 1939, quoting from a brochure to announcers:
    'Your voice and meaning...have to be carried only a few feet...This [announcing] is a public function but carried out in a private manner.'

9   This quote comes from the summary of the talk by the Director of Programmes. Elsewhere, Lloyd James takes a slightly different line:
    '...it is quite evident that we are not entitled to conclude that there is *one* standard pronunciation, *one* and *only one* right way of speaking English. There are varieties that are acceptable throughout the country, and others that are not' (emphasis his). (BBC 1928, p. 10)
    This formulation, which is much closer to the prevalent attitude in Germany (cf. Kohler 1970; Leitner 1980), would in fact allow the use of regional accents. But it is the more restrictive one above which succeeded.

10  Social distance relates to the concepts of *face* and *personal preserves*.

Goffman (1971) defines face as 'an image of self delineated in terms of approved social attributes'. Personal preserves include amongst others the conversational preserve and the information preserve. If these are defined widely, as is common among the upper middle class, then greater care must be taken not to infringe. If this is translated into speech behaviour it implies the use of more formal language, distancing address forms, cf. Brown & Gilman 1972.

11 As early as 1924, the Artistic Director said that 'the chief function of the Broadcasting Company, is as I see it, to disseminate Happiness and all those cheerful and invigorating qualities that go to make it up'. Although the Corporation redefined its objectives, this kind of attitude continued. See also note 8.

12 It was again the Artistic Director who most clearly expressed the connection between accent and usage. In a talk to announcers he contrasts: 'Miss Enid Beverly will sing you a group of songs. a) so and so...' with: 'You will all remember, I expect, Miss Beverly. She sang for us six weeks ago...She is now going to sing...' These recommendations are very close to those expressed in prewar Germany (cf. Leitner 1980).

13 Reith in a letter to station managers on 26 July 1926.

14 The switch to the 'personal approach' is much closer to the proclaimed policy in prewar Germany. There are, however, doubts as to how far this was implemented in Germany because there were continuous complaints about the 'Ansagebeamte' (announcers). In any event, the personal approach was interpreted on a *regional* communication pattern, thus favouring regional(ized) accents, whereas, in Britain, this was seen on a *national* (or, for local radio *local*) communication pattern, favouring more informal styles of RP.

15 The ACSE had in fact been dissolved in 1939 and the Pronunciation Unit succeeded it. Its brief was much more limited.

16 To date, there is no satisfactory phonological analysis of both styles. See Sinclair 1978 for examples on cassette.

17 There is very little work on speech styles which is useful here. Most works differentiate either along a generation scale, i.e. old, middle, young generation (Gimson 1970), or along a situation scale, e.g. reading, formal speech, singing, conversation (Jones 1969). This approach is useful in principle, but needs to be made more complex by incorporating factors like 'topic-in-situation' and prosodic and paralinguistic properties. Incidentally, these styles are often referred to as the 'demotic' voice, cf. Quirk 1980, p. 15; Burchfield *et al.* 1979.

18 The Annan Committee denies the claim that there is a bias to the right or towards employers, but they see problems in the way programmes are presented. They mention in particular the tendency to dramatize and to polarize points of view (1977, p. 279). This clearly confirms the importance of LOR.

19 Liddell is one of the most famous surviving newsreaders of the early

BBC. His criticisms are, however, marred by numerous errors. For instance, his belief that the coaching of announcers by Lloyd James translated the 'official' policy directly into practice is not confirmed by the analysis above and in Leitner 1979. He also mistakenly claims that the written word of the press does not intrude between message and reader, cf. Kress & Trew 1978.

20 This view was vehemently but unsuccessfully expressed during a debate at the Edinburgh Festival in 1979. Parts of it were broadcast on BBC Radio 4 under the title 'Words At A Festival' in August 1979.

21 I do not mean to imply here that the criticisms are completely wrong on factual grounds. However, by showing this link it may become apparent where models for a future LOR may be sought.

22 The Glasgow University Media Group (1980, part II) points to the high degree of predictability of news language and claims that this contributes to the creation of 'preferred readings', i.e. interpretations of reality. In other words, a functional interest in selection and codification is very closely related indeed to the interest in receptivity.

# 3

# Dominant discourse: the institutional voice and control of topic

CLAIRE LINDEGREN LERMAN

Language disguises thought...the outward form of the clothing ...is not designed to reveal the form of the body, but for entirely different purposes.

*L. Wittgenstein*

From the very outset we must...use language [*langue*] as the norm of all other manifestations of speech...It [language] is...a collection of necessary conventions that have been adopted by a social body to permit individuals to exercise that faculty [speech].

*F. de Saussure*

Although 'discourse' and 'conversation' are widely discussed in current linguistic writing, we have very limited knowledge about a question which is central to our understanding of the uses of language: How does the abstract *system* of language function in actual language use? — what really happens when people talk, or speak as or for an institution, as they so commonly do? In this paper, I will define a closed system of institutional discourse through two of its main elements, the Institutional Voice and Topic Transformation. These concepts are derived from a deliberately open and pretheoretical analysis of the Judiciary Committee transcripts of the Nixon White House conversations (Lerman 1981), of characteristic functions of language as it is actually used. Through this kind of analysis we can perceive discourse, not through the application of external theory, or the superficial level of 'words', but in terms of its own intrinsic language structures and processes, centring here on distanced identity (who is speaking?) and distanced topic (what is he really talking about?).

### The Institutional Voice and Topic Transformation

A model of the Topic Transformations of the Institutional Voice, a fragment of President Nixon's response to a difficult question, illustrates the form. The questioner asked:

Would it not be better *that you resign* and...*as a private citizen, answer all accusations?*

The Institutional Voice replied:

...and *I* will not be a party to *the destruction of the Presidency of the United States.*[1]

In this and the following examples, emphasis is added to mark significant portions of the text, not to denote intonational stress. The political leader's equation of his policies with 'national security' is a common form through which discussion of the factual basis for public policy is suppressed. Prime Minister Heath's statement about the miners' strike in 1972 is structurally and thematically the same:

I do not believe that we should tolerate anything which undermines [sic] our country and our way of life. And it is our country. (*Guardian*, 27 Feb. 1972)

The Institutional Voice and Topic Transformation are metaphors. But they are metaphors which are based upon and extend my empirical findings of a system of language and interactive structures through which speakers distance themselves from personally responsible 'I' statements (in many forms) and from a given topic, at the sentence level, in spontaneous conversation. The effect of distancing at the discourse level is to create a closed system of discourse, at the sentence level to create a closed utterance, or one in which a significant element is deleted:

John Dean:   Bud Krogh, in his testimony before the Grand Jury, was forced to perjure himself. [by the speaker, John Dean] (US Government Printing Office 1974b, p. 95)[2]

These examples illustrate distancing from self and topic at two very different levels of discourse. In this paper, I want to discuss institutional discourse in terms of these central structures of distancing, to generalize public discourse through its constitutive elements.

What are the general characteristics of the Institutional Voice (IV)? One who speaks in the IV is, like the member of the tribal council, skilled in 'the language game', The IV is a dominant and privileged voice. Its themes and discourse are uniquely its own; they can be stated *only* by one who speaks 'for the nation' or for any institution. Its arguments are unanswerable, both because of the impersonality and uniqueness of its role and voice and because of the structure of its transformed topics, which articulate ritual institutional values.

The Institutional Voice is equally, a constrained voice, trained in 'the priestly language' and limited by its discourse rules and traditions, for which it is the temporary spokesman. As the *selfless* personification of power and tradition, the IV has an inherent claim to virtue, a recurrent theme in its topics. Therefore, the IV uses the language of morality for the discourse of power.

Though I am focusing here on political language, I would include in the term 'institutional discourse' that broad category of language use in which the speaker is a representative of an institution, speaking not as 'I', the personal ego, but as a public identity or role. This includes, but is not limited to, the language of all the professions, such as law, medicine, the military, diplomacy, etc., the language of industry, of any bureaucracy. In some instances — for example, newsreading, or reporting in the media — the 'I' is inherently absent.

I am using the term 'topic' in a distinctive way. In the White House conversations, and I believe, in all serious discourse in real life, 'topic' is a multidimensional matrix of reference to an Underlying Topic (UT), which is rarely present in the surface of the talk. By 'serious' discourse I mean that which concerns topics of personal importance to the speakers. In the Nixon material, whose context is known, the UT is obvious. It is the pre-existing pervasive subject, the given in the discourse, the occasion for the talk. This topic, which may be generalized as the threatened loss of political power, is either so well understood or so threatening and 'unsayable' that explicit statement is consistently avoided.

In the taped conversations of the Watergate crisis, the interrelatedness of all of the events and their hundreds of referents in the talk to the Underlying Topic was perceivable in an objective sense because all of the surface referents co-occur with hesitation and profound disfluency. That is, 'danger statements' are functionally defined by disfluency, in otherwise remarkably fluent speech. These referents to UT concern the events of the Watergate: the Watergate investigations, the criminal acts, the cover-up and individuals or topics related to them.

The schematic topical structure illustrated by the Nixon conversations is then:

| | |
|---|---|
| Underlying Topic (UT) : | the threatened loss of political power. |
| Initial Topic (IT) : | referent to UT, occurring in the talk. |
| Transformed Topic (TT) : | distancing from personal voice to impersonal or Institutional Voice. Shift in topical focus (suppression of IT) to TT. |

Topic may be thought of as the 'psychological subject' fused with the logical subject — not of the sentence, but of the discourse (cf. Halliday 1971, p. 161).

Control of topic by the political leader is as old as the arts of rhetoric, 'the faculty of observing in any given case the available means of persuasion' (Ross 1971). R. Syme provides an historical example of a common, timeless theme, available only to the IV, the voice which personifies the state:

The *bribery of the troops* of the Roman State was coolly *described as the generous investment of a patrimony for the public good*...The higher legality is expressly invoked...namely, that all things advantageous for the State are right and lawful. (Syme 1939, p. 4)

Through Topic Transformation, any specific fact or action and personal reference is suppressed, superseded by the controlling, unanswerable topics of the IV. A new topic, distanced from the UT, distanced also from the personal self, replaces the Initial Topic.

The more complete statement of President Nixon's TT, cited earlier, shows the relationship between IV and TT (figure 1).

This spontaneous statement compresses the major argument of President Nixon's defence in the Watergate crisis which protected his power for almost two years. The charges of his personal criminal malfeasance in office were transformed and interpreted as attacks upon the Constitution and the Presidency. The common 'national security' theme is implicit.

*Figure 1    Topic Transformation through the Institutional Voice*

*Question.* Would it not be better *that you resign...* and [in] the public forum
*as a private citizen, answer all accusations?*

|  | Role | Features |
|---|---|---|
| *President Nixon:* | | |
| The nation and the world need a strong President...* | IV, leader | Institutional Voice |
| Now, personally, I will say... resignation is an easy copout... | Personal, self | Colloquial. Claim of bravery |
| Resignation of *this President†* | IV | Third person self-reference |
| on charges of which *he* is not guilty | IV, judge | IV judges and acquits self |
| would forever change our form of government. It will lead to weak and instable [sic] Presidencies in the future | IV, constitutional authority | Topic Transformation. Claim that IV's retention of office is essential to the strength of the nation |
| and *I* will not be a party to *the destruction of the Presidency† of the United States.* | Ambiguous. IV (+ 'I'?) Protector of Presidency | Charges against IV transformed to abstract issue. Fusion of personal identity with the office |

*Questioner:* Yes, sir.

(US Government Printing Office 1974a, p. 76: Executives' Club of Chicago,
15 March 1974)

* ...Indicates that fillers and asides have been deleted.
† Nominalizations facilitate reference to the self in the third person.

The essential link between the IV and its Topic Transformations is clear. *Only* through the IV can the President refer to himself in the third person as if he were speaking of another, judge and dismiss the charges against himself as insignificant, and define them as a threat 'to the nation and the world'. The Topic Transformation completely suppresses the Initial Topic, the 'accusations' and the resignation. The Transformed Topic dominates and controls the discourse.

Implicit in the TT is the assertion of a new substitute proposition — 'There is an attack upon the Constitution and the Presidency' — and the claim that accusations against the individual President threaten the nation.

Some of the general features of institutional discourse can be noted here:

1  Absence of the individual responsible speaker, 'I'. The inherently fused personal—institutional identity of the IV and the personal 'I', of self and role, are here disjoined. Only the 'selfless' IV can speak for the nation.
2  Topic Transformation and the deletion of the Initial Topic is achieved through the shift to the IV.
3  The direction of the TT is from the particular to the abstract. Such ritual themes are the exclusive prerogative of the IV.
4  The form of statement of the IV is superficially direct.
5  There is a double barrier against response. No responsible individual is speaking, the Initial Topic is suppressed.

In general terms, these features characterize distancing at the sentence level of conversation and at the discourse level, of institutional discourse. President Nixon did not create this style of discourse: it has a venerable history in the defence of any governmental policy. The generic similarity of the examples I cite below to 'the destruction of the Presidency' statement lies in their suppression of the Initial Topic of others, which is defined as a danger and replaced by a 'national security' TT. The statement of Prime Minister Heath, quoted above, went on:

But I talked of a double danger and in many ways the invisible danger is the more worrying...But when violence or the threat of violence [the miners' strike] is used...I can promise you that it will not be tolerated — wherever.it occurs...it is our country. (*Guardian*, 27 Feb. 1972)

Mrs Thatcher's statement in her successful campaign for leadership repeats this common theme:

The reasonable people must deal with the very, very unreasonable people who want to destroy our society. (BBC Radio 4, 2 Apr. 1979)

Its effects in suppression or avoidance of topic are the same as we find at the sentence level. For example:

Dean:    And I think that what *we* will do is *we'll* — /*there'll* be a logical, natural explanation for every single [illegal] transaction. (US Government Printing Office 1974b, p. 42)

Here, the speaker breaks off a beginning of a sentence (/) and shifts from 'we' to an impersonal form, '*there'll*', thus excluding himself from relationship to the topic. This shift produces a statement, not of 'what we will do', but of the result of an unstated action, which is the responsibility of a dummy subject, the impersonal pronoun, 'there'. By distancing himself from the topic, he has *changed* the topic, and describes a future action without an actor.

Through Topic Transformation, the IV asserts the right to define the terms and the level of the discourse, using distancing processes which are built in to the language system, constitutive of discourse. The Institutional Voice, raised in defence of any institution, asserts also 'the higher morality' of its arguments, which are thus insulated in yet another level of non-deniability. These themes are the ritual litany of power; they incorporate fundamental unquestionable values. They may be empty of content, yet evocative. Most importantly, they are unchallengeable. As Maurice Bloch has said:'Formalization is a form of power for the powerful' (1975, Introduction).

*Institutional self-reference: distancing and objectification of self*

The Nixon Conversations provide insight into the way in which identity shifts relate to Transformed Topics in public discourse. Of course, the Nixon case is an extreme one, in which these distancing processes suppressed accusations of crime. However, the structures of the discourse in which defence of personal power was equated with 'protection of the Presidency' are the same as those of any institutional discourse, in which the Underlying Topic is still the defence or retention of personal or political power. The fusion of identities which underlies every use of the governmental 'We' and the linguistic consequences of the 'selfless' IV are transparent and unequivocal in this extreme case.

Overt third-person self-reference (TPSR) is an uncommon characteristic of the Nixon style. It seems an inappropriate usage, especially in spontaneous intimate speech, in which its function is therefore most clearly seen. In talking with his aides President Nixon frequently used his title in referring to himself when discussing dangers to himself, that is, in distancing himself from the Topic:

...But the main thing, of course, is also *the isolation of the President from this.* (US Government Printing Office 1974b, p. 43)

You've got to *put the wagons up around the President* on this particular conversation. (Tape 25 Apr. 1973)

Ah, well, and *that will destroy him...It's his word against the President.* (Tape 25 Apr. 1973)

In most of this usage, he is viewing himself from afar, as the public figure. He is also, as here, speaking of danger and seeking the protection of his aides, not 'selfishly', but for the powerful figure, the President. Reference to the self as the office co-occurs with other forms of distancing: in the first two examples above the verbal action is expressed in metaphor, a common form of distancing from direct statement.

William Safire, a former member of his staff, relates that Richard Nixon used 'RN' for self-reference in his memos to his aides during 1968. He explains this usage:

Nixon came to refer to himself in the third person, not out of any...sense of the royal 'we'. He wrote often *as an observer*, watching 'RN' — himself — ... *handling himself as a kind of property.* (Safire 1975)

Third-person self-reference has many functions in the private talk. Its common usage, in discussing dangers to the President, is as an amulet, evoking the power and virtue of the office, denying the vulnerability of his position. It also directly asserts the loyalty system, the separation of 'the President' from the collective guilt; reminding his aides of their major function, loyalty to 'the President'.

In public, TPSR occurs most commonly in spontaneous speech, in press conferences and question periods, concentrated in difficult sections. The public usage asserts the power and virtue themes. It also distances the man from the situation: in a major speech, marked by first-person accounts of Watergate (the most convincing form for self-defence and justification), the President still made use of the distanced TPSR to describe his own intimate role in the investigation:

...the case was solidly within the criminal justice system pursued personally by the Nation's top professional prosecutor with the active, personal assistance of *the President of the United States*. (US Government Printing Office 1974a, p. 90)

Often, third-person self-reference is used protectively to claim the virtue of the role. As in these examples:

Many people assume that the tapes must incriminate *the President*, or that otherwise *he* would not insist on their privacy. (p. 84)

The basic question at issue today is whether *the President personally* acted improperly in the Watergate matter. (p. 85)

*I* want there to be no question remaining about the fact that *the President* has nothing to hide in this matter. (p. 85)

The tortuous problems of the IV's own perception of identity are illustrated by these peculiar forms of shifting self-reference. Who is the 'I' in this fused-split identity? What does '*the President personally*' mean? From my perspective, these strange forms of self-reference are implicit in the identity structure of the IV, though not usually expressed. In a time of crisis, when a system is disordered, the constitutive rules of the language game are more apparent.

To identify oneself as the institution, rather than the time-limited official, leaps a chasm of reference. Yet, this was the President's defence, and his language foreshadowed his new argument:

I, / but − Again, you really have to *protect the Presidency*, too. That's the point. (US Government Printing Office 1974b, p. 185)

The purpose of this scenario is to *clean the Presidency*. (p. 185)

This private usage expressed the essence of the public Topic Transformation, long before it was stated. The extension of the identity shift, from the individual President to the 'institution', provided a rhetorical sanctuary for the accused man. 'Cleaning the Presidency' (an abstract noun) invokes 'the higher legality' of Syme's Romans. The 'Presidency' arguments illustrate in an extreme form one of the most formidable discourse powers of the IV: *the IV uses the lexicon of morality*, to which it has a privileged claim, *for the discourse of power*.

'Protection of the Presidency' is unquestionably a virtuous theme. The files of President Nixon, subpoenaed for criminal investigation, are 'the files of the Presidency' (US Government Printing Office

1974a, p. 82) and sacrosanct. Through the TT the accused man is cast in a selfless, heroic role:

I also have another *responsibility*. I must think *not of myself*, but *I must also think of future Presidents* of this country, and I am not going to do anything, I am not going to give up to any demand that I believe would *weaken the Presidency of the United States. I will not participate in the destruction of the office of the President of the United States while I am in this office.* (p. 82)

In all such ritual statements the arguments of the IV are non-deniable. Individual identity and Initial Topic have been completely transformed; they are suppressed, deleted from the discourse. In this manner, the IV can transform discussion of any personal policy or action into a defence of a venerated institution.

Yet, the President must speak as 'the leader'. Anyone who writes or speaks with authority — the judge, the scientist, the doctor or any academic scholar — is required by the rules of discourse to speak in the IV of his role, in what may be called 'the priestly language'. Plato's 'noble lie for the public good' blends with a long tradition, summarized in 'A government of laws and not of men', and creates the realistic paradox, by assuming in each IV total selfless dedication (cf. Bok 1978, ch. 12). The valid claim of such language rests on its assumed transcendence of the merely personal: the IV may genuinely authenticate specialized knowledge and the power and responsibility of role. The tension in the Institutional Voice between its covert personal identity and the need to speak with 'selfless' authority is a central problem in the study of dominant discourse.

*The linguistic structures of Topic Transformation:*
*the markers of distancing*

In this section, I want to sketch the data upon which my description of distancing in institutional discourse is based. The linguistic significance of the distancing structures of the IV and TT is that they are an *extension* of empirically derived processes found at the intra-sentence level of spontaneous conversation. The replication and echoing of the same distancing structures in institutional discourse indicates the organic link between basic elements of the language system as it is used, and any level of speech.

'Good' data from speech communities are very difficult to obtain. The Nixon conversations are a unique record of natural language use, not only of spontaneous but of substantive talk (i.e., the speakers are talking about something, the Watergate crisis) among fluent speakers who are very accustomed to speaking together. Further, because of the size and nature of the record, both the developmental and situational context of the conversations were knowable.

Contrast is essential in linguistic analysis; it is through breaks in a customary pattern that we see the basic pattern. In this large, bewildering record of 'how people really talk when they are unobserved', two contrastive patterns emerged: (1) there were sudden breaks in the usual remarkably fluent flow of language and (2) very direct, explicit informative discourse contrasted with large sections in which it was impossible initially to know what the speakers were talking about. These contrastive patterns often co-occur; they were keys to my analysis.

The distancing structures which I describe here represent common, recurrent patterns in the conversations: the examples (see figure 2) represent hundreds of instances of similar usage. The markers of distancing were initially functionally defined; they terminate hesitation and disfluency, as the following exchange illustrates. The President is speaking to his attorney-general, Richard Kleindienst, in a section from a crucial and at times incoherent conversation:

|  | ...Now the point is, on the other hand, uh, that Baker wants − / what it means, / you know, / contacted, / and it really depends, |
| Disfluency | so − ...and so − / and, uh, you know, and I told Baker − I said (unintelligible) |
| Quotation | 'All right, now who do you want to talk to?' And he said, 'Klein- |
| Fluency | dienst,' and I said, 'Fine, he's the man.' And so I left it at that, and so he's, he's running down here − (US Government Printing Office (1974b, p. 153) |

The disfluency of the first section is terminated by the President's quotation of a past conversation, a very indirect form of 'commanding' a dangerous liaison by quoting the past words of Senator Baker.

This kind of resolution of hesitation occurs repeatedly throughout the text, with the markers of distancing functioning to make an indirect statement which is fluent. Of course, the distancing structures can also occur without association to disfluencies.

Figure 2 is a summary description of the markers of distancing identified in the conversations. This study and any analysis of natural speech forces awareness of the many forms of indirection in which we speak, distancing ourselves from our utterance. These are social conventions of language use, a mark of 'sociolinguistic competence'.

*Figure 2* Linguistic forms of distancing from self in utterance

| Form | Example | Comment |
|---|---|---|
| 1 *Nonagentive passive forms.* Suppression of 'I' and of Topic. | President: *You* could, *you* could get a million dollars. And *you* could get it in cash. I, I know *where it could be gotten.* (p. 94) [Compare with the direct form: I know where I could get it.] Dean: Bud Krogh, in his testimony before the Grand Jury, was forced to perjure himself [by Dean]. (p. 95) [Direct form: I forced Bud Krogh to perjure himself.] | These forms are the syntactic paradigms of all distancing and Topic Transformation. The non-agentive passive inverts the order of the direct declarative sentence and deletes its subject. |
| 2 *Nonagentive variants* distance the speaker from explicit statement of Topic. | Dean: He got a million seven dollars, [from whom?] uh, a million seven hundred thousand dollars to be custodian for. That *came down* from New York. It *was placed* in safe deposit boxes there.... The money *was taken* out to California. [by whom?]...(p. 96) ...I assume this was four hundred [thousand] that *went* to Wallace. (p. 97) | Most of these statements are transformations of a direct form: Someone (X): *gave* a million; *placed* it; *took* it; *knows*...etc. Subject-agent (actor) are deleted by use of a dummy impersonal pronoun subject, referring to 'the money', which becomes an '*animate*' subject: 'The money came down....The money went' – transporting itself. Again, the direct form would be: Someone (X) brought or took the money. |
| 3 *Overt revision* to distanced forms. | President: Then I'll repeat the fact that I – as far as the Watergate matter was concerned – there was no knowledge there. (p. 52) | Here, revision suppresses a direct statement: I [didn't know anything about the Watergate matter]. |
| 4 *Shift away from 'we'*, the customary pronoun usage in the conversations. | President: If...the thing blows and they indict Bob [Haldeman] and the rest, Jesus, *you'd* never recover from that, John [Dean]. (p. 106) [In context, this clearly means: *I* would be ruined.] President: *You*, on the money, if YOU need the money, I mean, uh, YOU could get the money. Let's say – Dean: Well, I mean I think WE'RE going – President: What I mean is, YOU could, YOU could get a million dollars. And YOU could get it in cash. I, I know where it could be gotten. [Passive form] (p. 94) | In the complete passage, the President excludes himself from pronoun involvement more than twenty times, in indirectly ordering payment of the blackmail money. |

| | | |
|---|---|---|
| 5 | *Speaking as another. Quotation of others.* Fused identity. Distancing self and utterance from discourse. | President: I shall go forward in a spirit perhaps best summed up a century ago by another President, *when he was being subjected to unmerciful attack. Abraham Lincoln said:* I do the very best I know how – the very best I can. If the end brings me out all right, what is said against me won't amount to anything...' (US Government Printing Office 1974a, p. 91) | The context of this quotation was a a major public speech, denying a subpoena for the Watergate tapes. |
| 6 | *Citation of authority* shields a statement in the talk. Speaking through another's words. Dean quotes his lawyer ('you' refers to Dean). | Dean: Well, my lawyer tells me that, you know, 'Legally, you're in, you're in damn good shape.'<br>President: Is that right?<br>∷ [After guessing what Dean's lawyer had said, the President continued:]<br>Huh? What does he say? (p. 193) | The propositions which are expressed in quotation of another cannot be challenged, they cite the words of another, who is absent. |
| 7 | *Speaking in an automatic figurative register. Metaphor.* (Avoidance of using one's own words.) | President: So forth and so on. And, uh, the, uh, I think, I think that's / Then we've got to, uh, *see what the line is.* Whether *the line is* one of, uh, continuing to, uh, run a, *try to run a total stonewall,* and *take the beat* from that... *In other words,* it would be if, uh, one of the uh, defendants, particularly *Hunt,* of course...might uh, *blow the whistle,* and he, he – / and *his price is pretty high.* but at least, uh, we should, we should *buy the time* on that, uh, *as I pointed out*...(p. 109) | Metaphor obscures meaning, avoids direct statement. Often, as in this example, metaphor and fillers are the only fluent speech in markedly disfluent utterance. Metaphor and fillers are underlined. |
| 8 | *Metaphorical expletives or profanity.* | President: It isn't worth it. It isn't worth it, *damn it.* It isn't worth – / *the bell with it.* What is the situation on your, /uh on the, on the little red box? Did they find *what the bell that,* that is? (p. 5)<br>[Profanity terminates disfluency]<br>President...And, uh, for that reason, I am, uh perfectly willing to uh – *I don't give a spit what happens*...(p. 183 + Tape); | These have the same function as metaphor. They provide an automatic expressive register which says nothing specific, and also an alternative to disfluency. |
| 9 | *Questions resolve disfluency.* They invoke the interactive level, turning the talk away from the speaker, to the other. | President: But that, /and that was,/ then we,/ but that was handled at, /by Mitchell. *Was that true or what the bell happened?* (p. 193) | The distancing markers may co-occur. Here, profanity and question in a single utterance. |

Symbols used in transcriptions:
– the abrupt termination of speech; a longer pause than is indicated by the comma.
/ a failed start of a sentence, and an incomplete form.
[] material not in the transcripts.
∷ a portion of the conversation has been deleted.
[unintelligible] portions of the tape which were not sufficiently clear for transcription.

Italics are added to mark features under discussion.
Page numbers refer to US Government Printing Office 1974b unless otherwise indicated.
Capitalized words indicate approximate intonational stress.

The distinctive feature of the Institutional Voice is that the speaker is virtually 'inanimate' in the terms of traditional grammars; personal identity is replaced by an interchangeable, institutional identity. The distanced IV has a standard repertoire of distanced Transformed Topics.

The immanence of personal reference (the 'I' who is actually speaking) in any speech, however distant, and of topic, however obscured, is essential to my method of analysis. A corollary is that self and topic are always related. Although it is methodologically useful to think of identity and topic as separate elements in order to analyse their variable relationship and dominance patterns, their inseparability is obvious in the analysis. In distancing from self, the speaker distances also from topic, and conversely.

The distancing from self and topic which occurs in these private conversations at the sentence level is replicated in institutional discourse. I am using two terms, 'focusing' and 'Topic Transformation', to differentiate the occurrence of similar, regular processes at the intra-sentence and macro-topic levels of discourse, respectively. The process through which an underlying, unwelcome topic, or its surface referent, is transformed to a distanced topic is the same, despite the level at which it occurs, and despite the variety of syntactic and grammatical discourse structures which may be employed.[3] The process is represented in figure 3.

*Figure 3    The process of focusing and Topic Transformation*

*Initial Difficult Topic*

(Refers to underlying topic. Often in association
with disfluency or pausing)

*Shift*

(Away from self or topic. Shift may take many different forms)

(Intra-sentence level)                          (Macro-discourse level)

*Distanced Form of Utterance*                    *Transformed Topic*

(Change in topical focus                         (Suppression of initial topic,
and/or speaker involvement)                      of speaker identification with
                                                 topic, or both)

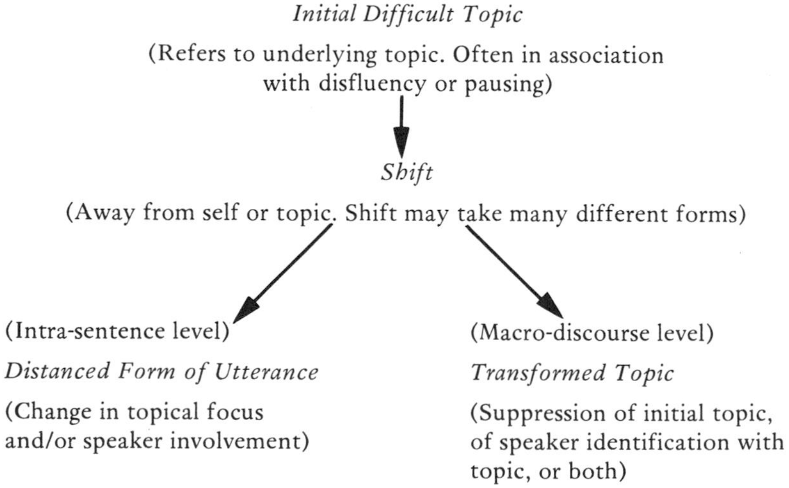

### The Institutional Voice: the Topic Transformation
### of 'the Presidency'

The public discourse of President Nixon concerning the Watergate affair shows the way in which the basic elements of distancing from personal identity and topic are expressed in institutional discourse. It is a particularly clear example of the closed structure of the customary themes of institutional discourse: through the arguments of the IV, the accused individual man protected his personal power in an unchallengeable system of Topic Transformations.

The themes of the President's defence are those which 'come with the office', in which national policy is traditionally justified. The network of TTs which shielded the President from any factual charge and the structural relationships in this discourse system are shown in figure 4.

In all of the examples I cite here, the Initial Topic (charges of criminal acts) is suppressed, transformed through the identity shift to 'the President'. Thus, the IV could defend suppression of evidence as a doctrine 'inherent in the Presidency' which he must follow because of his 'Constitutional responsibility to defend this principle' (US Government Printing Office 1974a, p. 90).

In a process analogous to quotation, citing 'history', the President invoked 'the Jefferson rule', in refusing to supply 'the documents of my Presidency', saying:

Now why did Jefferson do that? Jefferson didn't do that to protect Jefferson. He did that to protect the Presidency. And that is exactly what I will do. (p. 66)

When impeachment threatened, he proffered as evidence of his innocence a 1200-page bowdlerized set of transcripts, edited by himself, defining it as 'all the evidence needed to get Watergate behind us'.

Everything that is relevant is included...The facts are there...To anyone who reads his way through this mass of materials I have provided, it will be totally, abundantly clear that as far as the President's role with regard to Watergate is concerned, the entire story is there. (p. 90)

The 'defence of the Presidency' argument was elaborated into

*Figure 4    Structural features of Topic Transformation
in the Watergate discourse*

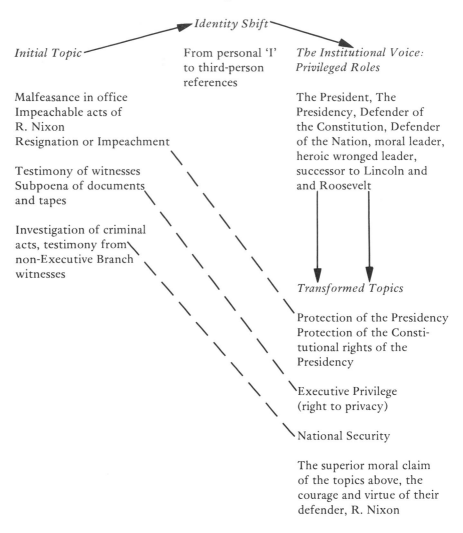

the necessary identity shift, through which topic is transformed. Only the Institutional Voice can formulate the Transformed Topics.

the relationship between Initial Topic and Transformed Topic, in general. However, they are interchangeably applicable.

many sub-topics; it was unanswerable. In speaking to his aide, John Ehrlichman, another voice discusses 'the Jefferson rule':

You should have the most godawful gobbledygook answer prepared. Just put it out, on executive privilege. Something that will allow us to do everything that we want. (National Archive Transcript Tape 845B)

In his Statement on Executive Privilege, he defined the doctrine broadly, to organically cover all of his staff, who were also implicated in crimes:

The manner in which the President personally exercises his assigned executive powers is not subject to questioning...members of his staff [should] not be so questioned, for their roles are in effect an *extension of the Presidency*. (US Government Printing Office 1974a, p. 6)

While evidence and witnesses were shielded from investigation by executive privilege, charges of crime were transformed to the topic-doctrine of *national security*. Where the doctrine is first applied, the rationale for ordering that the FBI stop the Watergate investigation is implicitly self-protection through 'national security':

President: Just tell him [CIA official] ...it would be a fiasco. It would make the CIA look bad...it is likely to blow the whole Bay of Pigs thing, which we think would be very unfortunate — both for the CIA and for the country...and for American foreign policy. (Tape 23 June 1972)

The President's arguments around the TT (distanced from the underlying facts, now suppressed) were reasoned and effective. He discussed his duty to protect national security.

These are difficult questions and reasonable and patriotic men and women may differ on how they should be answered...the Supreme Court said that implicit in the President's Constitutional duty is 'the power to protect our Government against those who would subvert or overthrow it.' (US Government Printing Office 1974, p. 37)

and gave assurances that his power would be honourably used:

I don't mean that we are going to throw the cloak of national security over something because we are guilty of something...where the national security would be disserved by having an investigation, the President has the responsibility to protect it and I am going to do so. (p. 37)

In the private conversations, the arguments are pragmatic. In discussing Howard Hunt's (the organizer of the Watergate burglary) threat to reveal the 'seedy things' he had done for the White House ('that' and 'it', in the text below), they construct an account:

President:     What is the answer on *that*? How do you keep *that* out?...Well, we can't keep *it* out if Hunt — if — ...
Dean:          You might, you might put *it* on a national security ground, basis, which *it* really, *it* was.
Dean:          Well, then the question is, why didn't the CIA *do it* or why didn't the FBI *do it*?
President:     Neither could be trusted...You see, with the Bundy thing and everything coming out, *the whole thing* was national security.
Dean:          I think we can probably get, get by on *that*. (US Government Printing Office 1974b, p. 112)

The Transformed Topics are interchangeable. In publicly explaining his private order to the Watergate Prosecutor not to investigate Howard Hunt or other illegal activities, the President said:

I was gravely concerned that other activities...of the Unit might be disclosed, because I knew that this could seriously injure national security...This is why I exercised executive privilege...(US Government Printing Office 1974a, p. 42)

The Watergate discourse reveals the potency and the unlimited applicability of the conventional themes of institutional discourse, which centre on the protection of the institution. The presumption of virtue inheres in Nixon's powerful role, providing another level of distanced topics. As the moral leader of the nation, the President defines political morality. He could deplore 'wallowing in Watergate', promise 'a new level of decency and integrity in America' (p. 37) and ask those who 'share my belief in these great goals' to give:

Your help to ensure that those who would exploit Watergate to keep us from doing what we were elected to do, will not succeed. (p. 39)

He could restate the moral themes of his administration:

...some of my goals for my second term as President...'To establish a climate of decency, and civility, in which each person respects...the dignity and God-given rights of his neighbor'. (p. 39)

and his fidelity to his Presidential responsibility:

These are great goals and I would not be true to your trust if I let myself be turned aside from achieving those goals [by the Watergate scandal]. (p. 39)

The role of the righteous, responsible leader provides privileged themes, uniquely available to the IV. They are the complement of the covert 'national security' Topic Transformations, asserting 'the higher morality' of power and office.

Through this network of Topic Transformations, an entirely new discourse was created at the institutional level. Its constitutional arguments could be answered, if at all, only by the judiciary. Although the legal charges of criminal acts and abuse of power grew, and could not be effectively suppressed, they were irrelevant to the 'Presidency' themes. Two antithetical streams of discourse coexisted, defining crisis. When all of his close associates had resigned under criminal charges and demands for his resignation grew, President Nixon was asked: 'Is there any limitation on the President...to compel the production of evidence of a criminal nature?' The IV, who stood at the fulcrum of the public opinion network, replied: 'The limitation on the President...is, of course, the limitation of public opinion' (Tape, News Conference 22 Aug. 1973).

### Controlling topics in political discourse

The Topic Transformations of the Watergate discourse exemplify the major themes which are available only to the Institutional Voice (and to any IV) speaking as or for its institution. These topics constitute a closed interchangeable network (which can be thought of as a circle). The examples of Topic Transformation in this section rest upon the same basic tenet of institutional discourse, the primacy of the institution, and its corollaries, summarized in figure 5.

The power of the IV derives from its unique position in this discourse system, in which the personal 'I' and the Initial or Underlying Topic are absent, distanced. At every juncture of this topical network that IV has the right to define the topics of 'others' within this conceptual framework, and thus to suppress their topics. While it is the legitimate responsibility of the IV to balance the views of a single group in terms of the larger community, underlying this power in democratic tradition is the assumption and the claim that the 'national security' arguments will not be used to suppress discussion or to obscure failure of policy.

*Figure 5    The Topic Transformations of the Institutional Voice*

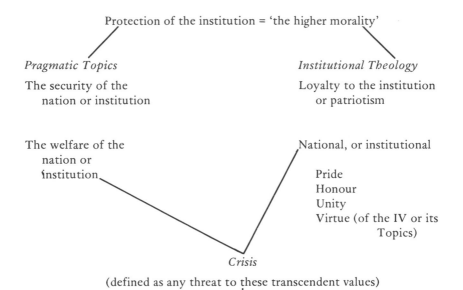

The primacy of the institution

Protection of the institution = 'the higher morality'

*Pragmatic Topics*                          *Institutional Theology*

The security of the                         Loyalty to the institution
   nation or institution                       or patriotism

The welfare of the                          National, or institutional
   nation or
   institution                                  Pride
                                               Honour
                                               Unity
                                               Virtue (of the IV or its
                                                    Topics)

*Crisis*

(defined as any threat to these transcendent values)

*Fear*

(of those who are defined by the IV as threatening institutional values;
the external enemy, the radicals or dissidents within)

*Protection of the Institution*

The controlling Topics are routine and conventional in the daily messages of the IVs. Whether the Initial Topic is malfeasance in office, a strike, a riot, the remarks of a political opponent, the seizure of an embassy, or nuclear weapons policy, the Controlling Topics are applied and prevail. They preclude substantive discussion of any issue: 'Defence' and a policy of 'nuclear balance' *are* national security. Discussion of economic policies is transformed to 'the theology of monetarism', as Norman St John Stevas has termed it, which promises the restoration of national greatness. Under this topic, the wage demands of unions are interpreted as dangerous.

Mrs Thatcher:    The Civil Service Union is putting personal gain before the
                 safety of the realm. (BBC TV 2, 12 Apr. 1981)

Political change in the Third World or Latin America is discussed
in terms of the threat of Communist hegemony, and as a danger
to the 'Free World'. In political campaigns, not 'issues' but fear of
the victory of the other party is often a dominant theme. The
rhetoric, as well as the conceptual categories, of the political campaign or of war dominates in the language of leadership. Topic
Transformations dominate the discourse, silencing factual discussion
of issues.

In this section, I will sketch brief examples of some of the themes
of the 'TT' process, necessarily removed from their context, to give a
view of the minutiae of the form.

*Fragmentation of topic* is a major element in the process, shifting
the focus to a single element of a larger whole, such as the seizure of
the American Embassy in Iran, the hostage crisis, as the sole issue in
the long history of US—Iranian relations. Similarly, in England, the
focus on IRA terrorism (and its sub-topics) obscures an even longer
history. Such restricted topical focus excludes the topics, the voices,
and the realities of 'the others', presenting any topic as *sui generis*,
having no antecedent history. During 1980, focus on the hostage
issue in the US media was matched by the discussion of US—Russian
relations after the Soviet invasion of Afghanistan, solely in terms
of the boycott of the Olympic Games. This topic extended international relations to the sports news. In Britain, fragmentation of
topic occurred in a similar way, as Mrs Thatcher's remarks in an
interview illustrate:

But, you know there is *Total* Control of News in Soviet Russia…If the athletes
to go Moscow…Moscow will *Use* it to say: '*Look*, we marched into Afghanistan
and the world comes to honour us in Moscow.'…What Else does she [USSR]
have to do before *Our* athletes, who enjoy *Freedom* say: 'We Cannot Go to this
country'? (Tape, BBC Radio 4, 4 April 1980)

(In the transcript of this interview — see also p. 97, and the interview on p. 99 — initial capitals and capitalized words indicate
approximate intonational stress. Arrows above mark each new
topical shift.)

The hostage crisis was dramatized by the American President's refusal on 'moral' grounds to campaign 'until our hostages are safe'. An NBC reporter reflected the general view:

The crisis are a cocoon that has restored his Presidency. He is a more forceful man than I have seen before. (14 Feb. 1980)

In the crisis, two Underlying Topics were suppressed: (1) the facts concerning the failure of US policy in Iran, or any facts relating to American foreign policy; (2) the Presidential election campaign, in which Carter had not been a strong candidate. During the crises, he experienced a great increase in popularity. 'Jimmy' became 'the Presidency', 'Our Commander-in-Chief'.[4] Although the circumstances were very different, the structure of the discourse was identical to that of the Watergate.

*The loyalty network of the Institutional Voices* is evident when one of them fails; a dramatic failure was President Carter's secret rescue mission to Iran. A chorus of protective sympathetic IVs shifted the topic. Writing of the abortive rescue attempt, a distinguished American columnist, Anthony Lewis, commented:

Americans will want to draw together with their President in such a time of trouble, and he is entitled to *sympathy...* [there is] *cause for concern about U.S. engineering and military maintenance, not political wisdom.* (*International Herald Tribune*, 29 Apr. 1980)

Although Mr Lewis's shift in focus is an absurd triviliazation, the sentiment is representative of the IV response. On the same day the London *Times* editorial headlined: NO TIME FOR RECRIMI-NATIONS, and the *International Herald Tribune* announced: 'The EEC foreign ministers have displayed wisdom and courage in standing by Mr Carter.' Secretary of State Vance resigned over the issue. However, he declined to discuss his reasons 'because it would contribute to dissension' and his resignation was discussed from the same perspective:

...Vance's resignation is unfortunate. It contributes to *the damaging impression* that after the failed rescue operation in Iran, the Carter administration is begin-ning to collapse. (*International Herald Tribune*, 29 Apr. 1980)

*Public opinion.* Mrs Thatcher, in an interview, denied the widely bruited view that President Carter's attempt to rescue the American hostages in Iran might have been related to the election campaign:

...it wasn't the election; it was the American People getting restless. And, indeed, if you look at the press and the media, that was very much so. And he felt, therefore, that he had, perhaps, to DO something, in response to AMERICAN OPINION. That's quite a different and much DEEPER thing, than any Election... (Tape, BBC Radio 4 Interview, 4 May 1980)

She went on to define the issue in terms of the humanity and power of the United States, invoking international law, modifying it to 'convention':

We have to make it Clear that there is a Difference between a rescue attempt and ...military intervention...to try to get out your Own People, who've been held contrary to Every International Law AND custom AND humanity...your Own people, who've been illegally held, flouting Every international convention, is quite different.

In the further development of the argument, responsibility for the President's action is shifted to his country (i.e. President Carter is equated with the United States):

...a very very Powerful nation being restrained for SIX MONTHS, for SIX months and I cannot blame a COUNTRY for trying to rescue its own people.

In this statement, we find the same shift in focus and suppression of subject, and its replacement by a dummy subject, which characterizes many of the markers of distancing at the sentence level. Note that President Carter is not mentioned by name. Responsibility for his actions shifts from the election (denied) to 'the people', to 'American opinion' and finally, to 'the country'. Each assertion justifies the President's action as virtuous.

The public opinion argument is an auxiliary Topic Transformation which can be applied anywhere in the TT network by the IV, who creates and interprets public opinion. The circularity of the public opinion argument is stated by Mrs Thatcher, in the same interview:

Interviewer:    Would public opinion push you into doing something...against your better judgement?
Mrs Thatcher:   ...Uh, [pause] no, [pause] I would hope always that we could *lead public opinion into the paths that we thought were right.*

It asserts a claim to virtue, whether the IV follows it, or resists it.

*Fear* is an immanent theme in the network of Controlling Topics.

The defence discourse is based on fear of the enemy, buttressed by fear of those who do not concur in the topics of the IV. In political campaigns, fear of the victory of the other party is a significant theme:

President Carter:    In this election, the American people will choose whether we have peace or war. (*International Herald Tribune*, 26 Sept. 1980)

This simple statement is an exponential Topic Transformation. Underlying it is fear of the external enemy. It implies 'My defence policy means peace' and 'Reagan's defence policy means war.'

The crises of 1980 effectively eliminated President Carter's Democratic primary opponents. When the strongest of them suggested that the government might have to negotiate with the Iranians, Carter replied: 'Senator Kennedy is threatening the nation and national unity with his criticism' (press conference, 14 Feb. 1980).

Implicit in all of the Controlling Topics is 'the higher morality' of the institutional values they assert, and the 'danger' of those who challenge them. Those who 'threaten the nation' are to be feared themselves, and ostracized. Fear of violating the rules of the discourse, knowing 'what can and *cannot* be said', protects the Transformed Topics.[5] In a British parliamentary debate on defence, when a Labour MP challenged government policy on the Trident missile, the Secretary of State, Mr Julian Amory, replied: 'Mr John's speech has repudiated years of the Labour Party's fine patriotic record on defence (Tape, BBC Radio 4, 2 Mar. 1981). Thus the TT is protected from open discussion by impugning those who challenge Controlling Topics as unpatriotic, and as dangerous.

*The power to define* those who challenge Controlling Topics is essential to the maintenance of the closed discourse system. Defining the issues of the other as a threat to national values suppresses the topics of the others, and articulates a skewed and unequal discourse in which those who are already so defined by the IV are either silenced or have a limited right to respond, within the frames of reference of the IV.

At the end of the miners' strike in Britain in 1972, Prime Minister Heath made a speech which is a classic in indirection. Denying that anyone had 'won', he described the miners' 'victory' as 'a double danger' and an 'invisible danger'. He began by defining the polity:

There is only 'us' — all of us...We expect sensible men and women to come to sensible decisions. But...not by force...It challenges what most of us consider to be the right way of doing things...and I can promise you that it will not be tolerated — wherever it occurs. (*Guardian*, 27 Feb. 1972)

In this extremely oblique speech, the exclusion and threat to those who are defined as not 'sensible' is clear. This form of speech suppresses any discussion of the events which had recently occurred, or of the miners' issues, replacing them with a statement of moral judgement.

In a radio interview, Mrs Thatcher defined the relationship of trade unions to the nation, and developing the theme, defined 'the militants' in the unions as the element lacking patriotism:

I'm not afraid of the trade unions [breath] which carry out the True ideal of trade unions, which is to get a Fair return for their members...and to help to raise the prosperity of this country.

Because the FACT IS that the only group of people in this country who are above the law in some respects Is the trade unions.

...Indeed the majority of them [trade union members] don't like it. We want to reduce the power of *the militants* in the trade unions to use the unions to THEIR advantage, and not to the advantage of the country. (Tape, BBC Radio 4, 17 Apr. 1980)

The Institutional Voice has the right and the responsibility to define and interpret complex issues in a manner which will be widely understood. In fact, the traditions of institutional discourse, of which the IV is the legatee, facilitate protection of the closed discourse system. Exclusion of those who challenge it from the pluralistic whole is common, as many of the examples above illustrate. Only the IV can define the terms of the discourse and claim the virtue of being the defender of the institution.

The Institutional Voice, distanced from personal self and accessible topic, is not speaking *with* the publics it addresses; it is, rather, engaged in a ritual soliloquy.

## The Institutional Voice of the media

I have been describing the political Institutional Voice in isolation, hoping to clarify the relationship of its structure to its discourse. But, of course, it does not exist in isolation; it speaks with and for a community of Institutional Voices, whose qualities are essentially the same, with one notable exception — the media IV. (Here I am using the term 'media' to apply to radio and television in the US and Britain.) The unique structural quality of the Media IV, in the crucial area of personal identity, is that it claims to have *none*. This claim is most strongly asserted in relation to its major function, the value-free reporting of the facts and analysis of the news.

The Media IV may be thought of as a pure case of the Institutional Voice. The constraints on those who present or comment on the news are obvious: a vast, heterogeneous audience and a discourse tradition which overtly governs what it may say. These constraints are those of any IV, restricting what it is possible to say; in general, formalization and constraint of discourse varies with the size and diversity of the audience. Further, the individual media IV is selected as an image of the institution; even the tone and dialect of its speech are regulated (cf. Leitner, this volume).

The normative function of the media is expressed in many of the BBC publications:

The BBC takes it for granted that the parliamentary democracy evolved in this country is a work of national genius to be upheld and preserved. The BBC's primary constitutional role is that of a supplier of new and true information...a newspaper has a point of view and a place of its own in the political spectrum. The BBC has none. (BBC 1976, p. 10)

A BBC Guide describes the relationship of the individual to the institution, even those who speak with a façade of individuality, such as news commentators:

Presenters, commentators, news correspondents, current affairs reporters and newsreaders have one thing in common. They are all in various ways the voice of the BBC. Each of them, for as long as he is on the screen or behind the microphone, is the BBC. (BBC 1971b).

Thus, the characteristics of the Institutional Voice are exaggerated in the Media IV, crucially in the area of identity. This IV, like its political affine, speaks for the society, from which it stands apart. It speaks with neutral authority.[6] But it has no personal identity, no overt message. Its task, in the transmission of the messages of other IVs, is to supply 'new and true information'. The Media IV speaks with anonymity *and* authority. *No one is speaking*, or if there is a personality displayed, we know that it is an artifice, distanced from the personal, conforming to certain rules which govern what it may say. Though it lacks the personal quality essential to credibility and sincerity, an individual who is free to 'speak his mind', it claims as its moral virtue this very depersonalization or objectivity.[7] Its paradox is that it creates and defines reality, while denying that it is doing so.

The neutral voice of the Media IV can be seen, from almost any sampling of it, to express attitudes, even at the sentence level, in the structure of its message. An immanent and conspicuous feature of its discourse is that it perceives events from an institutional perspective:

Park was a dictator *but* had modernized South Korea. Many Koreans are concerned about the future stability of their country. (Tape, BBC Radio 4, 16 June 1980)

A white South African *policeman has been killed* on the anniversary of *a riot in which hundreds of people died.* (Tape, BBC Radio 4, 16 June 1980)

South African police *have had to use* tear gas to disperse crowds. (Tape, BBC Radio 4, 11 July 1980)

After six hours, the police *had to use CS gas* to disperse the crowds [in Liverpool]. (Tape, BBC World Service, 7 July 1981)

Any news programme will provide further examples of lexical and syntactic choices through which the news is presented from the point of view of institutional authority. Awareness of others' institutional bias is rarely and selectively present. An interviewer, addressing a writer, Joe Smith, on the BBC:

Does the fact that you were supported by the National Union of Railwaymen affect your work?...Are you a good union man? (Tape, BBC Radio 4, 27 July 1980)

There is a symbiotic relationship between the Media IV and the Institutional Voices of the society; each is essential to the other. The IV *must* communicate; the Media IV *must* transmit the message, in a responsible and respectful manner. The inequality of this relationship is most evident in a crisis, such as the Watergate, when a leader flagrantly violates the rules. In this instance, the White House Press Corps, even unwillingly, served as the passive open channel for the President's daily 'public relations'.[8] Control of topic is effortless for a major politician, whose every statement is, by definition, news. The dominance of public discourse by Institutional

Voices and the limitation of 'the news' to frames of reference defined by them is manifest in every news broadcast.

The traditions and technology of the media exponentially augment the Topic Transformation process in many convergent ways. Fragmentation of topic and the distancing of any event from the context in which it has meaning arise necessarily from the constraints of time and 'objective fact'. We have detailed reports of battles, with no understanding of the war. Sports and entertainment, the most popularly appealing, unproblematic frames provide the thematic model for 'news'. Political campaigns and issues of public policy are reduced to personality conflicts, sporting contests, or battles; the focus, and the 'new and true information' is: 'Who's winning?' The metaphors of warfare and to a lesser degree, of sport, are prevalent. When 'issues' are discussed, two sides are presented, both from within a narrow spectrum. The opinions of the public are reported in polled responses to questions framed by the IVs: they are otherwise silent, except for the 'speech acts' of marches, strikes, riots, etc., symbolic speech whose meaning is interpreted by the IV network. The political IV or any public figure must communicate through this system, whose constraints both restrict and amplify its message.

Those who analyse discourse tend to see meanings which are not usually evident beneath the 'taken-for-granted' surface. The analysis of distancing at the sentence level provides a way of perceiving these same structures at the discourse level. It is based on a view of language best expressed by Saussure: 'But what is language [langue] ? It is *both* a social product of the faculty of speech and a collection of necessary conventions that have been adopted by a social body to permit individuals to exercise that faculty.' My description of distancing hopes to provide a way of seeing through the conventional disguises of language use, centring here on distanced identity — 'Who is really speaking?' — and distanced topic — 'What is he really talking about?' In this way we can generalize closed systems of discourse in terms of their own intrinsic structural processes.

## Notes

1  US Government Printing Office 1974a, p. 76. Nixon is speaking at the Executives' Club of Chicago, 15 March 1974.

2  These transcripts (*Transcripts of eight recorded presidential conversations* US Government Printing Office, Washington DC, 1974b) were carefully made;

*every sound* on the tape was transcribed. They were to be used in the possible impeachment trial of President Nixon, and should not be confused with those published by President Nixon, edited by himself. Other transcripts cited are from the Office of Presidential Libraries, US National Archives, Washington DC. All material marked 'Tape' has been transcribed by me.

3  Suppression of Underlying Topic through Topic Transformation is analogous to the process of metaphor, a fundamental lexical process. The suppression of literal meaning through its fusion into the figurative meaning is discussed in Ricoeur 1976. See also Lerman 1981, ch. 3.3, on masking metaphor in conversation.

4  John Pilger, *Daily Mirror*, 20 Feb. 1980.

5  For other discussion of conventional constraints on plain talk, see Tyler 1978; Rosaldo 1973; Labov & Fanshel 1977.

6  In the Akan of Ghana (and the subgroups, the Ashanti and the Aowin) the tribal king, whose word is truth, may not speak. This fallible task is entrusted to 'the linguists', who inherit the post and are trained to speak for the king. (Personal communication, E. Y. Benneh, Wolfson College, Cambridge.)

7  Other contributors to this volume discuss the media IV and its uses. See especially Leitner (chapter 2) and Corner (chapter 13). (Eds.)

8  Personal communication, Richard Pride, Vanderbilt University, Nashville, Tenn. Pride was an academic observer of the White House Press Corps during part of the Watergate period. See also, Lerman 1981, ch. 1.3.

# 4

# Cultural transformations: the politics of resistance

DAVID MORLEY

Mattelart has pointed to the fact that forms of popular resistance to, and subversion of, dominant cultures have rarely been studied. The point here, he argues, is that while the 'receiver' of communications is often considered as a passive consumer of information or leisure commodities, it is nonetheless true that the audience does not necessarily read the messages sent to it within the cultural code of the transmitters. The way in which the subaltern groups and classes in a society reinterpret and make sense of these messages is therefore a crucial problem for any theory of communications as a mode of cultural domination. At the macro level of international cultural relations, he argues, the consequences of a message being interpreted in a different way from what its senders intended may be quite radical. He asks:

In how many countries do the Aryan heroes of the television series, Mission Impossible, fighting against the rebels, undergo a process of identification which is the exact opposite of that intended by the imperialist code, and how often are they viewed as the 'bad guys' in the story? (Mattelart & Siegelaub 1979, p. 27)

Mattelart warns that any notions of ideological domination must be employed with great care and recommends that the idea that imperialism invades different sectors of society in a uniform way be abandoned in favour of an analysis of the particular milieux which favour or resist penetration.

In the domestic context, the argument alerts us to the relation between the dominant ideological forms of the media, and the

subcultures and codes inhabited by different classes and class frac-
tions within British society. Cohen and Robbins (1978) argue that
the specific popularity of Kung-fu movies within working-class
youth culture is to be understood precisely in these terms. It is an
instance of an ideological form securing some recognition and
purchase within a particular section of the media audience to the
extent that it 'fits' with the subcultural forms in which this class-
fraction understands and articulates its own particular experience:

The fascination of the content of Kung-fu movies for working class kids goes
side by side with their unconscious recognition of its narrative style or 'grammar',
as one which is identical with their own. They can read it effortlessly. (p. 98)

This is not simply a question of 'objective correspondence' between
situations protrayed in a given movie and 'the more subterranean
realities of living in a "hard" working-class area' which would allow
a simple process of identification at the level of content. These
authors maintain that the crucial factor in play is:

...the linkage of two forms of 'collective representation' which have radically
different historical origins and institutional supports. If the linkage is possible
at all, it is because there is an objective correspondence between some oral
traditions in working-class culture and some genres produced by the mass media.
It is a correspondence of form, rather than content, and where it doesn't exist,
the impact of the mass media on working-class consciousness is entirely negli-
gible. Finally, both in the history of the class, and in the life history of those
growing up into it, the narrative forms of oral culture pre-date those of the
mass media and constitute a kind of permanent infra-structure, which condition
and limit the effectivity of the latter. (p. 99)

This is to argue that the structures of imperialism and of class domination, when introduced into the study of communications, pose
the problem of audience responses to and interpretations of the
mass media as a critical area of research.


## Communications: a broken circuit?

We are faced with a situation in which there is a potential disjunction between the codes of those sending and those receiving messages
through the circuit of mass communications (cf. Hall 1973, pp.
18-19; Eco 1972, p. 121). The problem of (non-)complementarity
of codes at the production and reception ends of the chain of

communications is indissolubly linked with the problem of cultural domination and resistance. In a research project on Nationwide (a popular current affairs magazine programme on BBC television), we attempted to pose this as a specific problem about the degree of complementarity between the codes of the programme and the interpretative codes of various sociocultural groups. (Brunsdon & Morley 1978; Morley 1980). We were concerned to explore the extent to which decodings take place within the limits of the pre-ferred (or dominant) manner in which the message has been initially encoded. However, there is a complementary aspect to this problem, namely the extent to which these interpretations, or decodings, also reflect, and are inflected by, the codes and discourses which different sections of the audience inhabit, and the ways in which these de-codings are determined by the socially governed distribution of cultural codes between and across different sections of the audience — that is, the range of decoding strategies and competencies in the audience.

To raise this as a problem for research is already to argue that the meaning produced by the encounter of text and subject cannot be 'read off' straight from textual characteristics. The text cannot be considered in isolation from its historical conditions of production and consumption. And an analysis of media ideology cannot rest with an analysis of production and text alone.

The 'meaning' of a film is not something to be discovered purely in the text itself...but is constituted in the interaction between the text and its users. The early claim of semiotics to be in some way able to account for a text's functioning through an immanent analysis was essentially misfounded in its failure to perceive that any textual system could only have meaning in relation to codes not purely textual, and that the recognition, distribution, and activa-tion of these would vary socially and historically. (Hill 1979, p. 122)

Thus the meaning of the text must be interpreted in terms of which set of discourses it encounters in any particular set of circumstances, and how this encounter may restructure both the meaning of the text and the discourses which it meets. The meaning of the text will be constructed differently according to the discourses (knowledges, prejudices, resistances etc.) brought to bear by the reader, and the crucial factor in the encounter of audience/subject and text will be the range of discourses at the disposal of the audience. The crucial point here is that individuals in different positions in the social formation defined according to structures of class, race or sex, for example, will tend to inhabit or have at their disposal different codes and subcultures. Thus social position sets parameters to the range of potential readings by structuring access to different codes.

Whether or not a programme succeeds in transmitting the preferred or dominant meaning will depend on whether it encounters readers who inhabit codes and ideologies derived from other institutional areas (e.g. churches or schools) which correspond to and work in parallel with those of the programme or whether it encounters readers who inhabit codes drawn from other areas or institutions (e.g. trade unions or 'deviant' subcultures) which conflict to a greater or lesser extent with those of the programme.

This is to say that if a notion such as that of a 'preferred reading' is to have any value it is not as a means to abstractly 'fix' one interpretation over and above others, but rather to account:

For how, under certain conditions, a text will tend to be read in particular ways because of the way meaning is placed through the articulation of particular aesthetic, social and historical codes. (Hill 1979, p. 123)

It follows, then, that:

The task of ideological analysis is [that] of accounting for how meanings are generated for and through particular audiences...accounting for the processes of signification through which particular meanings are produced in specific contexts. (p. 123)

## The message: encoding and decoding

In outline, the premises on which we base our approach are as follows:

a  The production of a meaningful message in television discourse is always problematic 'work'. The same event can be encoded in more than one way.
b  The message in social communication is always complex in structure and form. It always contains more than one potential 'reading'. Messages propose and prefer certain readings over others, but they cannot be entirely closed around one reading: they remain polysemic.
c  The activity of 'getting meaning' from the message is also problematic practice, however transparent and natural it may seem. Messages encoded in one way can also be read in a different way.

Thus, the communicative form and structure of the encoded message can be analysed in terms of its preferred reading: the mechanisms which prefer one, dominant reading over the other readings; the means which the encoder uses to try to win the assent of the audience to his particular reading of the message. Special attention can be given here to the control exercised over meaning, and to 'points of identification' within the message which transmit the preferred reading to the audience.

It is precisely the aim of the presenter to achieve identification with the audience through mechanisms which gain the audience's complicity and 'suggest' preferred readings. If and when these identificatory mechanisms are attenuated or broken, will the message be decoded in a different framework of meaning from that in which it was encoded? Broadcasters undoubtedly make the attempt to establish a relationship of complicity with the audience (Brunsdon & Morley 1978) but there is no justification for assuming that the attempt will always be successful.

### The structure of the audience: decodings in cultural context

We might profitably think of the media audience not so much as an undifferentiated mass of individuals but as a complex structure of socially organized individuals in a number of overlapping subgroups and subcultures, each with its own history and cultural traditions. This is not to see cultural competence as automatically determined or generated by social position but to pose the problem of the relation between, on the one hand, social categories and social structure and, on the other, codes, subcultures and ideologies. In this perspective the primary relationships for analysis are those between linguistic and cultural codes and patterns of class (cf. Bernstein 1971; Rosen 1972), race (cf. Labov 1969) and sex (cf. Lakoff 1976; Spender 1980). We are therefore proposing a model of the audience, not as an atomized mass of individuals, but as composed of a number of subcultural formations or groupings whose members will share a cultural orientation towards decoding messages in particular ways. Individual members' readings will be framed by shared cultural formations and practices. Such shared 'orientations' will in turn be determined by factors derived from the objective position of the individual reader in the social structure. These objective factors must be seen as setting parameters to individual experience although not determining consciousness in a mechanistic way: people understand their situation and react to it by way of sub-cultures and meaning systems (Critcher 1975).

Bernstein's work on sociolinguistic codes and his hypothesis of a correlation between particular social (class) categories and codes is of obvious relevance to any theory of the media audience, in terms of how different sections of that audience may relate to different kinds of messages — perhaps through the employment of different codes of interpretation. However, Bernstein's scheme is highly simplified: it contains only two classes (working and middle) and two codes (restricted and elaborated), and no attempt is made to differentiate within these classes, nor within their 'corresponding' codes. Rosen attacks Bernstein for his mechanistic analysis of the working class as an undifferentiated whole, defined simply by economic positions, and argues that Bernstein ignores factors at the level of ideological and political practice which 'distinguish the language of Liverpool dockers from that of...Coventry car workers' (Rosen 1972, p. 9). Rosen is here attempting to extend the terms of the analysis by insisting on the operation of non-economic fac-tors. He rejects the argument that linguistic codes are determined by 'common occupational function' and presents a case for dif-ferentiating within and across class categories in terms of 'history, traditions, job experience, ethnic origins, residential patterns, level of organisation' (p. 6).

Bernstein's oversimplistic formulation of the relation between classes and cultural codes, and his neglect of cultural differentiation within classes, is to some extent paralleled in Parkin's attempt to produce a typology of 'meaning systems' in relation to class struc-ture. Parkin's treatment of class structures as the ground of different meaning systems (1971, ch. 3) is a fruitful if crude point of departure which provided some basic categories for Hall's (1973) hypotheses about typical decoding positions. The key question at issue is that of the nature of the fit between, say, class, socioeconomic or educa-tional position and interpretative codes.

Following, but adapting Parkin, we have suggested three hypo-thetical-typical positions which the decoder may occupy in relation to the encoded message. He or she may take the meaning fully within the interpretative framework which the message itself pro-poses and 'prefers': if so, decoding proceeds within, or is aligned with, the dominant or 'hegemonic' code. Second, decoders may take the meaning broadly as encoded; but by relating the message to some concrete, located or situational context which reflects their position and interests, they may modify or partially inflect the meaning. Following Parkin, we would call this a 'negotiated' position. Third, the decoder may recognize how the message has been contextually encoded, but bring to bear an alternative frame of interpretation, which sets aside the encoding framework and superimposes on the message an interpretation which works in a directly oppositional way — an oppositional, or 'counter-hegemonic' decoding.

Parkin elaborated these positions as three possible and typical positions of different classes in relation to a class-based hegemonic ideology. We have transposed them in order to describe possible alternative ways of decoding ideologically constructed messages. Of course, Parkin's conceptual framework is limited in that it provides only a statement of the three logical possibilities: that a given section of the audience may either share, partly share, or not share the dominant code in which the message has been transmitted (Morley 1974). If the three basic decoding positions have any sociological validity it will necessarily be at the very broad level of what one might call class competencies in the reading of ideological messages. Even at this level, further distinctions may have to be made: for example between a version of the negotiated position which reflects a deferential stance towards the use of the hegemonic code, or one which reflects a subordinate stance, as defined by Parkin, where messages cast at a general or abstract level are subject to negotiation when referred to a more limited or sectional interest.

Much of the important work in this respect consists in differentiating Parkin's catch-all category of 'negotiated code' into a set of empirically grounded subvariants of this basic category, which are illustrated in the sociological work on different forms of sectional and corporate consciousness (cf. Parkin 1971; Mann 1973; Nichols & Armstrong 1976). The crucial development from this perspective has been the attempt to translate Parkin's three ideal types (which are themselves a considerable advance on any model which sees the audience as an unstructured aggregate of individuals) into a more sensitive model of actual decoding positions within the media audience.

There remains, however, one critical problem in the attempt to integrate the sociological work of authors such as Parkin into a theory of communications. This is the tendency to directly convert social categories (e.g. class) into meanings (e.g. ideological positions) without attending to the specific factors which govern this conversion. It is simply inadequate to present demographic and sociological factors such as age, sex, race or class position as objective correlates or determinants of differential decoding positions without any attempt to specify *how* they intervene in the process of communication. The relative autonomy of signifying practices means that sociological factors cannot be 'read in' directly as affecting the communication process. These factors can only have effect through the (possibly contradictory) action of the discourses in which they are articulated.

*Audiences and ideologies:*
*methodological and empirical questions*

I will now attempt to illustrate some of these theoretical arguments by drawing on material from the Nationwide research project (see Brunsdon & Morley 1978 and Morley 1980 for a full account of this project). The research was designed to provide an analysis of the programme discourse and then to ascertain which sections of the programme's audience decoded in line with the preferred /dominant codes, and which sections operated negotiated/oppositional decodings.

Two videotaped Nationwide programmes were shown to 29 groups drawn from different social and cultural backgrounds, and from different levels of the educational system. Our procedure was to gain entry to a situation where the group already had some existence as a social entity — at least for the duration of a course. The videotape showings and the subsequent interviews were arranged to slot into the context of their established institutional settings as far as possible.

The groups usually consisted of between five and ten people. After the viewing session the discussion was taperecorded (usually about 40 mins duration) and this was later transcribed in full to provide the basic data for the analysis. The project used the 'focused interview' method originally developed by Merton and Kendal (1946). Thus the interviews began with non-directive prompting designed to establish the 'working vocabulary' (Mills 1939) and frame of reference of the groups, and the order of priority in which *they* raised issues, before moving on to a more structured set of questions based on our programme analysis.

We were particularly concerned to identify the nature of the groups' 'lexico-referential systems' (Mills 1939) and to examine how these systems related to those employed by the broadcasters. Our questions were designed to reveal whether audiences used the same words in the same ways as the broadcasters, in discussing different topics in the programme; whether the groups ranked issues and topics in the same order of priority as that given in the programme discourse; and whether there were aspects of topics not discussed by the broadcasters that were specifically mentioned by these groups. The decision to work with group rather than individual interviews followed from our desire to explore the extent to which individual 'readings' are shaped by the sociocultural groupings within which they are situated.

We attempted to work as far as possible with the raw data of actual speech instead of trying to convert responses into immediately categorizable forms. Although this choice raised problems which we cannot claim in any sense to have solved, it did allow us to bring into focus the question of the relation between the forms of speech employed by broadcasters and those employed by respondents.

We took as axiomatic Voloshinov's (1973) concept of the multiaccentuality of linguistic forms, the impossibility of establishing simple one-to-one correspondences between particular linguistic features and ideological structures.[1] Our main concern was the broader level of conceptual frameworks and perspectives, in so far as these (usually at the level of implication or assumption) could be detected from the actual linguistic usage of the respondents. Our main guide to this was an application of Gerbner's method of 'proposition analysis' (Gerbner 1964), which allows one to identify the patterns of argument and assumption, and the cognitive premises, underlying particular responses. This is done by reconstructing declarative statements in terms of the simple propositions which support or underpin them, thus attempting to explicate the assumptions which must be held in order for it to make sense to give particular answers to questions raised in the interviews.

While this is evidently a controversial area, where responses may be interpreted differently, we would argue that it must remain the primary level of analysis. This is because only when the baseline assumptions embedded in a particular discourse have been explicated, when we have some sense of its overall pattern, can we move on to an analysis of how particular forms or signifiers function within the context of that discourse. Thus, while there remains in this approach a problem about the sensitivity of the linguistic tools which the analysis employs, this focus on the underlying patterns of assumption is a necessary preliminary before more precise methods of formal linguistic analysis can be productively employed.[2]

*Classes, codes, decodings*

The problematic proposed here does not attempt to derive decodings directly from social class position or 'reduce' them to it. It is always a question of how social position, as it is articulated through particular discourses, produces specific kinds of readings or decodings. These readings can then be seen to be patterned by the way in which the structure of access to different discourses is determined by social position. The question is which cultural repertoires and codes are available to which groups, and how do they utilize these symbolic resources in their attempt to make sense of messages coming from the media?

Although the project as a whole investigated decodings made by groups across a range of class positions, I shall, in order to focus the comparisons more sharply, deal here only with the differences between the decodings made by three kinds of groups, all sharing a roughly similar working-class position or background. These groups were, first, young apprentice engineers and metallurgists, second, groups of trade union officials and of shop stewards, and third, young black students at a college of further education.

Of these groups it was the apprentices who most closely inhabited the dominant code of the programme. Their decodings were mostly closely in line with the dominant/preferred meanings of Nationwide. This seemed to be accounted for by the extent to which the lads' use of a form of populist discourse ('damn all politicians — they're all as bad as each other...it's all down to the individual in the end, isn't it?') was quite compatible with that of the programme. Although the dominant tone of these groups' responses to Nationwide was one of cynicism, a resistance to anyone 'putting one over' on them, most of the main items in the programme were, in fact, decoded by these groups within the dominant framework or preferred reading established by the programme. They tended to accept the perspectives offered by and through the programme's presenter. The situation here seems to be the converse of that outlined by Parkin: here we have working-class groups who cynically claim to be distanced from the programme at a general level but who accept and reproduce its ideological formulations of specific issues. The 'commonsense' interpretations which the programme's presenters offer seem 'pretty obviously OK' to these groups too, and Nationwide's questions are justified as 'natural' or 'obvious' — and therefore unproblematic: 'They just said the obvious comment didn't they?'

The groups involved in the activities and discourse of trade unionism produced differently inflected versions of negotiated and oppositional decodings, depending on their social position and positioning in educational and political discourses. There is a profound difference between the groups who are non-union, or are simply members of trade unions, and those with an active involvement in and commitment to trade unionism — the latter producing much more negotiated or oppositional readings of Nationwide. So the structure of decoding is not a simple function of class position, but rather the result of differential involvement and positioning in discourse formations.

Further, there are the significant differences between the articulate, fully oppositional readings produced by the shop stewards as compared with the negotiated/oppositional readings produced by the trade union officials. This, we would suggest, is to be accounted for by the greater distancing of the stewards from the pressures of incorporation which full-time officials experience, which thus allows them to inhabit a more 'left-wing' interpretation of trade unionism.

The trade union officials on the whole inhabit a dominant/populist inflected version of negotiated code and espouse a right-wing Labour perspective. They are regular Nationwide watchers and approve both the programme's mode of address and ideological stance — 'I find that quite interesting...there's something in that programme for everyone to have a look at...'; 'It seems to be a programme acceptable to the vast majority of people.' They accept the individualistic theme of the programme and accept the programme's construction of an undifferentiated national community which is currently suffering economic hardship: to this extent they can be said to identify with the national 'we' which the programme discourse constructs. However, this is at an abstract and general level: at a more concrete, local level — that of directly economic 'trade union' issues — they take a more critical stance, and specific items within this category are then decoded in a more oppositional way ( the classic structure of the negotiated code).

It is the shop stewards who spontaneously produce by far the most articulate, fully oppositional reading of the programme. They reject the programme's attempt to tell us what 'our grouse' is and its attempt to construct a national 'we' — 'They want "*we*"...they want the average viewer to all think "we"...' And they identify this Nationwide form of presentation as part of a general pattern: 'I mean, take Nationwide, add the *Sun*...the *Mirror* and the *Daily Express* to it...' This is a pattern in which: 'Union leaders are always being told "You're ruining the country!"'

Finally, the black students made hardly any connection with the discourse of Nationwide. The concerns and the cultural framework of Nationwide are simply not the concerns of their world. They do not so much produce an oppositional reading as refuse to 'read' it at all. These groups are so totally alienated from the discourse of Nationwide that their response is in the first instance 'a critique of silence'. In a sense they fail, or refuse, to engage with the discourse of the programme enough to deconstruct or redefine it. They are clear that it's not a programme for them, it's for 'older people, middle-class people'; it doesn't deal with their specific interests — 'Why didn't they never interview Bob Marley?' — and it fails to live up to their standards of 'good TV' defined in terms of enjoyment and entertainment (in which terms Today and ITV in general are preferred to Nationwide and BBC).

To this group Nationwide is 'so boring' it's not interesting at all': they 'don't see how anyone could watch it'. There is a disjunction between the discourse of their own culture and that, not simply of Nationwide in particular, but of the whole field of 'serious TV' ('BBC is definitely boring') and of party politics ('God that's rubbish'). Moreover, these groups reject the descriptions of their life offered by the programme. They can find no point of identification within the programme's discourse about the problems of families in Britain today — a discourse into which, the programme presenters have claimed, 'most people in Britain' should fit. Their particular experience of family structures among the black, working-class, inner city community is simply not accounted for. The programme's picture of family life is as inappropriate to them as that offered in a 'Peter and Jane' reading scheme:

It didn't show one-parent families...the average family in a council estate — all these people seemed to have cars, their own home...property...Don't they ever think of the average family?

Now this is precisely what Nationwide would claim to think of: the point here is that the representation of 'the family' within the discourse of Nationwide has no purchase on the representation of that field within the discourse and experience of these groups — and is consequnetly rejected.

However these are statements at the level of gross differences of orientation between the groups, and they should not blind us to the differences, divisions and overlaps which occur within and among these groups. For example, although the apprentice groups were generally in sympathy with the programme and identified with the perspectives on events offered by its presenters, they did at times find it hard to relate to the programme's style of presentation or 'mode of address' (Neale 1977). At this point they frequently invoked Nationwide's ITV competitor as being 'more of a laugh' or 'better entertainment' and were, to this extent, alienated from the discourse of the BBC programme.

Moreover, if we are to characterize the apprentice group as decoding in a dominant mode, we must recognize that this is only one version, or inflection, of 'dominant code': within the study there were groups from quite different social positions (bank managers, schoolboys, teacher training students) whose decodings shared some of the dominant characteristics of those made by the apprentice groups, but which diverged from theirs at other points. Thus the category of dominant code would need to be differentiated, in terms of the material in this study, to account for different versions (radical and traditional Conservative, deferential, Leavisite) of the dominant code.

Equally, we must distinguish between different forms and formulations of negotiated and oppositional readings, between the 'critique of silence' offered initially by the black students, the critical reading (from an educational point of view) articulately expressed by some of the higher-education groups (though this itself varied, with topic-critical readings being made by these groups on moral and social issues, but dominant code readings being made by the same groups on economic and trade union issues), and the various forms of 'politicized' negotiated and oppositional readings made by the trade union groups.

These are simply instances of a more general phenomenon of differentiation within and across the basic categories derived from Parkin's scheme which we would need to take account of in developing an adequate model of the media audience. We need to understand the process through which the multiplicity of discourses in play in any social formation intersect with the process of decoding media material. The effect of these discourses is precisely to lend variety to decodings. Thus, in each of the major categories of decoding (dominant, negotiated, oppositional) we can discern a number of varieties and inflections of what, for purposes of gross comparison only, is termed the same 'code'.

## Conclusions

This quick sketch of a large quantity of material at least allows us to see clearly the fundamental point that social position in no way directly, or unproblematically, correlates with decoding. The apprentice groups, the trade union and shop stewards groups and the black college students can all be said to share a common class position, but their decodings of a television programme are inflected in different directions by the discourses and institutions in which they are situated. In one case the framework derives from a tradition of mainstream working-class populism, in another from trade unions and Labour party politics, in another, from black youth subcultures. In each case the discourses in play inflect and organize the groups' responses to and decodings of the media material shown.

Any superficial resemblance between this study of television audience and the 'uses and gratifications' perspective in media research is misleading. In the latter, the focus would be entirely on what individuals 'do with' messages.[3] But the different responses and interpretations reported here are not to be understood simply in terms of individual psychologies. They are founded on cultural differences embedded within the structure of society; cultural clusters which guide and limit the individual's interpretation of messages. To understand the potential meanings of a given message we need a cultural map of the audience to whom that message is addressed — a map showing the various cultural repertoires and symbolic resources available to differently placed subgroups within that audience. Such a map will help to show how the social meanings of a message are produced through the interaction of the codes embedded in the text with the codes inhabited by the different sections of the audience.

## Notes

1  For some useful recent work in this area, which attempts to establish patterns of relation between formal linguistic features and ideological frameworks, see Kress & Trew 1978 and Fowler *et al.* (1979).
2  For a critical look at the use of the concept of 'codes' within cultural analysis, see Corner 1980.
3  Carey & Kreiling 1974 give an account of the relation between 'cultural studies' and the 'uses and gratifications' approach. The present work owes its main categories and concepts to the cultural studies tradition.

# Part II

# Printing and the Press

# 5

# Linguistic and ideological transformations in news reporting[1]

## GUNTHER KRESS

All reporting is a mediation. An event, of whatever kind, is mediated from a perceiver to someone who is assumed not to have been a perceiver of that event. Perception proceeds on the basis of given theoretical frameworks or schemata, which may be more or less well articulated. The mediation may take the shape of one of my children 'reporting' an incident to me. When the incident concerns some contentious issue between them, the relativeness of these schemata, and hence of perception, becomes apparent. The schemata interpose themselves (more or less consciously from the 'reporter's' point of view) between the event and myself, to whom the event is reported. As the recipient of this 'news' — and cast in the role of arbitrator — it is my task to reconstruct the initial event from the two differing reports which I have received. I may feel that I know the interpretative schemata of my children, and hence know how to 'read' the reports which they give me. That is, I assume that one will habitually report an event in a certain way while the other will report it in a predictably different way. Note that I am assuming that they are both telling 'the truth'. The reporter's interpreting may take a number of forms. For instance, the intention of the causer may be interpreted: an accidental bump, or a deliberate push; or the event itself may be classified differently: as a nudge or as a push.

The role of language consists in supplying the categories which may be imposed by the perceiver on the event, and in which the report is presented to me. The selection of one category (*nudge* rather than *push*) is guided by the schema which the perceiver brings to bear on the particular event. Indeed the same schema guides the selection of all the linguistic categories pertaining to the reporting of that event.

The reports and my attempts to 'read' them, to reconstruct the original event, involve language. Essentially, they are linguistic entities, though neither the causes nor the attendant events may have been linguistic. The reports exist only in and through language; my attempts to read them depend entirely on language. Indeed the schemata may exist only in language, or at least, become public and articulate only in and through language. However, the *formation* of the schemata, and their development and change, depends on linguistic and on non-linguistic factors. Clearly, non-linguistic factors enter into the process through the material conditions, experiences and situations in which we find ourselves. These can be either purely individual or social. Linguistic factors enter into the process at every point: articulated, 'talked about' experiences present events in linguistic form and already classified, so that the schema inherent in the text is 'there'. Even purely private experiences will be made articulate by us to ourselves through linguistic categories. An understanding of the schemata, of their effects, and in particular of their articulation in texts, involves linguistic skills of a complex kind. In hearing and reading, in inter-action, all of us bring these skills to bear constantly, though it is questionable whether we all do so with equal effect.

Of course, either of my children might not be telling me the 'truth', that is, rather than reporting the one event through different interpretative schemata they might be reporting a fiction to me: 'I wasn't even there!' In this case no degree of sophisitication in the use of linguistic skills will allow me to reconstruct the original event.

My simple example can be translated without too much difficulty to the media in general. The general framework remains useful, though it does become immensely more complex. In the media, the 'reporting' of an event is frequently a composite process, in which institutions and individuals participate to a different extent and with differing purposes. The more significant the event, the more likely it is that this is so. The initial perceiver/'reporter' may be a functionary of some institution; his or her report may be subject to amendment (again in accordance with interpretative schemata); the new report — given out by a 'spokesman' — may be taken over by a newsagency which performs its reworking of the report; it may then be used by a newspaper, which does its own, final, rewriting. It may be the case that the schemata of all the reporters (and re-reporters) along this chain are closely aligned, in which case only minor rewriting may take place. It may happen that the schemata are completely unaligned, in which case a total rewriting is necessary. From the preceding argument it is clear that rewriting is more than a mere tinkering with language. Rewriting is a shorthand term for a process which involves at least these stages: the deconstruction of the text, the reconstruction of the original event, its apperception in terms of the new schema, and its (re-)articulation in the linguistic categories appropriate to the new schema. Both writing and rewriting are practices which are firmly set in ideological structures, and are expressions of them.[2] The process is well described and carefully documented by Tony Trew in Fowler *et al.* (1979); also Kress & Trew (1978).

The three important points are (1) at each stage of re-reporting and rewriting the linguistic and ideological processes are in essence the same; (2) traces of these operations may remain in the final text; (3) the ideology used in constructing the text is expressed in the text, in the homology of ideological and linguistic structure. The first point implies that the same theoretical and methodological approach is valid in analysing each stage of rewriting as well as the final text, the product of all the rewritings. The second point implies that an appropriate methodology of 'reading' may help to reconstitute the original event. The third point implies that even if we cannot reconstruct the original event, if a 'lie' has been written, we can discover the ideology which gives content and structure to the 'lie'. That is, using some of the insights of linguistic theory may be an aid in uncovering the ideological layerings of meaning in a given text.

The contexts in which perception, writing and rewriting take place are of crucial significance in shaping the initial texts and their subsequent rewritings. They tend to be inaccessible to linguistic analysis, though some of the categories of linguistic theory may help in providing explanations. An example, from the Adelaide paper the *News*, a part of Rupert Murdoch's media holdings, can illustrate what I mean. Page 6 contains the editorial, plus two feature articles (see illustration 1). On this occasion (Wednesday, 6 August 1980) the editorial is entitled 'The road to 1983' and is an attack on 'red tape ...strangling us, choking industry, stifling enterprise'. It states that:

It is not only the cost of this massive indulgence in pen pushing that is alarming. What is also disturbing is the insidious way government pokes its nose into private affairs. This is true of business just as it is true of individuals in their private lives.

THE NEWS
EDITORIAL

## The road to 1984

RED tape is strangling us, choking industry, stifling enterprise.

Most of us have known that almost instinctively for years.

Now the Confederation of Australian Industry has put a figure on it — a staggering figure.

Complying with Federal and State Government regulations, feeding the bureaucracy with its pettifogging forms, costs business $3700 million a year.

Put another way that represents $900 per household a year and it is a good other way to put it since it is the Australian household which ultimately has to foot the bill.

It is not only the cost of this massive indulgence in pen pushing that is alarming. What is also disturbing is the insidious way government pokes its nose into private affairs.

This is true of business just as it is true of individuals in their private lives.

### Unnecessary

Some regulation is necessary, no doubt of that. But a lot is unnecessary, expensive snooping by little Hitlers.

The Confederation has proved anew that government by nature makes rules and regulations and bureaucracy by nature retains them and grows concerously to administer long after any original need has gone.

George Orwell seems to have had an uncanny sense of timing when he wrote about what kind of world that produces and called it 1984.

With 40 months to go, we are well on the way.

Louise Messner . . . "I would love him to resign."

Lady Laucke . . . "Tony Staley has made the right choice."

Mary Wilson . . . "I'm grateful Ian has had more time"

**❝I think it's a disease, once you're a politician — a horrible disease, and Mr Staley has cured it.❞**

By RANDALL ASHBOURNE

"I can tell you what I think of being a Federal politician's wife in two words — but I wouldn't want you to print them."

That is the view of Mrs Louise Messner, wife of SA Liberal Senator Tony Messner.

Her attitude to the political lifestyle is shared apparently by the Telecommunications Minister, Mr Staley, who will retire at the next election to spend more time with his young family.

Senator Messner warned before he called his wife if was a given chance to cancel and on the subject.

He said: "I've been in the Northern Territory for several days and didn't get home until six o'clock this morning.

"I had a shower, left again and won't be home until midnight."

Flying visits home have become normal since her husband won a Senate seat five years ago, according to Mrs Messner.

"I said to him this morning — 'Isn't Tony Staley's wife lucky?'

"I would love him to resign, but I would never pressure him to do it.

"The trouble is you can't be half hearted about being a politician, you have to give it everything.

"After five years I'm learning to cope with it.

"But we made the decision for him to enter politics together, and I'm not going to pressure him into giving up now."

MRS Ian Wilson's wife, Mary, says she has learnt to cope with pressures, and having a teenage family has eased some of the problems.

"I think the Staley's position was different from ours

# LUCKY MRS STALEY

**. . . say the wives of our Federal MPs**

because he's a Minister, so I have been grateful. Ian has had more time to spend with the family than a Minister would have.

"But the time away in Canberra from Monday to Friday does put pressure on the

"He's wonderful to be able to do something like that.

"I hope he enjoys ordinary life instead of extraordinary life. But whatever he does, we will be a happy family.

"It takes a lot to decide to give up the chase for power, especially when you have been in a position of power.

"I won't be making out a list of home duties for him.

"That would be too structured and Tony doesn't need that sort of thing to know what needs doing around here." Mrs Staley, yesterday

wife to take the role of both mother and father.

"We tend to save all the things we want to talk about until the weekend, when Ian is home."

One politician's wife who has lived through most of the problems over a lengthy period is Lady Laucke, whose husband, Sir Condor Laucke, has been commuting between Adelaide and Canberra for 25 years.

Her reaction to Mr Staley's decision was spontaneous: "I congratulate him! I congratulate him on knowing where his values should be.

"I think it's a disease. You know, once you're a politician — a horrible disease, and Mr Staley has managed to cure it.

"I know I found the lifestyle terribly hard. I cried as much as I laughed — and I found a lot of the women do the same.

"They go to and they think it's wonderful, but it doesn't take long.

"Our children understand now because they are older. But otherwise your home is not a home. It's a place where you come in, you eat, you sleep and you're off again.

"I really understand Tony Staley. I'm a family woman and I think he has made the right choice."

Mrs Clythe McLeay, the wife of the Administrative Services Minister, Mr John McLeay, believes her life has become a little easier since he became a Minister.

"The wife of a Minister can travel with her husband, whereas the wives of backbenchers are restricted to so many flights per session.

"I think that makes it difficult for them, but I enjoy the early years I had only one child who was really young. The other two were in their teens but, even so we had our problems.

"Then it was a very lonely life."

## Silencing the snobs

**Name-dropping is what one might call the snob's disease, with some people permanently afflicted and others suffering only intermittent mild attacks.**

But don't we all relish hearing how those who once have rubbed shoulders with the famous, avid for the details and always hoping to uncover secret foibles and small scandals?

The temptation for journalists who, like me, have worked and hobnobbed with royals, the rich, famous, notorious and influential is always there. It's frequently evident over television and radio that name-dropping is very alluring, tilt several prominent personalities are able to resist falling into the deplorable pit of name-drops.

It becomes a problem sometimes. How much is news, how much is of special interest to readers and listeners, and how much is simply showing off?

I could fill columns with the names of famous people with whom I am on friendly terms, with whom I've rubbed shoul-

BARBARA PAGE

ders and those I've simply met in the course of my work.

It becomes very tempting to weave them into my scribblings . . . just to prove to myself that I've been around. But is this news, or worth putting into print?

In a comparatively small, isolated city like Adelaide we're probably more prone to air our private knowledge of the Big Names of that vast outer world.

We're subjected to writers, radio and television personalities who feel impelled to talk about themselves, where they've been, what they've seen and whom they met.

If the material runs thin, then we get the tiresome details of their trips down to the last small scrap of their family's doings. It makes for

very boring entertainment, too save us from another domestic outpouring.

Every newcomer to Australia quickly discovers that "overseas" is a magic word. The "overseas" trip is a requirement of society and must be published to ensure the traveller is accepted into the social club.

There should be a special Bunther club, solely for those people who boast they've been there," so that they could sport a badge for all the world to see.

Only America perhaps equals Australia in its fierce desire for the "overseas" trip, almost a necessary qualification for any young person wanting to make an impression in his hometown.

Travel is very desirable, of course, and as a world traveller over many years I don't begrudge the young folk's odysseys.

It's the social merit badge sticking to these so-called socialites who feel compelled to broadcast that "they've toured the UK and Scandinavia, stayed with a cousin in Los Angeles and a sister in Hong Kong" that turns me off.

Is it news to hear that Mr and Mrs Another have spent five weeks in the UK, visited Oxford and went to the Henley Regatta?

Travel, and travellers are far removed from the social hoo-hah, and these days we have the whole world at our feet in print, over the air and on TV.

Professional travellers, explorers, adventurers . . . we can follow them every step of the way and, yes, we all want to go "overseas," and we want to rub shoulders with the famous people they meet.

We watch Parkinson and his personalities, we hang on to the Don Lane shows to share his intimacies with film stars and politicians, wanting a share of the secrets and glory. After all, we're simply human.

Name-dropping and place-name-dropping are irresistible, and we'll never be able to overcome that human failing of wanting to be in on the act.

But I always hope, optimistically, that we can rise above the pedestrian and the fatuous. Save us from those "overseas" boastings, spare us those domestic details, give us the fascinating tales and play down the social angles.

If you must drop the names, be sure you have something to weight them and make listening, watching and reading worthwhile for the less lucky folk who've never had the chance to rub shoulders with a Prince or a Duchess or a filmstar. Coming face to face with any one of these is rarely special these days.

Snot grapes? Well, as a professional travel writer, my "overseas" trips have been mostly work. Placenames have been my bread and butter.

Name-dropping I try to avoid, since my whole weekly life has been involved me with the rich, the famous and famous, the world-renowned personalities and real people.

I'm much more interested in talking about ordinary people, the patchwork of everyday life right here on our doorstep.

But, heaven help me, one day I may succumb and Tell All.

*Illustration 1    The Adelaide News, 6 August 1980, page 6*

Two questions arise: one is, what has caused this editorial?; the other is, is there a relationship between the editorial and the two feature articles on the same page — are all three parts of a single statement? First then, what is the event which is being discussed in the editorial? By coincidence the Australian Broadcasting Tribunal had at that time just begun a hearing into the acquisition by (Mr Murdoch's) News Limited of a television station in Melbourne, in seeming contravention of 'regulations' (the word is from the editorial) governing the broadcasting industry. By a further coincidence, the federal minister of Posts and Telecommunications had resigned on the fourth of August — ostensibly for 'family reasons'. There were allegations that he might have been aware of News Limited's intention to acquire the station, and of the controversial nature of this acquisition. The larger feature is a homily on the wives of federal politicians who sacrifice family etc. to the greater national good, and 'Lucky Mrs Staley', whose husband has declared his intention to renounce this life. It may have appeared in the paper, and next to that editorial, by mere coincidence. Its effect is to counteract rumours about possible political motivations for Mr Staley's resignation. The third feature, 'Silencing the snobs', is a chatty attack on snobbish name-droppers and returned travellers. The (woman) writer's head and name appear at the top. This links it with the photographs of four politicians' wives in 'Lucky Mrs Staley'. While the two articles seem quite clearly to be 'about' women, 'Lucky Mrs Staley' is certainly about men, the politicians in question. There is thus an interesting interplay between the three articles on this page. The editorial is reinforced by 'Lucky Mrs Staley' (both may well concern the same 'event') and at the same time it is made innocent by the homeliness of the article on politicians and their wives/families. The latter reading is further reinforced by the triviality of the third feature on this page.[3]

Hence editorial and features may well have had specific events as their source, and may jointly have had specific intentions. Linguistic concepts such as implication and presupposition may prove illuminating in an attempt to read this page, though a reading of this whole complex of motivation/event and statement is beyond the scope of linguistic analysis.

The mediation process, depending on language, is accessible to linguistic analysis and description. As ideological systems exist in and are articulated through language, the ideological system itself can be reached via an analysis of language. On one level this is well-known and uncontroversial. Words, for instance, represent categorizations of the world *from a point of view*. They exist within systems which are organized by, and represent, ideological systems. Hence a word such as 'freedom fighter', or 'terrorist', does not exist in a vacuum but in the context of sets of related words.

Such modes of reading have been and are used by lay or professional readers of media messages. This kind of reading can be extended, drawing in every linguistic feature, every linguistic process, extending it to all parts of the syntax of a text — both to the syntactic items and to the syntactic processes which have been applied in the construction of a text. At each point in the text choices are available to the speaker/writer, and at many points specific syntactic processes are employed. And at each such point we ask: Why was this form chosen, rather than one of the other available ones? Why was this linguistic process applied and not these other possible ones?

To make this somewhat more concrete, here is an example from the texts discussed below (pp. 130-1). First, to look at choices of linguistic items. The opening sentence of one report is: 'Telecom employees *are likely* to reimpose work bans...' The two italicized items are verb and (adjectival) complement, respectively. Together they function to convey the writer's felt degree of certitude about the events. The writer had two different kinds of choices to make: one, to select the appropriate modality, the right nuance of certainty/uncertainty; two, to express this modality either through the verb or through the adjective complement. The first sentence from the second text shows another writer taking other choices: 'industrial action *seems certain* to hit...' The two can be compared in this form:

|  | *Verb* | *Adjective complement* |
|---|---|---|
| Sentence 1 | are (certainty) | likely (uncertainty) |
| Sentence 2 | seems (uncertainty) | certain (certainty) |

That is, in each sentence there is an expression of both (degrees of) certainty and uncertainty. The writer may attach either to the verb, or to the complement. In (1), the writer expresses certainty that something *is*; that something is, however, uncertain. In (2), the writer expresses uncertainty about his own perceptual processes; the object itself of those processes is certain. The writer could have expressed certainty in both elements,

|  | *Verb* | *Adjective complement* |
|---|---|---|
| Example 3 | are (certainty) | certain (certainty) |
| Example 4 | seem (uncertainty) | likely (uncertainty) |

that is: 'are certain to reimpose work bans...'; 'seem likely to re-impose work bans...' Other possibilities exist: 'will reimpose work bans', etc. The overall effect of the two sentences may appear to be the same, but the analysis reveals that there is a difference to be explained. In perceptual terms the complement probably has the greater impact. That is, a relation is established between an object and a quality, and as readers we are more interested in the quality of the object, than in the mode in which that relationship is established (though clearly some readers may pay more attention to the mode of the relationship). One writer, by modalizing the perceptually less prominent verb, is able to use the complement 'certain'; the other writer modalizes the adjective complement 'likely'. Hence one report manages to convey a stronger degree of certainty about 'industrial action' than the other, without doing violence to the reality of the situation. It is clear that the one mode of presenting the event will fit into a given view of industrial relations more easily than the other — a mere likelihood of industrial action both fits less well into a confrontational view of industrial relations than the certainty of action, and at the same time may conform better with the paper's view of what its readers may want (or what it wants for its readers).

As far as linguistic *processes* are concerned, the second sentence of one report can serve as an example: 'effects will be felt in South Australia...' This sentence is in the passive voice. The writer had the choice of either presenting the event in the active or the passive voice, and he chose to apply the linguistic process of passivization to the sentence. The result is to place emphasis on *effects*, and to delete mention of whoever may be feeling these effects. Given that the writer had the choice of passivizing the sentence or not, we are entitled to ask why he chose to do so.

In the analysis below, a number of syntactic features and processes will be examined from this point of view. Each in isolation gives a certain amount of insight into the meaning of a given sentence, or the intentions of the writer. However, the analysis depends on the consideration of all the features and processes of a given text *together*, as the articulation of an ideological system *in toto*. That is, while items and processes do have meaning in isolation, they acquire new, additional and even different meanings when they occur as part of a new system. Ultimately they derive their specific meaning from the place they occupy in the total system of items and processes which were selected to form the text.

In addition to the meaning which linguistic items and processes have as parts of systems, it is also necessary to consider the meaning which each item and process has *as such*, inherently and intrinsically. Taking the verbs of the first two sentences, 'seem' and 'are', we noted (1) that they share the function of relating an attribute (expressed by the adjective) to the subject noun of each sentence; and (2) that they are involved in expressing 'modality': [*employees reimpose work bans*] is 'likely' and [*industrial action hits the nation*] 'seems certain' (where the proposition is in square brackets). They differ in that 'seem' establishes that relation as the judgement of some beholder (that is, *it seems to someone*), whereas 'are' establishes the relation as an existential statement. In ideological terms there is a considerable difference between the two modes of establishing relations.

As far as the inherent meaning of linguistic processes is concerned, the second sentence quoted above can illustrate the point. The passive form has a number of features which contribute to its meaning. If we contrast 'someone felt the effects' with 'The effects were felt' we note that the focally significant first position is occupied by the subject of the action in the active, and the object of the action in the passive. That is, the focus has switched from subject/actor to object/goal. In the active form the action seems closely connected with the subject; in the passive form the action has become attached to the object, as a kind of resultant quality or attribute of the object. This is so much the case that one can go one step further and talk of the 'felt effect', where the attributive adjectival nature of 'felt' is complete. Similarly, whereas the verb has its process/event meaning in the active, in the passive the verb is adjective-like, quality-like, state-like. These are not all the meanings and effects of the passive but they suffice to indicate the ideological significance of the form: focus on the affected entity; representation of the action as a quality/state, and as an attribute of the affected entity; the possibility of deleting the subject/agent of the sentence.

A comprehensive analysis of any text will provide at one and the same time (1) a full syntactic/grammatical description of the text, and (2) a statement of the ideology which guided the selection of the linguistic features and processes. A reading of this kind may reveal meanings which are additional to a reading of the surface alone, or it may reveal ideological contradictions and tensions within the text. It can be an aid in reconstituting the original event.

In what follows I apply this methodology to two newspaper reports. My intention is twofold: on the one hand I wish to give an example of the application of the methodology; on the other I wish to draw out the ideologies which shaped the construction of (and are contained in) the text, in order to recover something like the original text.[4] My comments are organized under three headings, according to the broad linguistic function of the linguistic items and processes:[5]

1    those features which express the speaker/writer's perception and classification of events and their attendant participants — the expression of experiential meanings;
2    those features which express the speaker/writer's attitude towards the proposition and towards his audience — the expression of interpersonal meanings;
3    those features which express the speaker/writer's wish to structure the information which he presents — the expression of contextual meanings.

The two texts (pp. 130-1) deal with the same topic, namely an impending strike by telecommunications technicians. Text one is from the Adelaide afternoon paper the *News*; text two is from the Melbourne morning paper, the *Age*. The latter has the reputation of being 'the best' Australian paper, while the former has a distinct down-market reputation.

Below I provide an analysis of a number of sentences from the two reports, under the three headings mentioned. I offer some comments on the significance of the linguistic and ideological transformations contained in the reports.

### *The expression of experiential meaning*

Sentence 1, the *Age*: 'Telecom employees are likely to reimpose work bans or strike within a week unless their demands are met on pay negotiations.' Processes (actions, events, states) may be presented in two ways: by verbs, or by nouns (nominalizations) which express verbal action. Here we have both. The verbs are: 'are', 'reimpose', 'strike', 'met'. The nouns which express verbal action are: 'work bans', 'demands', 'pay negotiations' (and possibly 'employees'). English has the facility to express verbal action, as well as the actors, objects and other entities involved in these, either as full sentences or as single nouns, by the process of nominalization. Thus 'work bans' is systematically related to *Someone bans work*; 'demands' to *Someone demands something*; 'pay negotiations' to *Someone negotiates about pay (with someone)*. In reconstructing the full sentence form from the nominalization it becomes clear that while we can recover the types of entities which were involved in the action, their specific identity is generally irrecoverable. From an ideological point of view this is significant: it may be that we are interested in these participants only as types or roles (so that their individual identity does indeed not matter); it may be that the writer does not know the identity of the participants, and the nominalization provides a way of avoiding such mention; it may be that the identity of the participants is important (indeed, frequently this does happen, as when negotiations become problematic), but we are not provided with that information.

The two alternative forms of reporting one event (nominalization or full sentence) have other significant implications. A sentence must always be situated in time (at the very least the verb must express past or present tense); a nominalization need not. By expressing an event in nominal form it is at once taken out of time, and can therefore be readily assimilated to 'timeless' sets of categories. The event is taken out of the world of the specific, concrete, and placed in the world of the general, abstract. In this way events can be assimilated to a pre-existent paradigm or ideology of *industrial action, pay negotiations, demands, work bans*, etc. From a reporter's point of view both the fixed categories and the ideology are necessary to clarify the event, and certainly more manageable than the classification of shifting elusive issues through the more specific and fluid full sentence forms.

However, the sentence contains both verbs and nominalizations. We may ask which events are reported in verbal and which in nominalized form. Of the four verbs only 'strike' expresses a concept at the heart of industrial conflict ('reimpose' derives its meaning from its nominalized object); all three nominalizations express concepts which are at the centre of industrial conflict. It is interesting that the crucial actions are expressed in a linguistic form which presents them as objects, entities.

Some of the participants in these events and processes are recoverable: 'Telecom employees' is subject/actor of 'reimpose', '(work) bans', 'demands', 'strike'. The participants of 'pay negotiations' may

*Industrial disputes*

## TELECOM STRIKE THREAT

1 Telecom employees are likely to reimpose work bans or strike within a week unless their demands are met on pay negotiations.

2 The federal executive of the 26,000-member Australian Telecommunications Employees Association drew up a plan for a fresh industrial campaign after a seven-hour meeting yesterday.

3 The recommendations will be put to members in Sydney today, in Brisbane, Perth, Adelaide and Hobart tomorrow, and in Melbourne next Tuesday.

4 Action could be taken as early as tomorrow or Friday, because the executive could then have the necessary support of three States and a majority of members.

5 The executive is also seeking rank-and-file support to withdraw from Arbitration Commission Full Bench hearings on the union's wage claim.

6 The plans for industrial action and a boycott on bench hearings would be put into effect unless the union gets 'genuine' wage negotiations with Telecom.

7 The union's assistant federal secretary, Mr Mick Musumeci, said last night the Federal Goernment's 'phantom' industrial co-ordinating committee had prevented Telecom from negotiating freely on the side of wage increases.

8 Negotiations before Arbitration Commissioner E. J. Clarkson broke down last week after Telecom had offered a $7 increase.

9 The union is seeking about $20.

10 Commissioner Clarkson referred the talks to the Full Bench last Monday to set an arbitrary increase.

## WORK BANS

11 The ATEA, hearing that the bench would award a rise of only about $8, failed to persuade the bench to send the parties back to the negotiating table with Commissioner Clarkson.

12 The bench is due to sit again next Wednesday.

13 The union imposed work bans in June in support of its original 20 per cent pay claim, causing widespread disruption to national telecommunications.

14 The bans took about three weeks to have a serious effect, because breakdowns in the system were gradual.

15 Mr Musumeci said last night he expected that members would support the recommendation.

16 He claimed the settlement terms of the June-July dispute had been flouted by Telecom's limited negotiating ability.

17 Telecom had also failed to give proper recognition to comparative wage rates in private enterprise when studying ways of applying increases.

*TV men vote to stay on strike*

18 There is no end in sight to the 13-day-old strike by commercial television production workers.

## Text 2    From the News

---

### PHONE CHAOS LIKELY NEXT WEEK

*TV strike continues*

1 Industrial action seems certain to hit the nation's telecommunications network from early next week.

2 Effects will be felt in South Australia — where more than 2500 Telecom workers will meet tomorrow.

3 Most likely action is bans on new business phone installations, bans on maintenance and bans on repairs to call-recording equipment.

4 In Sydney today a meeting of striking television production workers voted to continue their strike and meet again at mid-day tomorrow.

5 The meeting was told the deputy president of the Arbitration Commission, Mr Justice Robinson, had called for a compulsory conference of all parties in Melbourne this afternoon.

6 The Professional Radio and Electronics Institute, whose members have been working throughout the strike, have called for a meeting tomorrow where an executive recommendation for a 24-hour stoppage will be put.

7 Adelaide Telecom workers, members of the Australian Telecommunications Employees' Association, will meet at the Dom Polski Centre, Angas St at 12.15 pm tomorrow.

8 They are upset at a decision to refer their claim for a 20 per cent wage rise to the Arbitration Commission.

9 The union's federal executive met in Melbourne yesterday and decided on mass meetings throughout the nation to back a protest campaign of industrial action.

10 A final decision which rests largely with meetings in Melbourne and Sydney during the next two days, will be decided by an aggregate vote of members.

11 The workers are expected to be asked to endorse immediate industrial action if Telecom refuses to negotiate on their wage demands.

12 The dispute has been brewing for some months, with protracted negotiations between the union and Telecom failing to find common ground.

### HEARING

13 The dispute apart from hitting telephone services, especially STD calls, could also hit telex operations and data processing systems.

14 The Full Bench hearing is expected to be held from next week, and already it has warned the union it could forfeit backpay on its demands if it takes industrial action.

seem equally recoverable, that is 'employees' (or their representatives) and 'Telecom management'. However, the fact of the situation
was that 'Telecom management' (itself a nominalization) insisted
that they were not permitted by 'government' and the rules of
arbitration procedures to negotiate. This shows the effect of nominalizations: a reader may feel that he or she can easily recover the
deleted entities; a reporter can readily shelter behind this unfounded
expectation on the reader's part.

Similarly, the deleted actor of the passive 'their demands are met'
is not recoverable: the identity of this actor was precisely what was at
issue in the dispute — management, government or arbitration court?

Sentence 2, the *News*: 'Industrial action seems certain to hit the
nation's telecommunications network from early next week.' The
processes here are: verbs — 'seems', 'hit'; nominalization — 'industrial
action'. Neither 'seems' nor 'hit' is a verb which expresses or explains
concepts of industrial relations; 'hit' becomes imbued with meaning
only in the context of its subject/actor and its object/goal (unlike
'strike', 'work ban', etc.). The nominalization, 'industrial action',
does express such a concept; however, it is of such generality that
it encompasses all aspects of the subject within itself. It is a concept
at the highest level of generality; and so indeed is the object of the
sentence, 'the nation's telecommunications network'. The nominalization 'industrial action' is more complex than those just considered.
It stands in a relation to a sentence of the form *The action is industrial (action)*; *action* itself stands in a relation to *someone acts on
someone/something.* It is quite obvious that the identity of both
*someones* or *something* are entirely irrecoverable. The nominalization dissolves in a haze. The relative specificness of the *Age* sentence
emerges by comparison with the *News* sentence.

In a seeming paradox, the *News* uses a physical, action verb, 'hit',
but with a subject/actor of the highest generality, 'industrial action',
and with an object/goal of equally high generality. 'Hit' must therefore either take on an equally abstract meaning (not the physical,
aggressive *punch*, but the abstract, vague *affect*), or else readers
are expected to interpret 'industrial action' and 'nation('s telecom
network)' in a concrete, physical, personal form. If the latter, then
the *News* is inviting its readers to view abstract events on the national
political plane in terms of a bar-room brawl. It is clear that the two
statements immediately impose distinctly different paradigms on the
events. (The fact that both are the opening sentences is most significant in this connection.)

In the *Age* sentence human actors (those which are stated and those which can be recovered) perform actions which are part of their sphere and within their power — striking, demanding, negotiating. In the *News* sentence a subject/actor of the highest generality performs (?) an action which is at once general and metaphoric or, on the literal plane, not within its power (whatever that means here).

Sentence 2, the *Age*: 'The federal executive of the 26,000-member Australian Telecommunications Employees' Association drew up a plan for a fresh industrial campaign after a seven-hour meeting yesterday.' As in the first sentence, the crucial actions are presented in nominalizations — 'plan', 'industrial campaign', 'meeting'; the verb 'drew up' is empty, deriving its meaning from 'plan'. The subject/actor of 'plan' and 'meeting' is an institution (though as such still a plausible actor); the subject/actor of 'campaign' is presumably but not certainly, 'employees'.

Sentence 2, the *News*: 'Effects will be felt in South Australia — where more than 2500 Telecom workers will meet tomorrow.' The verbs are: '(will be) felt', '(will) meet'; the nominalizations: 'effects', 'workers'. The 'experiencer' of 'felt' is not given (it is the deleted subject of the passive), though there is a 'surrogate' experiencer, 'in South Australia'. That is, rather than naming the people or institutions who will be affected, the reporter suggests that it will be 'felt [by everyone] in South Australia'. This was patently not the case, though given the paradigm which the reporter has invoked in the first sentence and which is continued here, it is a necessary linguistic and ideological device for him to use. *Effect*, like *action*, is difficult to decode with any degree of accuracy: it is not clear precisely what will affect precisely whom.

Sentence 3, the *Age*: 'The recommendations will be put to members in Sydney...' The central action is expressed in the nominalization which probably derives from *The executive recommends some things*. The passive form has been used to delete mention of the subject/actor of 'put'.

Sentence 3, the *News*: 'Most likely action is bans on new business phone installations, bans on maintenance and bans on repairs to call-recording equipment.' The sole verb in this sentence is 'is'; all other action is expressed through nominalizations: 'action', 'bans', 'installations', 'maintenance', 'repairs', 'recording equipment'.

The pattern is clear, and repeated in the remainder of both reports. The difference between the two reports is equally apparent. Both reporters[7] use a specific ideological grid which they impose on the events. In the case of the *Age* it is a broadly pluralist ideology of industrial relations[8] (as well as specific views of the function of management, including 'union management'); in the case of the *News* it is an ideology of essential conflict, less a model of industrial relations than of class struggle. The two ideologies determine the reporting of the event, that is, they structure the linguistic presentation of the event. In the one case the (nominal) categories of one kind of industrial relations theory are imposed on the world. Within this model most processes are absorbed into abstract nominal concepts. Some processes are presented verbally, with causal powers attributed to individuals or institutions ('employees', 'executive'). In the other case highly abstract categories of contention and conflict at the largest social level are imposed on the same world. It is not possible to say that this conflict is overtly presented in class terms: indeed the largest grouping, the nation (Australia) and the next largest, the state (South Australia), are portrayed as unified wholes, affected as wholes by the oppositional 'industrial action'. (In other words, a unified society vs. industrial action which is extraneous to that society.) While the *News* report does become more specific, the oppositional structure is adhered to; similarly, the *News* report prefers to assign agency to the largest possible or most abstract entity. So in sentence 4 it is 'the meeting' which votes, rather than the 'production workers' (that is, *production workers voted at a meeting...* would be perfectly possible linguistically, but less in line with the ideological framework).

### The expression of interpersonal meaning

The expression of the writer's attitude towards the proposition contained in a sentence has been briefly discussed above. On the face of it this seems to have nothing to do with interpersonal meaning. That is, if speaker/writer and hearer/reader are related by a message, we expect some reference (however implicit) to aspects of the speaker—hearer relation. However, the situation is one where the paper speaks to its readers with the intention to inform them, ostensibly at least. Hence one aspect of interpersonal meaning is to achieve solidarity between the paper's point of view and the reader's. In such a framework it is clear that the writer's expressed attitude to the proposition does have interpersonal effect. It represents an attempt to structure the reader's interpretation of the event, and to bring him or her into agreement with the paper's ideology.

All those linguistic forms which express modality in various ways have such interpersonal function: modal auxiliaries (might, would, can, etc.); adjectives expressing certainty/uncertainty (possible, likely, certain, etc.); verbs which express mental process (...*seems* that..., ...*think* that..., ...*feel* that..., etc.). Many of these are present in the two reports. A simple check reveals a difference between the two reports, with the *Age* making greater use of modal auxiliaries than the *News*. Modality is not only conveyed by the presence of modal particles, the absence of these also expresses modality. So, to write 'They are upset...' (sentence 8, the *News*) expresses modality as much as *They seem* (*seem to be, are likely to be*) *upset*... The former conveys 'unproblematic certainty'. By not showing overt signs of modality the meaning may be the more effective.

These forms permit the paper a degree of distancing from or identification with the events which are reported. This has ideological motivations and effects — that is, the paper is able to present material as being more or less close to its own ideological position. Readers perceive such identification or distancing, and will interpret the information accordingly. One of the most prominent forms of such evaluating of information is by the use of quotation marks. Sentence 6 (the *Age*): '...unless the union gets "genuine" wage negotiations...' The quotation marks signal that this is someone else's word, an importation from someone else's text, and not to be read as part of the *Age*'s ideological/linguistic system. Similarly, sentence 7 (the *Age*): '...the Federal Government's "phantom" industrial co-ordinating committee..., represents an allegation by the union, which the paper does not wish to make its own.

The effect of this device depends on the assumption that for both parties the item would constitute an element from a foreign ideological system. The device takes such a coincidence of position for granted and therefore it coerces (even if only temporarily) readers (who might not share the paper's view) into accepting it, or at least into regarding the item in question as 'strange'. A telecom employee reading about the dispute in his union's journal would not find either 'genuine' or 'phantom' in quotation marks. Within the union's ideology the offered negotiations are not genuine, and there is no doubt that the government operates a phantom industrial coordinating committee. The conflict between the two ideologies and forms of discourse becomes overt in both papers' treatment of key terms. When the *Age* present 'genuine' in quotation marks it is an attempt to prise an important element out of one ideological system; when the union journal presents 'genuine' without quotation marks it is an attempt to present that element as a natural, unquestionable part of presented reality.

A number of other devices have a similar effect: attributing a statement to a person (sentence 7, the *Age*: 'The union's assistant federal secretary, Mr Mick Musumeci, said last night...') has a specific effect depending on the ideological 'valuation' of that person in the paper's ideology. The use of 'claimed' rather than *said* (sentence 16, the *Age*: 'He claimed the settlement terms had been flouted...') works similarly.

The use of these devices represents the transformation of events or texts in accordance with the ideological framework of the writer or the paper, just as much as the use of the linguistic devices for the expression of experiential meaning does. In the latter case, the initial classification and subsequent transformation of events proceeds as though it were based on physical reality — that's what it is, that's what happened. In the case of interpersonal meaning, the social bases of classifications and transformations are more apparent. It is a case of the contention of social forces for the possession of meaning, of discourse.

Ultimately, both are equally social. For instance, using nominalizations to express verbal actions reflects an attitude of fundamental significance towards the world, and consequently to the reader. Deleting all references to the agents who are causally responsible for certain processes expresses an attitude both to the world, and to the reader.

### The expression of contextual meanings

The expression of experiential and interpersonal meaning has effects which include the expression of contextual meanings. All are responsive to the context of the reported event and of the situation in which the report is received. Conversely, the structuring of the message from its formal aspect has effects on experiential and interpersonal meanings. As mentioned earlier, the order in which events are presented in the report immediately 'sets the stage' for the reading and interpretation of the rest of the report. Comparing the two reports briefly, it is clear that the *Age* tends to choose as first elements in the sentence (a focal position in the sense of announcing 'what the sentence is about') personal or institutional actors involved in the dispute. The majority involve workers or their institutions. This is so in eleven out of sixteen sentences. A further three are passives, where an abstract noun involving action comes first. The *News* tends to choose abstract nouns involving action or the location of action as the first element in the sentence. This is the case in seven out of fourteen sentences; five sentences are passives, where workers are the passive subjects of actions initiated by other forces. Only in three out of fourteen sentences are individuals or institutions in first position.

*Allocation of first position in sentences*

|  | *The* Age<br>*No. of sentences: 16* | *The* News<br>*No. of sentences: 14* |
|---|---|---|
| Personal/<br>Institutional<br>Actors | 11 | 3 |
| Abstract Action/<br>Effect<br>(including passive<br>subject) | 4 | 10 |

It is apparent that the two reports differ significantly from this point of view. The ideological paradigm which is at work in each report clearly guides the structuring of the formal aspects of the message. In one case individuals and their associations are the focus, in the other abstract actions and their effects. In the former, individuals and institutions are presented as the potent forces in the conflict; in the other they (and especially workers) appear as the affected participants, secondary to the large, abstract social forces which are not so much in action as in opposition.

## Notes

1  I wish to thank Heather Annear, who first used the two extracts in a student essay, and John Flower for his helpful comments on a draft of this chapter.

2  My use of 'ideology' instead of 'schema' from here on is deliberate. While schema implies the systematicness and structuredness of categories, ideology implies that such systems and structures are organized from a point of view. This may be known to the writer/speaker or not, consciously offered to or imposed on others, or not. For a discussion of this use of ideology see Tony Trew, 'Theory and ideology at work' and ' "What the papers say": linguistic variation and ideological difference' in Fowler *et al.* 1979; also Kress & Trew 1978.

3  A full reading of the page itself as an utterance would need to consider oppositions such as private—public, male world (politics)—female world (home and family). The effect and meaning of the use of photographs of four women (wives of politicians) in 'Lucky Mrs Staley', which separates the editorial from the feature (politics from family, public from private), the opposition of the photograph of Mrs Staley and the three other photos would need to be examined, as indeed a whole range of other factors such as general layout, type-faces etc.

4  The analysis is not an exhaustive one; I concentrate on the most immediately significant features. For more detailed analyses see Fowler *et al.* 1979. The theory underlying these analyses is outlined in Kress & Hodge 1979.

5  The linguistic theory drawn on here is that of M. A. K. Halliday: see Halliday 1971, 1979.

6  The text as printed here does not preserve the layout in columns, etc., but it does preserve the 'paragraphing' of the originals. That is each numbered section (sentence) corresponds to a 'paragraph' in the originals.

7  Throughout I have used reporter and paper interchangeably. That is no doubt an oversimplification, though it is equally clear that reporters adapt to the 'style' of a paper. The force of my argument is to suggest that 'style' is far from being an ideological neutral term.

8  See e.g. Wood & Elliott 1977.

# 6

# 'The economy': its emergence in media discourse[1]

## MIKE EMMISON

In a recent article Foucault (1979, p. 11) has drawn attention to how the modern conception of government has its origins in the extension of the idea of government of the family — the practice of oeconomy. He writes that what is at stake:

in the establishment of the art of government is the introduction of oeconomy into the area of political practice. This is the case in the 16th century and will still be so in the 18th. In Rousseau's article on Political Economy the problem is still posited in the same terms. He says, roughly: the word 'oeconomy' can only refer to the wise government of the family for the common welfare of all, and this is its original meaning: the problem, writes Rousseau, is how to introduce it, mutatis mutandis, and with all the discontinuities that we will observe, into the general running of the state. To govern a state will therefore mean to set up an oeconomy involving the entire state that is to exercise towards the citizens, the wealth and behaviour of each and everyone, a form of surveillance, of control which is as watchful as that of the head of a family over his household and his goods.

An expression which was important in the 18th century captures this very well: Quesnay speaks of good government as an 'economic government'. This notion has by now become tautological, given that the art of government is just the art of exercising power in the form and according to the model of the economy. But the reason why Quesnay speaks of 'economic government' is that the word 'economy'...is in the process of acquiring a modern meaning, and it is at this moment becoming apparent that the very essence of government, that is the art of exercising power in the form of economy, is to have as its main objective that which we are today accustomed to call the economy.

I have quoted Foucault at some length, for although I am in essential agreement with him, research of my own indicates that the relation between the development of the modern conception of government and the origin of the expression 'the economy' is in need of some clarification.

This paper therefore addresses two related issues: the specific circumstances of the appearance of the term 'the economy', and the fetishistic character of the discourse in which it is located. At a mundane level the language, icons and structure of economic discourse must be theorized as hegemonic, in that they serve not merely to describe but to legitimate the capitalist economic order. Seen in this way the conception of 'the economy' as an abstract object is an example of the process of reification — the generalized ideological counterpart to a commodity-producing society.

The paper reports on a content analysis of a variety of newspapers and magazines, the object being to discover when the category 'the economy' first appears in media discourse. The introduction of the term in fact occurs at a specific historical conjuncture long after the formal emergence of this discourse in the late eighteenth century. Its appearance, it is argued, is related to the rejection of neoclassical economic theory in the 1930s and the onset of large-scale state intervention in the economic affairs of the nation.

I begin by considering the question of the meaning of the term 'economy' as discussed in recent literature in economic anthropology, because this debate has implications which are also significant for an understanding of the emergence of the term.

## The meaning of economy

One of the more persistent themes which have recently been debated in the field of economic anthropology is the applicability of a model derived from market economic systems to an understanding of traditional economic organization. The issue became known as the formalist-substantivist debate after the two opposing meanings of the idea of economy that were to emerge. Briefly, the formalist school held that the meaning of economy was to be found in the logical character of the means—end relationship, that involving questions of choice over scarce or limited resources. The formal meaning of economy is entailed in terms such as 'economizing' or 'economical' as these are currently understood, and it was this market model of economic behaviour which formalists regarded as being equally applicable both to an understanding of the economic life of traditional societies and to the modern economic system to which it owes its origin. The substantivist position, on the other hand, was based on the view that there was a wider meaning to the notion of economy which, in the words of the leading advocate of this position, Karl Polanyi:

derives from man's dependence for his living upon nature and his fellows. It refers to the interchange with his natural and social environment insofar as this results in supplying him with the means of material want-satisfaction. (1971, p. 139)

For Polanyi the substantivist and formal meanings of economy are poles apart: 'the latter derives from logic, the former from fact'. Accordingly, substantivists hold that their meaning of economy is of greater analytical use in examining all types of economic systems. They do not deny that a *substantive* economy might be organized predominantly on *formal* lines; their case is that it is mistaken to infer from this that the formal notion of economy is the only one possible. The problem is that in the case of modern market-regulated economic systems the distinction between the formal and substantive meanings is not clear, with the result that the formal meaning is dominant. As Polanyi argues:

As long as the economy was controlled by such a system, the formal and the substantive meanings would in practice coincide. Laymen accept this compound concept as a matter of course; a Marshall, Pareto, or Durkheim equally adhered to it. Menger alone in his posthumous work criticized the term, but neither he nor Max Weber, nor Talcott Parsons after him, apprehended the significance of the distinction for sociological analysis. Indeed, there seemed to be no valid reason for distinguishing between two root meanings of a term which, as we said, were bound to coincide in practice. (p. 141)

A full account of the formalist—substantivist positions is outside the scope of this paper. In fact, the original controversy has now been largely resolved or more accurately dissolved. However, the distinction between the two meanings of economy is crucial to an understanding of changes in economic discourse and specifically, the emergence of the category 'the economy'. Before considering this it is first necessary to look at another aspect of Polanyi's work which is of relevance to these later comments.

Polanyi introduced the idea of a distinction between an embedded and a disembedded type of economy. This is in part related to the distinction previously made between the formal and substantive meanings of economy, but it also raises the more interesting question of the 'visibility' of economic life. The distinction between embedded and disembedded economies also parallels that of the more familiar sociological dichotomies, status and contract, Gemeinschaft and Gesellschaft. Rather than being organized around a distinct institutional sphere of exchange, the market, an embedded economy is one which is characterized chiefly by reciprocity and redistribution. By implication:

As long as these latter forms of integration prevail no concept of an economy need arise. The elements of the economy are here embedded in non-economic institutions, the economic process itself being instituted through kinship, marriage, age-groups, secret societies, totemic associations and public solemnities. The term 'economic life' would here have no obvious meaning. (p. 84)

Now this is crucial. The idea of a historical transition, from embedded to disembedded types of economy, provides a sociological perspective on the question of the emergence and development of the discipline of economics. Put simply, only when economic activity becomes disembedded and conducted through separate institutional spheres can it become visible and thus available as a topic of discourse.

The consensus reached by historians of economic analysis, both orthodox and radical, is that the discipline emerged in its modern form in the late eighteenth century, with its birthdate typically given as the publication of Adam Smith's *Wealth of nations* in 1776. As Therborn has put it: 'Economic discourse emerged as a concomitant of the rise of what this discourse was about: the capitalist economy' (1976, p. 77).

A detailed discussion on the emergence of economics per se is outside our scope, given our concern with the more mundane aspects of economic discourse.[2] However, there is a second aspect of the embedded/disembedded distinction which is of direct relevance and which relates to the question of legitimation of an economic system, the manner in which the arrangements of that system come to be accepted and justified. Where economic activity is conducted through other institutions the means of legitimation are provided by the already existing obligations of kinship and religion.

Wisman, drawing extensively on Habermas, refers to this process as 'tradition steering':

In traditional societies...the economy is not viewed as a separate institution but rather as embedded in the total social fabric. In such societies economic activity is principally steered by tradition. Accordingly, there neither exists, nor is there a social need for a distinct body of economic thought. Just as the economy cannot be viewed by its participants as a separate social institution, so economic thought cannot be viewed as distinct from total social knowledge. (1979, p. 295)

But what legitimates a disembedded economy, one whose arrangements have become separated from other institutions and which as a result are, or at least should be, visible? Wisman's position is that the legitimation for this form of economic activity is provided first by a belief in the natural laws of motion of the market, 'market steering', and then later through the belief in the neutral, technical role of the state which he refers to as 'administrative steering'. This analysis is not necessarily incorrect but it does not go far enough. For what is common to both 'market steering' and 'administrative steering' is that each is part of a distinct body of discursive practices which articulates knowledge of what economic activity entails, of the conditions of its existence and reproduction, of the possibilities and constraints that affect all the agents engaged in this activity. At a far more fundamental level, a mechanism of legitimation for a disembedded economy is provided by the structure of the very discourse that describes it. Put differently, the potentially visible arrangements of this type of economy have become opaque and mystified, one might almost say invisible, as a result of the reified imagery of discourse, whether this takes the form of economic processes 'naturally' controlled by the laws of the market or of an object-like economy subject to neutral state intervention and guidance.

Such a formulation of legitimation clearly does not exhaust all that could be said about such a vast topic. Nor is this merely to repeat what a number of writers on the history of economics and economic philosophy have argued, namely that economic theory is inescapably ideological because as a practice it bears the marks of its social origins.[3] I am referring rather to the more mundane ways in which the economic life of a nation is conceived and conducted, in everyday language in particular. It is at this level that an ideological effect can be discerned.

### Fetishism, language and 'the economy'

Throughout his work Marx accorded a prominent place to the analysis of the relationship between material conditions and the categories through which people become conscious of these conditions. Marx first drew attention to the way in which under the capitalist mode of production the social relationships between the producers and consumers of goods are masked; instead the 'real' relationships appear to be between the material objects that labour has produced. He calls this the 'fetishism of commodities', arguing that it stems from the specifically dual character of the commodities — things which have use for their possessors (use value), but which also have value in exchange (exchange value). Where production for exchange dominates (i.e. capitalism) it is commodities which appear as if in a relationship through this exchange mechanism and not their producers. This notion of commodity fetishism is at the core of Marx's method, the manner in which he systematically moves from surface appearances to their underlying realities. For Marx the entire sum of capitalist activities appears as a vast and elaborate network of appearances every one of which in some way or another hides the true nature of the social process which is its essence. Together this constitutes:

the complete mystification of the capitalist mode of production, the conversion of social relations into things, the direct coalescence of the material production relations with their historical and social determination. It is an enchanted, perverted topsy-turvy world in which Monsieur le Capital and Madame La Terre do their ghost-walking as social characters and at the same time directly as mere things. (Marx 1959, p. 830)

Marx notes in the above passage how capital is not only regarded as a thing, but even appears to come to life and acquire human powers. I would like to suggest that perhaps even more so than in Marx's time, examples of fetishistic thinking are widespread. David Goldway's comments are appropriate here:

Commodity fetishism is not just an intellectual abberation of those who examine commodity economics. Rather it is a way of looking at things that is built in; everyone living in a commodity society is subject to its hypnotism.... The intervention of the market between the act of production and the act of consumption of necessity obscures the social productive process and develops the magical power of making material things 'get up on their hind legs to the labourer'. Our very language becomes infused with fetishist metaphors. A coat is not a coat but a 'good buy'. A superior commodity 'commands' a high price. The market itself comes alive; the newscasters tell us daily that the market is healthy or ailing, vigorous or sluggish, bullish or bearish. And who among us doesn't know that 'money talks'? (1967, p. 435)

To Goldway's list must be added the very term 'economy', for as in the manner of the earlier reification of capital and the market, we now have 'the economy' as something with powers and needs of its own. Indeed we seem to have reached the apotheosis of commodity fetishism in that the totality of the nation's economic activity has come to be regarded as a vast object or machine which 'gets over-heated', is 'off the rails', 'steering the right course' and so on.

Let us consider this central question of the emergence of the expression 'the economy'. Commodity fetishism can account for the category's general appearance but its emergence at a specific historical moment calls for empirical investigation.

### The emergence of 'the economy'

Apart from some minor disagreement over timing there is a fairly well established consensus on the origins of economic science. According to this view, modern economic discourse has a history of approximately two hundred years, so it is surely remarkable that the category which one might think to be the object of this discourse, 'the economy', does not appear until some considerable time later. This is perhaps even more surprising given the popular and widespread usage of the term today. Indeed, its very taken-for-granted status can perhaps be gauged from the fact that no dictionary of economic terms or textbook on economics that I have found to date contains an explicit definition of the category. Raymond Williams's (1976) otherwise admirable collection of the *Keywords* of culture and society equally fails to offer any comments on this term.

In an attempt to discover when the term enters into public usage I undertook a content analysis of a number of newspapers and magazines. The research proceeded along qualitative rather than quantitative lines in that once the point of emergence was roughly located no attempt at enumeration was made. Instead attention was paid more to the term's context of use: for example, which word or phrase was used prior to its emergence and had any changes occurred since then? The analysis is based on material from the London *Times*, the *New Statesman*, the *New York Times*, *Time* magazine and *The Economist*, although comparative checks with some Australian periodicals were made. The results of this exercise are summarized in figure 1.

*Figure 1*   *'The economy': vocabulary and usage*

| Time period | Vocabulary | Context of use |
|---|---|---|
| Up to 1930 | 'economy' in formal sense of economizing — a state of affairs | Formal |
| Laissez-faire and the transition to monopoly capitalism | 'The economic system' — as synonymous with capitalism | Descriptive |
| 1930-45 | 'The economy' — with qualifiers | Substantive |
| Keynesianism and large-scale increase in state involvement | e.g. 'The economic machine' 'The national economy' 'The economic structure' 'The general economy' | Passive connotation |
| 1945-80 | 'The economy' — fewer qualifiers and use of mechanical/biological metaphors | Substantive |
| Postwar boom to recent crisis | e.g. 'working flat-out' 'ailing' 'off the rails' 'needs priming' | Active connotation connotation, increasing anthropomorphism extending to other items in economic discourse |

It is not until the 1930s that the term 'the economy' makes the first appearance in its contemporary usage. Prior to the 1930s one finds many references to the notion of 'economy' but these are all in the formal sense of the word discussed earlier. Examples of this are found throughout the nineteenth century:

railway companies are acting out of motives of economy rather than passenger safety (*Times*, 10 Sept. 1840)

'make an economy in space' (leader on planning for the Great Exhibition, *Times*, 23 Nov. 1850)

'an article of luxury not of economy' (*Times*, 6 December 1855)

Economy is seen as a state of affairs achieved by rational people in the various spheres of their lives, be they private citizens, business leaders or politicians. It is the classical formal sense of economizing which is dominant.

It is possible to cite a number of candidate words or phrases which might be regarded as forerunner to the modern use of the term. There are numerous references to 'The Revenue', 'The State of Trade', 'The State of British Finance', but, as I will argue later, it is misleading to regard these as linguistic equivalents. Closer to the contemporary usage would be expressions such as 'the economical and industrial conditions of the country' (*Times*, 24 June 1885), but still the formal sense is apparent.

Usage of the notion of economy in this way continues after the turn of century, as indeed it still does today:

actual economies in our personal consumption of commodities (*New Statesman*, 17 July 1915)

something done for economy (*Economist*, 5 Oct. 1929)

An expression which appears towards 1920 is 'the economic system'. This is a phrase which today has, in some usages, an equivalent status to that of 'the economy'. Its preferred referent, however, is still its initial usage, in which it appears more as a synonym for capitalism, as a particular mode of production. Thus:

even the complete abolition of all 'excessive profits' whatever they mean, if it were possible within the present economic system, would not really effect a very substantial or lasting reduction in the prices of most necessaries of life. (*New Statesman*, 26 June 1920)

It is not until the mid-1930s that the category 'the economy' in its modern sense is coined. Its appearance I argue is closely tied to developments in theoretical economic discourse, most obviously the writings of Keynes. The earliest media reference I have discovered is in 1936, the year of the publication of Keynes's *General theory of employment, interest and money*. The term is in fact used by Keynes in the book, although along with a number of similar expressions. What is important here, it seems to me is not to puzzle over a precise and incontrovertible date of appearance but rather to consider what political and ideological circumstances were responsible for this particular category emerging as dominant.

Foucault is correct in suggesting a connection between the emergence of the term and the conception of government as manager of the economic affairs of the nation, but conceptually he would appear to locate the origin of the expression far earlier. My own interpretation is that Keynesianism represents an 'overdetermination' of the

recognition of the connected series government/management/
economy and that the emergence and subsequent adoption of
this expression relates to the manner in which the Keynesian critique
of the prevailing economic orthodoxy is made.

Consider the years immediately prior to the publication of *The
general theory*. It is in this period that the notion of formal economy.
the cornerstone of neoclassical theory, comes to be viewed with
increasing suspicion, at least in the left-wing magazines. Throughout
the early months of 1933 the *New Statesman*'s editorials contain
numerous increasingly vitriolic references to the idea of economy,
and to those still arguing that economy, frugality and thrift are
the solutions to the nation's unemployment. Thus the *New Statesman*
claimed on 14 January 1933, under the heading of 'The "Economy"
Madness' that: 'the false god of "economy" blinds his devotees even
to their own interests'. And on 25 February 1933: Mr Chamberlain
and Mr MacDonald are so obsessed with "economy" that they can
make no distinction between miserly hoarding and indiscriminate
prodigality'. Keynes himself, in an article in the same magazine on
4 February 1933 entitled 'A programme for Unemployment', similarly treats the notion of economy with some suspicion, confining
it within the now obligatory inverted commas.

I want to argue that the introduction of the term in its modern
usage is inextricably bound up with the rejection of the tenets of
neoclassical theory in the 1930s which owes so much to Keynes.
For it was Keynes's lasting achievement that he was able to show
that the economic wellbeing of a nation could be vastly improved
by the then heretical notion of acting in ways that had up to that
time been considered formally uneconomical. Formal economic
orthodoxy, with its divination of the laws of supply and demand,
could only conceive of individual economic agents, be they firms
or people, all subject to the market mechanism. Keynes's suggestion
was that there existed a level to economic analysis other than this,
in fact a national economic structure that was capable of being, and
indeed should be modified by government action. Keynes does not
reject formalist assumptions outright. Rather, he argues that it is
necessary to conceive of formal economic action but to do so in
terms of a wider substantive notion of economy. Linguistically, to
facilitate the expression of this idea, he begins to refer to 'the
economy' as an abstract entity, as something more than the combined activity of all the individual economic units.

Clearly, the whole Keynesian revolution in economic thinking
cannot be reduced to a minor change in terminology. But there is

sense in which a change in linguistic usage was a necessary feature of the ideas he had developed. Neoclassical economic theory was built around the reification of the laws of supply and demand — 'the market'; in rejecting the assumption of the inviolability of this mechanism, Keynes replaces one reified notion with another. The whole economic structure — 'the economy' — becomes the new focus of economic wisdom.

What Keynesianism heralds, to refer to Wisman again, is legitimation of economic activity through 'administrative steering'. Linguistically, this entails a change in the conception of this activity. For the state has to be able to steer some 'thing', hence the introduction of the definite article, an apparently innocent grammatical convention but one which is ultimately ideological.

Grammatical convention probably accounts for some of the attenuation of the qualifiers which accompany 'the economy' in the early years of its appearance. Yet the term is frequently linked with others until the postwar period and on occasions after that. One finds, for example, qualifiers such as 'the economic structure', 'the national economy', 'the British national economy', 'the general economy' and so on. Keynes himself uses 'the economic machine', 'the economic scheme', 'a monetary economy' amongst others in addition to 'the economy' by itself.

There is, however, a further grammatical change which has an important ideological component. Between the onset of the use of the term, with or without qualifiers, and about the beginning of the postwar period (it is not possible to date this precisely) the dominant metaphorical usage is essentially of a *passive* object. The economy is something which has things done to it or is shaped by other forces. Thus:

The British national economy has been converted from one based on competitive free enterprise into one whose strategic centres are controlled. (*Economist*, 3 Aug. 1940)

It is increasingly clear that our economy is taking its shape from the war. (*Economist*, 27 July 1940)

In the postwar period, however, there begins to appear a further change in metaphor. The change is not abrupt, nor is it total, but it certainly is there and it is one which has clearly accelerated in recent years. It consists in a move from a passive conception — the economy which has things done to it — to an *active* conception — an economy which has the capacity to act by itself, has needs of its own and which ultimately acquires an almost anthropomorphic status. Thus:

If the British economy is to be given the room to manoeuvre on which its efficiency depends...

and:

...to the needs of the economy as a whole...(both in *The Economist*, 5 Jan. 1952)

An important part of this new conception of the economy is the wholesale adoption of mechanical and biological metaphors to depict economic activity:

The economy was working at such high pressure that any additional burdens ...were bound to blow price valves. (*Time* magazine, 10 Jan. 1944)

Since the U.S. economy came through the first quarter full of vigour expressions of doubt about its health for the rest of 1957 all but disappeared last week. (*Time* magazine, 15 Apr. 1957)

...what the economy can produce going full out. (London *Times*, 11 Apr. 1967)

During this period, but increasingly since 1970, similar metaphors to those noted by Goldway have been applied to other items in economic discourse. Thus we are said to be fighting a war against 'the disease of inflation'. Units of currency too are endowed with health or sickness — 'the dollar is ailing', 'the yen is strong', 'the pound had a bad day' and so on. But it is in references to the economy that this process is best seen. The following remarks made recently by Australian politicians are revealing:

We were too optimistic about what we or the economy, working in partnership could perform. (Prime Minister Fraser, *National Times* 25 Aug. 1979)

The economy can employ more people. (Minister for Employment and Youth Affairs, Mr Viner, ABC radio, 20 Nov. 1979)

The economy urgently needs tax reductions. (Queensland Premier, J. Bjelke-Petersen, ABC radio, 4 Jan. 1980)

Here the economy has become a business partner, an employer and a taxpayer. Its anthropomorphization could hardly be more complete.

## Ideology and 'the economy'

It was suggested earlier that the changes in usage which have been identified have ideological implications. They stem not merely from the fetishistic character of the discourse but from the way in which the elements in the discourse are structured and from the overall ordering of its themes, I want to illustrate this by making some comments on the two cartoons reproduced in illustrations 1 and 2 for what is depicted in the cartoon images provides a remarkably concise illustration of some of the theoretical points made earlier The cartoons, spanning a period of just over fifty years, each endeavour to depict the workings of the economic process — the principal agents involved, their obligations, constraints and so on — in a way which reflects the dominant assumptions which were current at the time of their production.

In Partridge's *Punch* cartoon of 1921 we see Capital confronting Labour, with the state nowhere to be seen. 'Economic Law', the prize fighter, is ready to step in on Capital's behalf if this should be necessary. In one image Partridge has juxtaposed the essential ingredients in neoclassical economic doctrine. The idea of 'the economy' is still to be formulated and instead it is the market mechanism which is presented anthropomorphically. The ideological component of Partridge's cartoon scarcely needs any decoding; the economic process is to be seen as straightforward and compelling. From the use of the older categories of political economy to the sneer on 'Economic Law's' face the message is clear: those who defy the Holy Grail of economic orthodoxy will meet an untimely fate. The caption simply underlines the point.

In contrast, the Pickering cartoon taken from the *Australian* in 1976, apparently more innocuous in appearance, has its message more deeply embedded. Here the economic process has shifted squarely into the arena of state intervention. 'The economy' is now with us as a somewhat unpredictable snake, and economic mangagement is depicted as being too much for Treasurer Phillip Lynch to handle. The snake swallows both him and Prime Minister Fraser, and they join the already ingested Labour Prime Minister Whitlam in the economy's bowels. There is no apparent ideological side being taken here. All that is important now is the economy's growth and successful management.

Nevertheless, the use of 'the economy' in this way serves an important political function. For the economy is cast as something more compelling and powerful than given political and sectional

UP AGAINST IT.

CAPITAL TO LABOUR. "YOU MAY SUCCEED IN KNOCKING ME OUT, BUT DON'T FORGET THAT THEN YOU'LL HAVE TO FIGHT A CHAMPION THAT NO ONE CAN STAND UP AGAINST."

*Illustration 1*   Punch *cartoon, 13 April 1924*

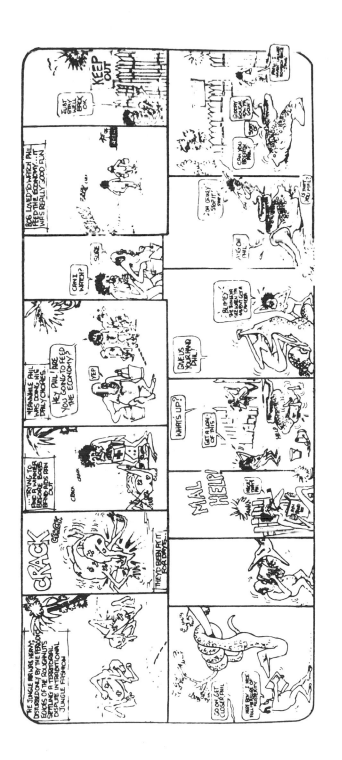

*Illustration 2   Larry Pickering cartoon appearing in the Australian, 11 September 1976*

demands. The economy has here become an example of a linguistic sign to which 'the ruling class strives to impart a supraclass eternal character' (Voloshinov 1973, p. 23). The economy, in short, appears to be on no one's side. In this way unpopular political decisions and policies can be taken and justified whilst avoiding the charge of class- or self-interest. The nation's economy is apparently more important than its citizens.

We have all grown accustomed to hearing the economy referred to in such a manner by politicians. The fact that the term is employed by spokesmen from both the right and the left (although in different contexts and with different 'recipes' for health and sickness) should warn us against an interpretation of such usage as simply a political strategy. This view of the economy is such a basic feature of a capitalist society that the language and indeed cartoons which serve to constitute it are produced without reflection. It has become the 'natural' way to see economics. Although this paper has concentrated almost entirely on a single category, 'the economy', similar movements can be seen in a much wider variety of economic discourse in that they semantically convey a world of normality, a set arrangement that cannot be usefully challenged. As Stewart Clegg has argued:

even in moments of severe structural crisis in the economic sphere, such is the opacity and embeddedness of a people's ordinarily available ways of theorizing…that the consequences of crises in the economic system remain more or less taken-for-granted. Little effort is expended in critique or counter-strategy because the weapons of critique are not available. Unemployment, inflation or wage-cuts can come to be accepted as normal, as natural, as something which could not have been otherwise, as their sense is constituted in and through hegemonic forms of theorizing. (1978, p. 19)

### Conclusion

Any programme concerned with the understanding of forms of control in bourgeois society must include analysis of the everyday, the routine, the normal. This paper has sought to demonstrate both theoretically and empirically that an important aspect of the legitimation of capitalist social formations is to be found in the mundane features of the discourse which depicts our economic activity. There is now a growing literature[4] concerned with the relationship of ideology and everyday cultural practices. It is hoped that the diversity of tradition which is informing this work is matched by an equally innovative outcome.

## Notes

1  I wish to thank Paul Boreham for his helpful comments and advice on an earlier version of this paper.
2  For a recent study which seeks to reappraise the question of the emergence of economic discourse, in particular the assumption that there is a continuity that can be readily granted to successive texts, see Tribe 1978.
3  See, for example, Meek 1967; Robinson 1964; Dobb 1973; Eagly 1968.
4  See, for example, Barrett et al. 1979; Glasgow University Media Group 1976, 1980; Kress & Hodge 1979; Kress & Trew 1978; Williamson 1978; Woolfson 1976.

# 7

# 'Reality' East and West

WALERY PISAREK

Journalistic information is based, to a large extent, on the use of words. By means of words, newspapers present chosen phenomena, events, people and subjects to readers and influence their attitudes to them. If this is true, an analysis of the words used in newspapers will allow us to reconstruct the image of the world presented by the press and the attitudes propagated by it.

The style of the socialist press has been on many occasions a matter of interest to Western linguists and political scientists, but analyses of socialist newspapers have been misued for antisocialist propaganda. Descriptions and analyses of language phenomena have the same features as those found in most Western studies of social phenomena in socialist countries. By such features I mean, first, the feeling of superiority towards the described phenomena; second, the belief that for 'obvious reasons' science in a socialist country cannot deal with given phenomena freely; third, the implication that the researcher uses only reliable sources, and that his or her work is factual and objective; fourth, a biased choice of cases and presentation of unnatural phenomena as typical; fifth, attempts to show, or mere suggestions of, similarities between reality in socialist countries and that in totalitarian countries; sixth, a selective emphasis on superficial phenomena without any attempt to go to the heart and origin of the matter.

From such studies one can learn that, for example, the language of the socialist press has a tendency to overuse solemn words and expressions, exaggerated metaphors and comparisons, and in general a tendency to use emotional vocabulary often of religious origin (Rossbacher 1966). Such language does in fact occur in some journalism, but it is a big mistake to see this tendency to solemn and emotional expression as the essence of the language of the socialist press, since this is to take for a vital feature what is of marginal and superficial importance. The mistake is particularly serious when one wants to draw conclusions about philosophy and attitudes towards life from a language analysis.

## Stylistics

Similarities and differences in the stylistics of press publishing in various countries have been a fruitful subject for comparative studies. Stich has accurately demonstrated some of the variation in his article on persuasive functional style. According to Stich, despite the fact that 'social and ideological change often brings about a radical reorientation in the repertory of the persuasive functional stylistic stratum...stylistic differences between the persuasive functional style of individual languages are still quite distinct, both between languages that are typologically far removed from one another and languages, like the Slavonic group, that are genetically related' (1973, p. 65). These differences have been conditioned historically and culturally. Many features of various styles which were formed in very early times have survived until the present day and are now only a national form which embraces entirely new contents. There are many simple and convincing examples to be found in vocabulary. Thus, in the slogan 'military service is the holy duty of a citizen' Polish speakers use the adjective 'holy', which is a word of religious origin, but in current usage it does not mean that the user is a believer. If we started drawing similar conclusions from an etymological analysis of words forming the basic vocabulary in the Polish press we might come to the conclusion that the press is destined not only for deeply religious people but also for very warlike people who at the same time earn their living from capital resources. Words belonging to the military vocabulary are very commonly used, and the metaphors 'to put it on somebody's account', 'to discount something', etc., occur with similar frequency.

However, it is the image of the world presented in press reports and not the analysis of style that is the subject of this chapter. I wish to show how the lexical surface of the language of a journalistic text reflects and at the same time impresses upon a reader a specific image of the world and a particular attitude towards reality. This image of the world and the attitude towards reality as presented by the press are, in my opinion, basic factors in its educational role, which is a historical and national role of far greater importance than the temporary propaganda function of the press.

Material for the analysis is provided by four dictionaries of word frequencies in the contempoary Soviet/Russian, Czechoslovak, Polish and West German press.[1] Three of them represent the press of socialist countries, one the press of a capitalist country. All dictionaries were published at about the same time and are based on press texts from the same period (1961-67). All have many common features both in the area of functional (grammatical or structural) vocabulary and in the area of words with a full meaning.

In all four dictionaries the preposition *in* clearly has a high frequency of use. The preposition is used in expressions locating an action in space (e.g. *in* Warsaw) or in time (e.g. *in* 1968). Unusually high frequency of use of this preposition is a feature which distinguishes newspaper language from other variants of national language and particularly spoken language as used in everyday speech and the language of *belles-lettres.* This feature of press language is most visible in news texts, where the preposition *in* comes before the conjunction *and* (in Polish and Russian, *i*; in Slovak, *a*; in German, *und*).

The frequency of use of names in the word count is an indication of similarities and differences in the degree to which the newspapers of the four countries are interested in the affairs of other countries. The name of the mother country is the name most frequently used in all cases, i.e. the name Poland is most often used in the Polish press, Slovakia in the Slovak press, and the Federal Republic of Germany in the West German press. Moreover, the names of the two biggest world powers, the USSR and the USA, and also of a few other industrially developed countries such as France, Great Britain and the Federal Republic of Germany, are used particularly often. It can be seen from the comparative analysis of vocabulary that the Polish and Slovak press pay more attention to Central European socialist countries than do the Soviet and West German press, i.e. Polish journalists write relatively often about the GDR, Hungary and Czechoslovakia and the Slovak press contains more about Poland and Hungary. The interests of the Soviet press — and also the Polish press — are, to a large extent, worldwide: the names of Vietnam, Middle Eastern and African countries and the so-called Third World countries in general can be found quite often in their pages.

All these conclusions should however be treated with great caution. Although the dictionaries used in the analysis are based on press texts from approximately the same period, whether or not a piece of information on a country will be printed may be a matter of weeks or even days rather than a matter of years. That is why the most trustworthy observations in this analysis are only those on the widespread interest of the press in news from the USSR and the USA, on the definite interest of the Polish, Slovak and West German presses in problems of neighbouring or not too distant countries, and finally the observation on the special attention given by the Soviet press to Third World countries. Findings about the frequency of occurrence of the names of smaller countries should be treated as no more than a source for hypotheses.

## Noun frequencies

In order to find the subjects and the concepts which are of particular interest to the press let us compare thirty word lists of the most frequently used nouns. The procedure will also make it possible to find out similarities and differences between press texts from the four countries. Let us start from the common features:

1   the noun most frequently used in the newspapers of all four countries is the word corresponding to the English 'year' (Pol. *rok + lata*; Sl. *rok*; Rus. *god*; Germ. *Jahr*);
2   the words dealing with time play an important role in all press texts (Pol. *rok, czas, okres*; Sl. *rok, den, čas*; Rus. *god, vremya*; Germ. *Jahr, Zeit, Zukunft, Monat*);
3   the words dealing with place belong also to the category of highest frequency in all four collections of press texts (Pol. *kraj, miasto*; Sl. *krajina, miesto, svet*; Rus. *strana, rayon, mir, oblast*; Germ. *Welt, Land, Stadt*);
4   Besides the above-mentioned 'year' the other most frequently used words in all four collections of texts are: 'country' (Pol. *kraj*, Rus. *strana*, Sl. *krajina*, Germ. *Land*); 'party' (Pol. *partia*, Rus. *partya*, Sl. *strana*, Germ. *Partei*); 'man' (Pol. *człowiek*, Rus. *chelovek*, Sl. *človek*, Germ. *Mensch*); 'problem' (Pol. *sprawa*, Rus. *delo*, Sl. *otazka*, Germ. *Frage*); 'time' (Pol. *czas*, Rus. *vremya*, Sl. *čas*, Germ. *Zeit*).
5   In each of the thirty word lists the most frequently used word (i.e. first on the list) is used approximately five times more often than the noun occupying the thirtieth position on the list, i.e. *god:oblast* = 4.7:1; *rok:zväz* = 4.6:1; *rok:okres* = 4.6:1; *Jahr:Seite* = 4.5:1.

Descriptions which name places and dates and locate the problems of countries and people are a basic feature of press texts notwithstanding the sociopolitical conditions in which they function.

Every fifth word in each of the four noun lists has its precise semantic equivalent in the remaining three lists. At the same time, the three lists representing the press of socialist countries reveal distinct differences from the West German list. The West German list contains as many as 15 words out of the total number of 30 which have no equivalents in any of the three remaining lists. The Polish list contains only four such words (*przykład, kultura, konisja* and *okres*), the Slovak list eight (*republika, deň, umenie, mládez, žena, konferencia, literatura, koruna*), and the Russian list seven (*rayon, zhizn, borba, mashina, kolkhoz, komanda, oblast*). Moreover, the Russian list includes 17 words with equivalents in the Polish list, 16 words with equivalents in the Slovak list and only 10 words with equivalents in the West German list. These subtotals include the above-mentioned six words which are common to all four 30-word lists.

Comparison of the most frequently used words appearing only in the West German list with the most frequently used words from the three remaining lists which are not included in the West German list is especially significant. Most important are the words from the top of the two lists. It is hardly accidental that the word *DM* (*Deutsche Mark*) tops the West German list and the words for *work* are at the top of each of the socialist lists. These two words -- DM and work — can be regarded as the keywords in the vocabularies of newspapers representing the capitalist and socialist word. They tell much more about the press, its language and the sender's attitude than culturally conditioned figures of speech. The keywords revealed in the analysis enable us to define the image of the world presented by the capitalist press as money-oriented, and by the socialist press as work-oriented.

From the remaining words, one can contrast at least four pairs of concepts characterizing different political systems and different ideologies, namely: *Regierung* (government) and *AG* (joint-stock company) in the West German press with *rada* (council), *organizacja* (organization), and *naród* (nation) in the socialist press; *Fall* (chance) and *Markt* (market) in the West German press with the *zwiazek* (relationship) and *plan* (plan, task) in the socialist press.

The first of these two contrasted sets of words shows differently acting subjects, the second, the mechanisms of activity. In the world presented by the capitalist press, apart from *governments*, the *joint-stock companies* are the main operating institutional subjects (heroes); in the world represented by the socialist press the *councils* and the *nations* are the heroes. *Market* plays a very important role in the world presented by the capitalist press while *plan* and *task* occupy the important place in the world presented by the socialist press.

The preparation of the material from the four dictionaries for a comparative analysis of adjectives proved to be very complicated. Each of the dictionaries is based on different principles and the particular problems included in them were solved in a different way. Thus, for example, in the Polish dictionary, the forms *dobry* (good) and *lepszy* (better) are treated in separate entries but the forms *nowy* (new) and *nowszy* (newer) are placed in the same entry, while in the Russian dictionary the form *luchshiy* (better) is given in the entry *khoroshiy* (good). Preparation of the material from the German dictionary was particularly laborious. Here it was necessary to gather together the scattered forms of the cases and the degrees of comparison. Moreover, in a number of cases it was impossible to distinguish between adverbial and adnominal attributes.

We cannot exclude the fact that, despite many efforts, some inconsistencies remain, but they do not seriously distort the general pattern of usage of adjectives in the contemporary press. While the frequency of use of nouns indicates the subjects of greatest interest to the press of particular countries, the analysis of the frequency of use of adjectives enables us to find out which descriptive elements are stressed by the press of those countries.

Comparing the four lists of the most frequently used adjectives one cannot help noticing their similarities. They do, after all, originate from texts which have similar functions. The common features of all four lists reflect this fact.

1   At the head of each of all four lists we find adjectives denoting the newness and size of a subject. These are the Russian adjectives *noviy* (new) and *bolshoy* (great, big), Polish *nowy* (new) and *duzy* (big); Slovak *nový* (new) and *velky* (great, big); German *neu* (new) and *gross* (great, big).

2   At least half of the total frequencies in each of the four lists are accounted for by the adjectives denoting the *newness, size, scope* and *importance* of the described subjects. They are as follows: In the Russian list. *noviy* and *posledniy*; *bolshoy, visokiy, krupniy, velikiy, shirokiy, mnogiy, narodniy, obshchestvenniy, natsyonaliniy, mezhdunarodniy, mirovoy*; *vazhniy, glavniy, osnovnoy, tsentralniy,*

*verkhovniy*. In the Polish list: *nowy* and *ostatni*; *duży, wielki, wysoki, szeroki*; *społeczny, narodowy, ogólny*; *ważny, podstawowy, główny, poważny*. In the Slovak list: *nový, posledny, ostatny*; *velky, vysoký, mnohý*; *narodný, spolecenský, statny, ludski, svetovy*; *hlavny* and *zakladny*. In the West German list: *neu, früh, letzt*; *gross, hoch, viel, lang*; *international*; *wichtig*.

3    Although equivalents of some of the West German adjectives cannot be found in any of the socialist lists, they still appear in two or at least one of them. They are as follows: *politisch, weiter, eigene, nächst, ganz, gesamt, einzeln, alt, jung, klein, militärisch, technisch*.

The differences between the four lists are no less significant than the similarities. In particular, the West German list is strikingly different from each of the socialist lists, which have much in common with each other. Here are the most important differences between the socialist lists and the West German list:

1    The cumulative frequency of adjectives denoting importance is nearly equal to the cumulative frequency of adjectives denoting newness in each of the socialist lists; in the West German list the total number of usages of adjectives denoting newness is several times higher than the total number of usages of adjectives denoting importance.

2    The cumulative frequency of adjectives denoting the social character of the subjects described by the socialist press at least equals the cumulative frequency of adjectives denoting newness; again in the West German list the cumulative frequency of adjectives denoting newness is several times higher than the cumulative frequency of adjectives indicating the social character of the described phenomena and subjects.

3    In contradistinction to the West German list, in the socialist lists (usually in all three but always in two) there are adjectives which correspond to the English adjectives: socialist, national, social, scientific, working.

4    In contradistinction to the West German list, the socialist lists contain a number of adjectives testifying to the economic orientation of the socialist press; adjectives which correspond to the English words: economic, productive, agricultural.

5    The expressions denoting the uniqueness of a subject, like

*einzeln, einzig, besondere,* play a more important part in the West German list than in the socialist list.

As can be seen from the above, the socialist newspapers stress the significance, the social character and the economic side of the described elements of reality. In other words, a socialist journalist is interested not only in the notions 'new', 'big' and 'unusual', but above all in what can claim to be of social and economic consequence.

## Conclusions

The comparative analysis of words most frequently used in the newspapers is an appropriate method for displaying the main contours of newspaper content and for reconstructing the image of the world portrayed by the press.

The analysis entitled us to put forward the hypothesis that all press texts exhibit certain common features which are independent of the social system. Among these features there are, for example, an interest in the superpowers, definite location of the described subjects in time and space and an interest in novelty and large-scale phenomena.

On the other hand the image of the world embedded in the vocabulary of the socialist press is decidedly different from the image of the world in the vocabulary of the capitalist press. If work, followed by organization, nation and plan, prevails in the socialist image of the world, then money, followed by government, joint-stock company and market, dominates the capitalist image. The socialist newspapers write first of all of what is seen to be important, socially and economically, whereas the capitalist newspapers write of what is seen to be unusual and exceptional. Thus the educational function of the language of socialist newspapers is most clearly revealed, not in its characteristic use of metaphor, but in its stress on the importance of work and in showing the significant, social and economic aspects of human activity.

## Notes

1 Soviet/Russian: Polakova & Solganik 1971 (as the dictionary of Polakova and Solganik does not take into account proper nouns, in our comparative

analysis the Soviet press was represented not by the names of the countries but the adjectives based on them). Czechoslovak. Mistrik 1968: Polish: Lewicki *et al.* 1971. West German: Rosengren 1972.

# Part III

# Advertisements

# 8

# Myth in cigarette advertising and health promotion

SIMON CHAPMAN AND GARRY EGGER

Well he can't be a man cause he doesn't smoke the same cigarette
as me...

*M. Jagger & K. Richards, 'Satisfaction'*

There is no logically necessary link between smoking and manhood.
In fact one might suggest the opposite.[1] Yet the ironic certainty in
the Rolling Stones' lyric illustrates the power of an image forged
through deliberate and consistent association. Advertising is perhaps
the most prolific vehicle for such image making in capitalist societies.
It is made more efficient through the built-in process of evaluation
obtained through sales records, which are often used to 'fine-tune'
subsequent messages.

Advertising is often used to promote and sell products and services
which in the long term may be harmful to human health. On the
other hand it has been used sparingly in promoting health, probably
because the reaction of health professions in general to advertising
has been to regard it as 'soft', 'pop' and without an established base.
Yet it should be through awareness rather than disdain of these
techniques that health promoters operate.

Health education and promotion in the mass culture of the 1980s
require efficient public health communication. An understanding of
the principles and techniques involved in commercial advertising
could provide a potentially powerful means of improving those
modern health problems such as smoking that have a large behavioural component. If people can be persuaded to take up smoking
by advertising, perhaps they can be also persuaded to give it up.

In this paper, we show that advertising can be subjected to structural analysis that focuses on the role of myth; we examine five examples of current cigarette advertisements that have been used in Australian print media; and we conclude with a description of an adaption of the mythical process to the development of a positive mythical status for non-smokers. The example discussed here has been used as a theoretical basis for aspects of the North Coast (NSW) Healthy Lifestyle Campaign begun in early 1979.[2]

## Myth in advertising

Advertisements can be argued to have a mythical dimension which parellels aspects of the nature and functions of myth in traditional societies. In modern society, the place formerly occupied by traditional and overt mythology has been supplanted by many disguised mythologies (Eliade 1957; McLuhan 1959). The correspondence in popular commitment to old and modern myth systems is clear — advertising surely influences as many people today as were influenced by traditional myths in pre-industrial societies. As Maranda has explained, there is little difference in the metamorphosis of a beast into a handsome prince whether it be communicated as a fairy story or as a deodorant advertisement (1972, p. 16).

Advertising is one of the richest sources available for surveying the state of modern mythology. The truncated form that advertising takes necessitates a concentration of symbolism and imagery for the sake of economy in communication. This enables one to quite readily attempt to dissect the essence of the communication because of the relatively small number of elements being used. It is of course possible to analyse a mythical dimension in any public form or institution — fashion, humour, the news etc (Smith, R. R. 1979).

In popular usage, the word 'myth' is often used to refer to beliefs or opinions that are demonstrably false. In anthropology, it is used independently of any truth function. We are using 'myth' in the latter sense to refer to any real or fictional story, recurring theme or character type that appeals to the consciousness of a group by embodying its cultural ideals or by giving expression to deep, commonly felt emotions. In this way, to describe an element of social life as 'mythical' is to refer to the way that it is somehow *culturally distinctive* as both a meaningful and expressive element of the culture or subculture in question. Myths vary in content from culture to culture, so that for example the story of Excalibur (essentially, the story of the 'chosen' person) or of David and Goliath (the triumph of mind over matter, or of the underdog) will be told in different guises or not at all in different cultures depending on a particular culture's *need* to express the essence of the myth.

Just in the way that Hamilton (1975) asserts that the myths revealed in the popular Australian children's book *Snugglepot and Cuddlepie* represent culturally distinctive themes about pairs of men and an attached female in Australian society, we hope to show that the mythical dimension of tobacco advertising is similarly illuminating of the particular phenomena and roles of smokers and tobacco in our society. And just as Dorfman and Mattelart (1975) have argued that the Disney cartoons function as a vehicle for US imperialist ideology, so too do we hope to demonstrate that the imagery of tobacco advertising functions through being chosen to legitimize and perpetuate certain world views that are commercially advantageous to the industry. Mythological analysis can in this way, serve as one approach to the description of social ideologies. Like Lévi-Strauss we are 'concerned to clarify not so much what there is *in* myths' as the function of myth in 'conferring a common significance or unconscious formulations which are the work of minds, societies and civilisations' (1969, p. 12).

## Promises for problems

Of all the illustrations, photographs and words that might be used to make up copy in advertising, why is it that particular scenes and actors in their special poses are selected rather than all possible others? In turning the pages of a magazine or watching a 30-second commercial, the 'reading' of an advertisement and the myths within it are 'exhausted at one stroke' (Barthes 1973a) or read 'at a flash' (Goffman 1978, p. 27). Like traditional myths, they aim at causing an immediate impression. 'It does not matter if one is later allowed to see through the myth, its action is assumed to be stronger than the rational explanations which may later belie it' (Barthes 1973a, p. 128).

In tobacco advertising, like all advertising, the fundamental problem that an advertisement seeks to redress is that, for whatever reason, not enough people are choosing the product of concern. It will seek to redress this either by bringing the product to the consumers' attentions, or by trying to change the impression of the product and its associations. Conceptually, the whole venture of developing an advertisement may be considered in terms of there being a *problem* to which the advertisement will need to offer a *promise* which will be energized or made salient by a *myth* (Chapman 1979).

*Figure 1   Framework for decoding advertisements*[3]

|  | In product | In user of product |
|---|---|---|
| Problem | negative qualities or associations in product as seen by consumer | negative qualities or associations in user or potential user of product (popular views about smokers of particular brands; common personal worries; anxieties) |
| Promise | positive aspects of product | positive aspects of user of product and the product's part in attaining these aspects |
| Myth | the role of the product expressed as a metaphor for a cultural myth | the essence of the sort of person who uses the product, their basic qualities, needs and place in the world: as such, a mythical portrait |

The problem that an ad will offer a promise about may be one or a combination of two things:

a    negative qualities or associations of the actual product;
b    negative qualities or associations in or about users or potential users of the product.

So for example, cigarette sales may be down or not high enough because of widespread beliefs about their role in the aetiology of cancer, their stale smell or their role in halitosis. Such facts or beliefs about tobacco are problems to the company in the sense of (a) above. Similarly, in the sense of (b) above, there may be some consensus that smokers of particular brands characteristically behave, dress, or simply *are* a certain way that is felt as negative by people who are not (or hope that they are not) that way themselves. Schoolchildren have little difficulty in dramatizing differences between 'Mr Marlboro' and 'Mr Benson and Hedges', which may mean that many have internalized stereotypes for such smokers. Advertising may influence brand loyalty either positively or negatively: positively in the case of those attacted or identifying with an image; negatively in the case of those who are turned off or away from a brand by its image.

The third aspect to this framework is the part played by myth, and may be best approached by asking of any advertisement: 'Why does this particular promise *work* for this readership.' Generally speaking, a literal interpretation of any advertisement is commensurate with the promise being offered, while a metaphorical interpretation shows the way to the mythological force behind the promise that makes it culturally distinctive and meaningful to its reader. This deeper, mythological aspect of the process may sometimes be unconscious in the work of the advertiser. Interviews with former employees of the industry have revealed that the mythological/ideological aspects of the advertising process do not always occur to those involved in the production of advertisements. Their perception of their work concurs with Hall's comments on the day-to-day practical/technical routinizations of their tasks whereby supposedly ideologically neu-tral considerations of graphic design, good taste or 'eye-catchiness' govern what is finally produced (Hall, 1977). The process is better understood not as any attempt at deliberate, sophisticated manipu-lation of mythological themes, but rather as a case of the advertiser bringing his own humanity and socialization into the process through use of the 'naturally' appealing, taken-for-granted things of life, the way things *are.*

### Myth resolves contradiction

Why is it that only *some* objects, relations or character types become mythical? Why are there themes that are over-represented in adver-tising (Maut & Darroch 1975; Prather & Fidell 1975; (Goffman 1978)? Mythical content emerges by appropriation: it must be relevant to the dealings of a people in their interactions. While there are age-old myths, there are no eternal ones that are inevitably a source of suggestiveness, because it is human history that converts reality into an oral or expressive state (Duncan 1972; Barthes 1973a).

Comparative mythology shows that the subjects of myth are immense in variety and cannot be reduced to any single motif or theme. Cassirer believes, however, that in a sense the development of mythical thought can be reduced to a single motive: that of *expression* (1946, p. 37). Language symbolically objectifies sense-perception, and myth is developed in order to objectify emotion.

The conglomerate of images presented by all brand advertising covers the range of somking personae encompassed by all different smokers of different brands. Brand advertising and the consumer behaviour that may be generated by it fulfils a totemic function in differentiating smokers and others' perceptions of them. As pointed out by Williamson:

Advertisements appropriate the formal relations of pre-existing systems of differences. They use distinctions existing in social mythologies to create distinctions between products. (1978, p. 27)

How and why would tobacco companies benefit from participating in the mythical process by providing expressions of sentiments meaningful to smokers? What is there in such expressions that results in new recruitment of smokers and increased brand loyalty? Myths may be studied as either *mirroring* or *constituting* a social condition (Armstrong, 1959). Cassirer's notion of the function of myth as expression may be explained a stage further by the introduction of this idea: that in the mass expression of commonly held sentiments or character ideals, the public form thus acquired serves as a mirror that can only be said to be somehow intrinsically gratifying to those who see their desired self-image or sentiments on various issues reflected back to them.

Further explanation would necessitate resource to psychoanalytic theories of the human condition — of why mirrors (metaphorical/ social and literal/glass) are so popular. Lévi-Strauss, for example, makes an appeal for a 'group instinct': 'Just as music makes the individual conscious of his physiological rootedness, mythology makes him aware of his roots in society. The former hits us in the guts; the latter we might say appeals to our group instinct' (1969, p. 28). So when a smoker views an advertisement that *appeals*, one might explain this as perhaps a process of his being gratified through seeing certain aspects of real or sought-after self-identity, attitudes and fantasies objectified and somehow made more real through virtue of the constitutive nature of the physical advertisement itself.

Lévi-Strauss, in *Structural anthropology*, argues that the purpose of myth is to provide a model of thought capable of overcoming contradiction generated by society or human condition. This notion is compatible with the problem-promise approach to understanding advertising described earlier, and with Langholz Leymore's use of the Exhaustive Common Denominator (ECD), a basic structuralist analytical process involving the reduction of signifying surface presentations to binary opposite substructures. Langholz Leymore writes that, like myths, advertising:

acts as an anxiety reducing mechanism. This is done first by re-stating, on the deep level, the basic dilemmas of the human condition; and second by offering a solution to them. It re-iterates the essential problems of life — good and evil, life and death, happiness and misery etc. and simultaneously solves them. (1975, p. 7)

Cigarettes, their use and their users are rife with contradictions which advertising attempts to resolve by placing their resolution in apposition to the product or user. Cigarettes (that are easy to obtain) are placed in apposition to cherished or desired values, moods or situations (that are difficult to obtain or experience). The desirable values, moods and situations are located within certain social settings, e.g. the sophisticated, international 'world' of the jet-setter, or the rugged, free, masculine 'world' of the cattle-rancher. These social settings or 'worlds' are *referent systems*.

Elements of content of the advertisement that evoke the referent system are called *signifiers* by Saussure. Thus in the examples above of the sophisticated, international world of the jet-setter and of the rugged cattle-rancher the signifiers may be a Concorde jet, and a horse, cowboy gear etc. respectively. It is pointed out that any given advertisement has theoretically an inexhaustible number of signifiers, but that invariably only a limited number are selected out in the decoding process as being significant. For example, in the Marlboro advertisement (illustration 2, p. 176) we list four signifiers (Marlboro man; cowboy hat; stables; and Marlboro smoking gesture). It could be argued that more pertinent signifiers are shown but not listed as significant by us. Why have we not listed his sideburns, his poker face, the hair on the back of his hands and so on?

Our selection is really a shorthand approach in recognition of Goffman's elegant description of this methodological impasse that would otherwise plague all decoding of photographs with copious listings. He writes:

The student can exploit the vast social competency of the eye and the impressive consensus sustained by viewers. Behavioral configurations which he has insufficient literary skill to summon up through words alone, he can yet unambiguously introduce into consideration. His verbal glosses can serve as a means to direct the eye to what is to be seen instead of having to serve as a full rendition of what is at issue. The notion of a 'merely subjective response' can then be academically upgraded; for clearly part of what one refrains from studying because the only approach is through verbal vagaries has a specific nature and is precisely perceived, the vagary being a characteristic of one's literary incapacity, not one's data. (1978, p. 25)

In decoding advertisements one can use the three-tiered 'problem—promise—myth' framework (figure 1) as a guide in following the steps of the makers of advertisements. This will be best achieved by first examining the advertisements for *signifiers* which will then allow for extrapolation to *referent systems*. In utilizing this approach, it is necessary to constantly project one's thinking into the various realities of people reading these advertisements, into part of what folklorists and mythologists call the 'ethnographic context'. One must imagine oneself as both pleaser and pleased: as those offering solutions and those in need of them. Barthes would approve. He wrote:

If one wishes…to explain how [myth] corresponds to the interests of a definite society, in short, to pass from semiology to ideology…[one must focus on] the reader of myths who must reveal their essential function…If he receives it in an innocent fashion, what is the point of proposing it to him? (Barthes 1973a, p. 129)

*Example 1: Winfield*

Winfield has been the leading brand on sale in Australia for some years (currently 20 per cent of Australian market).

Three elements central to this advertisement are:

*1 Paul Hogan, the character seen in all Winfield advertisements.* Who is Paul Hogan? Many Australian people would be aware of Hogan's recent off-camera biography — that he was a painter on the Sydney Harbour Bridge prior to appearing in his first Winfield advertisement. Now he is known nationally as a multi-media personality, with his own TV variety programme, and as someone who has travelled the legendary path from rags to riches. He was 'discovered' on a TV talent show doing the sort of humour routine that is 'so bad, it's good'.

The Sydney Harbour Bridge could not be more evocative as the definitive Australian image; the choice could have only been matched by choosing someone like the curator of Ayers Rock (which, incidentally, has been used in recent Winfield cinema advertisements). The Harbour Bridge as a significant element in the 'chosen' Hogan's biography also serves as a signifier of a certain degree of danger and devil-may-care outlook. Many would regard working high up on the

*Illustration 1*
*Winfield advertisement*

Bridge as an occupation fraught with considerable peril. People, after all, occasionally use it as a suicide platform. Hogan therefore could well represent some degree of heroism.

Hogan's passage from obscurity to fame is an indispensable element in his appeal. This aspect of his life is akin to the cherished myth that abounds in our culture which may be encapsulated in the expression 'the chosen one.' Many people harbour fantasies of their number being drawn to win the lottery, of their face being picked out in a crowd for a future of stardom in the public eye, of their contributions being selected above all others and against all odds for attention. Hogan's much-publicized biography shows that this can be a reality.

*2   Hogan wears a dinner suit.* In many Winfield advertisements Hogan is shown wearing a dinner suit. This feature was first seen when Hogan conducted an orchestra that played a Tchaikovsky symphony. What does this mean?

Clearly there is a juxtaposition between Hogan's working-class lowbrow culture, his proud philistinism and the highbrow culture signified by dinner suits and classical music. Hogan conducts the orchestra with aplomb and confidence, he doesn't appear to care if he makes *faux pas*, and he doesn't appear awkward or ill-at-ease in his penguin suit. At the same time he does not forsake his working-class roots by talking 'with a plum in his mouth' or by making intellectual smalltalk.

This element of the advertisement gives us insight into who Winfield's promotions are aimed at. Winfield is most likely being promoted to working-class men who are shy of high culture, who are intimidated by formality and who are self-conscious at their *gaucherie* when placed in such situations. Hogan provides a model of someone like them who can thumb his nose at high culture and emerge triumphant. Above all he does not sell out on his origins. He perpetuates the idea of the solidity of the Australian national character, confident and uncompromising in international culture.

3   The word 'anyhow'. Every Winfield advertisement features the word 'anyhow'. Clearly the word is pivotal for important elements of Winfield's appeal.

Generally the word may be seen as a synonym for the Australian expression 'she'll be right', which is usually taken to connote a fatalistic outlook on the world, slightly optimistic in the face of adversity or hopelessness. Why should this word be used to sell cigarettes? Here it is vital to ask: 'To sell cigarettes to who?' If Hogan appeals to working-class people, then the word 'anyhow' is probably intended to act as a pat on the back to people on low incomes, with high mortgages, with bad marriages, with bleak prospects etc. It is saying 'yes, we know your life is dull/bleak/wearying/unrewarding, but…anyhow…'

There is another function for this word that concerns the now well-known harmfulness of cigarettes. Most people are aware of the relationship between smoking and lung cancer and this represents a potential marketing problem to tobacco producers. The word 'anyhow' can be seen as a more specific form of fatalism in this regard: 'Frightened of lung cancer? Be assured that it won't happen to you! But still, a little worried? Forget it! we've all got to die from something! Anyhow have a Winfield.'

SUMMARY

| | |
|---|---|
| *Signifiers:* | Paul Hogan in dinner suit; the word 'anyhow'. |
| *Referent system:* | the legendary path from rags to riches. |
| *Problems:* | working men's lack of high culture and refinement; |
| | feeling awkward in social situations demanding *savoir-faire*; |

|                              |                                           |
|------------------------------|-------------------------------------------|
|                              | bleak prospects;                          |
|                              | trapped in the suburbs;                   |
|                              | boring life;                              |
|                              | worries about lung cancer.                |
| *Promise:*                   | be confident and succeed in any situation. |
| *Myths:*                     | poor boy makes good (Cinderella story);   |
|                              | product as talisman against alienation, oppression; |
|                              | the chosen person (cf. the legend of Excalibur); |
|                              | she'll be right.                          |
| *Binary opposites:*          | success : failure;                        |
|                              | happy : unhappy;                          |
|                              | confident : unconfident;                  |
|                              | *savoir-faire* : social incompetence;     |
|                              | active : passive.                         |
| *Exhaustive common denominator:* | Winfield smokers : others <br> ≃ winners : losers. |

*Example 2: Marlboro*

The recurrent signifiers in Marlboro ads are the 'Marlboro man', horses (usually being rounded up), open spaces and the distinctive smoking gesture of the Marlboro man's mouth. All of these signifiers are found in the mythical 'Marlboro country', a place that is better understood as a metaphor for freedom than as any literal rural Utopia.

Most people who see Marlboro advertisements (and who smoke Marlboro) are urban dwellers. The advertisements are not designed for people who are like the Marlboro man, but for those who would like to be like him. Marlboro advertising is perhaps the most blatantly escapist of all cigarette advertising. It offers translation of the harried, rushed and crowded urban man to the open spaces, freshness, elemental toughness and simplicity of Marlboro country.

The Marlboro man himself is a man of few words. Unlike Hogan of Winfield, or the sophisticates of Benson and Hedges, he displays neither wit nor sophistication but is rather the 'strong, silent type' with quiet confidence and inner resources. As such it is likely that he acts as a model for many men who have little to say in social situations: lighting up a Marlboro signals to others and reassures the

*Illustration 2*
*Marlboro advertisement*

smoker that he is really a person of some depth: like a Zen master, he only speaks when absolutely necessary.

It is in this context that the Marlboro 'way' of smoking is particu larly interesting. If one asks a group of schoolboys to role-play 'how a Marlboro smoker smokes' and 'how a Benson and Hedges smoker smokes', we see that the task almost always presents no difficulty, and the differences are marked. The Marlboro smoking style is full of determination, facial grimacing and suggests that a drag from a Marlboro is not child's play. One definitely knows that a 'decent' cigarette is being smoked. In short, it is a tough smoke for tough men.

Schoolboys probably choose Marlboro for its escapist promise as well as its promises of power and control. The Marlboro man rounds up horses that haven't seen man for months (so one advertisement explicitly claims). They are quite wild, yet are rounded up helplessly. There is an analogous role reversal portrayed here in the schoolboy situation. They see themselves as young men being belittled, ordered about, rounded up, placed in uniforms and made to conform by teachers and parents who still view them as children. The role of the Marlboro man is obviously an attractive alternative.

SUMMARY

| | |
|---|---|
| *Signifiers:* | Marlboro man; cowboy hat; stables; Marlboro smoking gesture. |
| *Referent systems:* | wide open spaces;<br>the touch, free life of the cowboy. |
| *Problems:* | trapped in urban artifice;<br>rushed, ordered, powerless, insignificant;<br>lost for words. |
| *Promises:* | freedom;<br>power;<br>signal to others one's inner strength. |
| *Myths:* | product as restorer of freedom and potency; |
| *Binary opposites:* | free : trapped;<br>strong : weak;<br>independent : dependent.<br>powerful : powerless. |
| *Exhaustive common<br>    denominator:* | Marlboro smokers : others<br>$\simeq$ winners : losers. |

*Example 3: Hallmark*

Hallmark is a low-tar brand of cigarette with a popular reputation for being very mild in taste. Low-tar brands are considered less dangerous to health than higher-tar brands, and the emphasis on safety is clearly the rationale behind Hallmark's marketing theme.

Hallmark is being promoted as the 'thinking person's' cigarette. This image serves as a resting place for those people who have taken some cognizance of the smoking/health argument: they can rest assured that they are smoking 'intelligently'. They don't want to give up smoking, as this is very difficult, but they wish to stay healthy, so Hallmark supports their wishful thinking that smoking and health are not incompatible.

The characters portrayed are all self-made well-to-do types, whose opinions cannot be ignored. Hallmark becomes a symbol of informed opinion.

Low-tar brands are often sneered at by smokers through hyperbole such as: 'You have to drag so hard to get any flavour that you wind up with a hernia.' The currency of this sort of opinion suggests that these sort of cigarettes are comparatively flavourless. The comments of the pictured Hallmark smokers all concern its flavour or taste: this is an attempt by the advertisers to give informed opinion (by

*Illustration 3*
*Hallmark advertisement*

thinking people) that this belief is quite wrong. A wine consultant adds his wine buff's mystique to this strategy.

SUMMARY

| | |
|---|---|
| *Signifier:* | well-to-do people with opinions worth printing. |
| *Referent systems:* | affluent, pleasurable lifestyle; connoisseurship. |
| *Problems:* | worry over cancer; <br> non-smokers thinking that you are foolish for smoking; <br> little taste in low-tar brands. |
| *Promises:* | Hallmark is the low-tar that tastes high-tar; <br> be identified as an intelligent smoker. |
| *Myths:* | cigarette as IQ rating; <br> sorting the officers from the other ranks; <br> cigarettes for smoking buffs (cf. wine buffs). |
| *Binary opposites:* | wise : foolish <br> knowledgeable : ignorant; <br> discerning : indiscriminate. |
| *Exhaustive common denominator:* | Hallmark smokers : others <br> ≅ winners : losers. |

*Illustration 4*
*Chesterfield advertisement*

*Example 4: Chesterfield*

This advertisement is all about how Chesterfield has not changed over the years. Chesterfield is promoted here in a similar way to the usual advertising of port, sherry and many pipe tobaccos. It is a cigarette for conservatives — for the sort of people who feel intimidated and confused by the pace of life and seek reassurance that their perceptions and values are not obsolete, but have endured, still remaining worthwhile or competitive despite the rigours of the passage of time. Chesterfield has not fallen by the wayside. It has not been made redundant by newer, more refined tobaccos, new-fangled smart-alec brands etc., because it has, like old port, an enduring quality that stands the test of time (like its smokers).

SUMMARY
*Signifier:*              1920s characters, costumes.
*Referent System:*        times past; the gay life.
                          the pace of modern life — things don't endure, are ephemeral;
                          the feeling of being obsolete;
                          young people have all the fun.

| | |
|---|---|
| *Promises:* | preserve your stability and conservatism; |
| | feel anchored to your past; |
| | comfort in the hurly-burly of life; |
| | remember you were young once too. |
| *Myths:* | the good old days; |
| | cigarette as time machine; |
| | cigarette as talisman against change, as a keepsake; |
| | things that stand the test of time; |
| | a security blanket. |
| *Binary opposites:* | conservative : radical; |
| | lasting : transitory; |
| | substantial : insubstantial: |
| | stable : unstable; |
| | old : new. |
| *Exhaustive common denominator:* | Chesterfield smokers : others |
| | ≃ winners : losers |

## Example 5: du Maurier 25s

Du Maurier are packaged in burgundy and gold, colours that reflect wealth and sedate opulence. But this advertisement is paradoxical in that amongst this it makes an appeal to penny-pinchers, offering five extra cigarettes at no extra expense. The paradox is resolved by the depiction of an eccentric. The well-heeled central character may be down on his luck compared with his neighbours in their Rolls Royces, but he is down with definite style in his chauffeur-driven BMW motorcycle (the so-called Rolls Royce of motorbikes). Du Maurier offer the style of their more traditional and well-known rival brands but cost less. Moreover they give their smokers a touch of eccentricity.

SUMMARY

| | |
|---|---|
| *Signifiers:* | bowler hat; |
| | chauffeur; |
| | Rolls Royces; |
| | BMW motorbike. |
| *Referent systems:* | opulence with style; |
| | keeping up appearances in hard times. |
| *Problems:* | the high cost of keeping up appearances; |
| | the need to show you're different. |

With 5 extra du Maurier at no extra expense,* times can't be all that hard.

du Maurier 25's

*Illustration 5*
*Du Maurier advertisement*

| | |
|---|---|
| *Promise:* | show some panache while privately clutching your extra change. |
| *Myths:* | gentry fallen on hard times; keep the flag flying; cigarette as pedigree. |
| *Binary opposites:* | eccentric : ordinary; real style : borrowed style; thrift : wastage. |
| *Exhaustive common denominator:* | du Maurier smokers : others ≃ winners : losers |

### Hero Myths

Heroes typically rise from the common ranks and achieve success as winners. As Henderson (1964) has pointed out however, mythological heroes are of many and varied form. Their function is to assist the immature ego through a trying stage of development to where it can stand alone. As such, different types of heroes have different appeal at varying stages in ego development. Henderson uses North American Winnebago mythology to illustrate the appeal of the trickster myth as exemplified by the hare and the fox to the early adolescent Trickster characters are subtle, fun-loving, mischievous, unthreatening and uncomplicated. Unlike the superhuman image of some hero myths, the trickster is more accessible as an identity model to the perceiver. He is not extra-ordinary. Yet he can compete with the extraordinary or superhuman and invariably come out on top. Because he is not superhuman, the trickster is easily identifiable by the young adolescent who can not yet relate to power and strength beyond his or her own capacity.

The Winfield appeal is primarily through the trickster character of Paul Hogan. He lacks the superhuman powers of an athlete or the virtues of a health buff. Yet he invariably wins (*Win*field, after all). In classical mythology his counterpart might be Odysseus.

The Marlboro man, on the other hand, is a winner through inner strength. Like Hercules of classical mythology, the Marlboro Man conquers the odds expected on a voyage to maturity by meeting them head-on. The Marlboro appeal is likely to be to the older adolescent (i.e. 15+), whilst Winfield appeals largely to those younger (i.e. 10-14). This appears to be borne out in part by a recent Sydney survey of brand preference in 9-14 year-olds, where Winfield emerged as the overwhelming favourite (Dunoon 1980). This is not to say that either brand is not purchased by adults or other market segments.

### Myth and anti-smoking campaigns

Health appeals aimed at attacking advertising appeals are doomed to failure. The Winfield slogan 'anyhow' and the trickster Hogan are rebuttals to the overwhelming might of health evidence against smoking. Orthodox health appeals, with their theme of delayed gratification (i.e. postponement of premature death perhaps 40 years hence), and their incitement to those identity-seeking young wishing to show strength by defying the odds, must suffer the fate of Goliath in the hands of the all-conquering David. A number of conclusions about anti-smoking education arise from this.

First, it should be obvious that rational information-based appeals aimed at preventing smoking amongst adolescents will not succeed (Thompson 1978). Adolescents know from their own experience of smoking that its adverse consequences will arrive, if at all, in the distant future. 'Future rewards for current deprivations' is the antithesis of the essence of advertising (except perhaps insurance and

and bank advertising), which promises instant gratification.

This is not to suggest that informational approaches do not work with more mature audiences. The decline in smoking amongst Australian males over 30 (Gray & Hill 1977) may be explained in part by this approach. But the increase in smoking from 33 per cent to 45 per cent amongst 15-16 year olds in New South Wales since 1971 (Egger & Champion 1978) suggests that anti-smoking education to date has been ineffectual. The implication for future campaigns therefore may be that while research shows a definite need for still more health information related to smoking, this should be aimed at a more mature audience, i.e. over 30 years of age. Appeals directed at the young need to be more concerned with image and less with knowledge.

Second, while every effort should be made to restrict cigarette advertising that appeals to the young, there is little to be gained by attacking the image perpetuated by cigarette promoters. The trickster has a thick skin and the hero, by definition, always wins. Non-smoking appeals can aim to replace these images, not destroy them. They can utilize similar techniques to develop an image around the non-smoker, although not one in which adult motivations (i.e. health, longevity) are used to appeal to sub-adult audiences. The adolescent who chooses not to smoke, unlike his smoking peer, has no established mythological image structure with which to identify. The task is to develop one.

As part of the North Coast Healthy Lifestyle Program begun in NSW in 1978, both information and image approaches are being used through the media in the region. The following is a transcript of a 30-second television spot that has been developed by a commercial advertising agency after consultation with one of the authors (GE). The spot is an attempt to deliberately forge a positive mythological role for non-smokers in 'winner' terms. Full evaluation of the program is currently under way.

*Transcript of 'winner' TV spot* (30 seconds)

| *Content* | *Words to music* (sung in plaintive, ballad style voice) |
|---|---|
| Close up of young man, looking lonely – drags on cigarette; | *Only a smoker knows the feeling* <br> *Only a smoker knows the score* <br> *How you've given up on giving up* <br> *A dozen times or more* |

camera draws back to show
party scene, happy young women
in foreground, lonely young
man in background;

*How you couldn't help but notice*
*All those girls and blokes*
*Who'd somehow kicked the habit*
*An' weren't dying for a smoke*

young man takes another drag,
glances about, looks 'left out'.

*Feelin' kind of lonely*
*Feelin' kind of tense*

Stubs out cigarette, stands up. Young
Young women turn to face him —
acceptance gestures.

*Till you MADE A STAND*
*MADE A STAND* (given emphasis)

Successive scenes follow:
young man passes rugby ball;
surf skis; older man bowling;
family scenes    mother kisses
child; father hand-in-hand
with kids.

*And GOT DOWN off the fence*
   (Change of beat)
*You're a born non-smoker*
*We knew you had it in you*
*We knew you could do it*
*We knew you were a winner*

Return to young man jogging
through hills and pastures,
runs into close-up.

repeat chorus (with more throat)

fade chorus

'Quit for Life' across screen.


A structural analysis of the TV spot is as follows:

*Signifiers:*            party situation;
                         boy alone;
                         girls in group;
                         people active, in control.

*Referent systems:*      the trial of boy meets girl;
                         freedom, control, success, enjoyment;
                         adolescent lack of confidence;
                         smoking turns people off;
                         no crutch without a cigarette;
                         smokers seen as weak, unconfident —
                         losers.

*Promises:*              be confident without a cigarette;
                         show your prowess and inner strength by
                         giving up smoking.

*Myths:*                 non-smokers as winners;
                         smokers as losers.

*Binary opposites:*        acceptance : rejection;
                          company : loneliness;
                          desirable : undesirable;
                          success : failure;
                          appealing : unappealing.
*Exhaustive common*        non-smoker : smoker
  *denominator:*           = winner : loser.


## Notes

1  Evidence shows that whilst a decreasing proportion of adult (over 30 years old) men now smoke, there is an increasing proportion of youth (under 17 years old) smoking (see Gray & Hill 1977).
2  For a complete protocol on the North Coast Program see Egger *et al.* 1978.
3  In the case of pharmaceutical advertising, where the doctor, as reader of the advertisements, acts as a third party between advertiser and the eventual consumer (the patient), a third heading to this decoding framework can be placed on the horizontal in figure 1: 'in supplier'. Problems will concern doctor as supplier of drugs, doctor as therapist generally, or doctor as human being. See Chapman (1979) for full exposition.

# 9

# How is understanding an advertisement possible?[1]

TREVOR PATEMAN

## Introduction

Anyone who reads this will routinely accomplish the identification, understanding and criticism of advertisements encountered while watching TV, listening to radio, sitting in the cinema, reading a magazine, walking past billboards, and so on. Here I offer an analysis of some neglected conditions of possibility of this routine accomplishment, and I do so because it seems to me that failure to undertake such an analysis or to realize (and even deny) its significance is a serious limitation upon the value of the hermeneutics and critique of advertisements which has been produced within broadly structuralist and semiological paradigms, say from Barthes's essay, 'Rhetoric of the image' (Barthes 1977), through to Williamson's *Decoding advertisements* (1978). These tend to take for granted important conditions of possibility of the routine accomplishment, proceeding directly to a hermeneutics or critique which consequently has an unnecessarily hazardous character, inviting the question 'How do you know?' Specifically, they tend to ignore those conditions of possibility which distinguish instances of *la parole* (speech; utterances) and their comprehension from *la langue* (a language), to recall the Saussurean distinction (Saussure 1959; Barthes 1967, ch. 1), and so analyse utterances as if they were languages, which they are not.

What I am sketching out in this essay belongs to a wider endeavour by many theorists to rethink the theory of the (formal) *organization* of texts and images in terms of a theory of the active *comprehension* of text and images in context,[2] and thereby to complement theories of formal systems (linguistics, semiology) with a general theory of communication, itself part of a general theory of action. Such a general theory of communication has as one of its central problems 'to build a coherent picture of the clearly heterogeneous processes by which utterances are interpreted' (Smith & Wilson 1979, p. 150).

## Identifying advertisements

In general, it is easy to identify something as an advertisement, and much less easy to say how it is done, might be done, or must be done. Identification is even easier than I suppose in an earlier study (Pateman 1980a), for advertisements are rarely identified *in isolation* and *retrospectively*, but rather they are identified *in a context* where they have been *anticipated*.[3] For example, if we are watching commercial TV, we know that sooner or later we will be taken through a commercial break. In other words, viewing, like most or all human activities, has an anticipatory character in the sense that it has expected future components, and having the expectation of the occurrence of those components is part of what it means to be engaged in that activity.

A model for what is involved in this kind of projective activity is provided by Schank and Abelson's theory of script-based understanding. They describe a script as follows:

A script is a structure that describes appropriate sequences of events in a particular context. A script is made up of slots and requirements about what can fill those slots. The structure is an interconnected whole, and what is in one slot affects what can be in another. Scripts handle stylized everyday situations. They are not subject to much change, nor do they provide apparatus for handling totally novel situations. Thus, a script is a predetermined, stereotyped sequence of actions that defines a well-known situation. (1977, p. 41)

Because we actively anticipate that something will occur to fill a script-defined slot, we can use minimal and diverse cues to decide that something now occurring fills a slot in a script. This is certainly recognized by advertisers: they certainly do not have to do much to get us to perceive anything appearing on the back cover of a Sunday colour supplement *as* an advertisement. All the same, it should be stressed that however 'obvious' it may be that something is an advertisement, there is always an inference to be made from the cue to the decision that something does indeed fill an advertising slot (i.e. count as an advertisement). Even when an advertisement is labelled with the word 'Advertisement', the reader has to add the premise or assumption that the word is being used with its literal meaning, to perform an act of classification, etc., in order to conclude that the word 'Advertisement' labels an advertisement, for the word could be used otherwise. (The word 'Advertisement' incorporated in a fine-art poster does not label an advertisement.)[4]

No doubt it is because identification of advertisements is so easy and 'automatic' that its mechanisms are taken for granted in many analyses. I have said something about these mechanisms just because I want to argue that if we did not accomplish the identification of an advertisement *as* an advertisement it would be strictly impossible for us to understand or criticize it. This is a claim I attempt to sub-stantiate in the next two sections.

### *What is advertising? and what is an advertisement?*[5]

Various sorts of knowledge about the kinds of thing which fill a slot in a script can and will be accessed and used in the analysis of a particular slot-filler, if it is analysed at all (for often we skip past slots filled by advertisements).

This knowledge will be (part of) our knowledge of advertising as a practice or *activity type*, to borrow a concept from an impor-tant paper by Levinson, who describes it as follows:

I take the notion of an activity type to refer to a fuzzy category whose focal-members are goal-defined, socially constituted, bounded, events with constraints on participants, setting, and so on, but above all on the kinds of allowable con-tributions. Paradigm examples would be teaching, a job interview, a jural interrogation, a football game, a task in a workshop, a dinner party, and so on. (1978, D-5)

— to which list I am adding advertising.

Now it is clearly the case that each of us knows different things about any given activity type, and that on different occasions, dif-ferent bits of our knowledge are accessed. In the case of advertising, it is often argued in justification of media studies courses that the more we know about it (history and structure of the advertising industry, production processes, campaign strategies, visual and verbal techniques, etc., etc.), the better off we are in understanding and criticizing individual advertisements as we encounter them. Doubtless this is true. However, what I want to stress is the (minimal) knowledge about advertising without which we would not be able even to get started on the business of understanding and criticizing advertisements. Such (minimal) knowledge forms part of the competence of most of the world's population, very young children included, and does not have to be taught in school.

This (minimal) knowledge concerns the point or purpose of advertising, which assigns the point or purpose with which any individual advertisement is produced. This point or purpose is, of course, to sell products. Individual advertisements are paradigmatically a means whereby the sale of particular products is promoted, and through the advertisement the (anonymous) advertiser addresses (or interpellates: Althusser 1971) any actual reader or viewer as a potential consumer of the product in question.[6]

This minimal knowledge is required to get started on understanding and criticizing an individual advertisement. Of course, we also require knowledge of a *language* and knowledge of a *culture* in order to accomplish an interpretation of an advertisement. But knowledge of a language and a culture are insufficient to understand an advertisement; we must also assign the point or purpose with which we believe a given text or image has been produced, and to understand such a text or image *as* an advertisement is precisely to assign it to the activity type, *advertising.*

It is often argued that a text or image must possess certain 'formal' properties in order to count as belonging to a particular genre – say, haiku or limerick. However, even if necessary, such formal properties are not sufficient to classify a text in a particular genre, for one can have 'accidental' haikus and limericks because the formal properties of a text can be mapped into a genre regardless of authorial intention or activity type. More radically, it can be argued that it is only because of the genre assignment that we pick out certain formal properties as the *relevant* properties which then confirm or disconfirm our initial genre assignment. This is the position I want to defend in the next section, by showing that the relevant 'formal' properties of texts and images used in advertisements can only be *specified* on the basis of the recognition that they are being produced in advertisements, that is as belonging to the activity type, *advertising.*[7]

### Examples

In this section I give examples to show how identification of something as an advertisement is involved in specifying the operative structure, meanings and illocutionary force (see Searle 1969; 'illocutionary force' is roughly equivalent to 'function') of texts and images used in advertising. And I begin with an example which shows how identifying something as an advertisement can allow the reader or viewer to complete an incomplete text or image.

## The absent product

To know that something is an advertisement is to know that it is an advertisement *for* something (some product). Because of this, advertisers are able to leave out of advertisements the name or any icon of the product they are advertising, relying on the reader or viewer to make a 'default assignment' (Schank & Abelson 1977, pp. 38-42) and infer the name of the product being advertised on the basis of whatever clues are provided by the advertiser in the text or image, together with knowledge about the world of products, past advertisements, etc. Recent examples are provided by Guinness (illustration 1), White Horse whisky and Benson and Hedges cigarette advertisements (see chapter 10 for an example). As far as I can see, this default assignment of a product, prior to further interpretation of the explicit text or image, is strictly incomprehensible within the structuralist or

*Illustration 1    Guinness advertisement*

semiological frameworks which have generally been employed in media and communication studies.

One facilitator of the process of default assignment is the reader's or viewer's knowledge that an advertisement is a thoroughly *prepared* act of communication which is unlikely to have omitted a product's name by mistake (as a 'performance error' to use Chomsky's expression), but rather deliberately, and that to be compatible with the point or purpose of advertising, the advertisement will contain deliberate clues permitting the recovery of the product name. This makes the process of default assignment a rational (and often enjoyable) activity in which to engage (compare Pratt 1977 on the preparedness of literary texts).

From the point of view of further understanding of the advertisement, identifying the product is indispensable, for it is around the product that the discourse of the advertisement is built. The product is thus a structuring principle or function as is shown in the examples that follow.

### Jingle bells this Christmas

Suppose the four words and full stop 'Jingle bells this Christmas.' were given to you, written on a piece of paper, and you were told

*Illustration 2     Buzby poster, British Telecom*

that they were a transcript of a continuous stretch of writing occurring in an undefined context (so the situation is like Katz's (1972) 'zero-context' semantics). Several surface structure syntactic analyses of this fragment are possible, including at least two — (2) and (3)[8] —

which yield a well-formed sentence, and one (1) which renders a well-formed noun phrase:

| | Jingle | bells | this | Christmas |
|---|---|---|---|---|
| 1 | nominal (song title) | | deictic | noun |
| 2 | imperative (verb) | noun (direct object) | deictic | noun |
| 3 | imperative verb | noun (vocative) | deictic | noun |

Now, if the four words appear (as they did: see illustration 1): (a) on billboard poster; (b) at Christmas time (1979); and (c) accompanied by the Post Office's Buzby character, I would argue that *sufficient* information has already been provided to allow a reader to assign analysis (2) to the words 'Jingle bells this Christmas' as the operative reading in this instance, and this may be the only reading which occurs to readers, though they would have missed something if they did not also see that the words 'Jingle bells', which often appear as a nominal compound or 'fixed syntagm' (Saussure 1959) have been given an unusual (and amusing) operative syntax, semantics and pragmatics by the Post Office.

In a moment, I shall consider what difference is made by the further textual material — 'Make someone happy with a phone call.' — and the fact that Buzby is holding a telephone. For the present, consider how even without this material, reading (2) rather than reading (3) can be assigned, in virtue of the fact that among other things[9] we (as readers) know that:

i   'Jingle bells this Christmas' appears in an advertisement, and advertisements are attempts to get us to do something, paradigmatically, to buy products;

ii  the Post Office (identifiable as the advertiser from Buzby alone) sells telephone calls, and 'bells' can be analysed as metonymic for telephone calls.

This analysis can be *novel*; we don't need a dictionary of metonyms. In contrast, the Post Office has no interest in appealing to bells to ring, which is what reading (3) is about.

Now in (i) above we refer to facts about *advertising* and in (ii) to facts about a *product* advertised. Neither of these are facts about *language*, but (if I am right) they are sufficient to decide (or disambiguate) the operative syntax, semantics and pragmatics of a text. In the present case, they could have determined what is the operative syntax ('Bells' as direct object rather than vocative); the operative semantics ('Jingle bells' means '(you) Jingle bells!', rather than naming a song or meaning 'Let bells jingle'); and the operative pragmatics (the textual utterance is addressed to us who read the advertisement rather than to bells).

Against this line of analysis, it can rightly be pointed out that the advertisement I am considering contains both a disambiguating text ('Make someone happy with a phone call!) and a disambiguating icon (Buzby is holding a telephone). These double the message of 'Jingle bells this Christmas', and 'anchor' its operative meaning (cf. Barthes 1977, esp. pp. 38-40). So even if 'Jingle bells this Christmas' could be understood in the way I have suggested, it can also be understood in the way semiologists have suggested — through semantic material (text and image) actually present in the advertisement. For some readers, this material may be *redundant*, in the sense of information theory, but that is just their particular good fortune or bad luck, depending on how you evaluate the possession of competence in decoding advertisements.

However, it seems to me that an account which says that one text or image 'anchors' or 'disambiguates' another is vulnerable to a set of objections consistent with the alternative approach I am sketching in this article. In particular, how do we *know* that 'Make someone happy with a phone call' disambiguates 'Jingle bells this Christmas' and does so in just the way required? First, it is necessary to see the two texts as connected and then to see them as connected in a particular way. Here we make use of our pragmatic knowledge about texts in general and advertisements in particular. And, second, far from the second text disambiguating the first, which would require that in some mental dictionary 'Jingle bells' was entered as a semantic equivalent of 'Make...a phone call', it is rather *because* we can work out pragmatically that 'Jingle bells' means 'Make a phone call' that we can use the second part of the text to *confirm* a reading of the first part. In other words, the disambiguation has *already been done* by the time we are able to say that one sentence disambiguates another, and the 'anchorage' one text provides for another is essentially illusory, since 'anchorage' is only of use to those who know how to anchor (compare the earlier remarks on

genre, p. 190, and note 7), and remarks below, p. 198, on the
Dictionary Fallacy. It is, of course, entirely possible that some
advertisers have the same mistaken theories of textual understanding
as some analysts of advertisements, and this would account for the
fact that they put into advertisements material which apparently
provides evidence for the analysts' theories.

The fact that Buzby is shown holding a telephone can be analysed along the lines indicated in the preceding paragraph and in
the next section.


## Pragmatics of the photographic image

Parallel arguments apply to iconic — or analogic — material in advertising, of which photographs form a sub-class.[10]

Imagine a typical still-life painting — say, a composition of apples,
cheeses, a pheasant, a wine-bottle, etc. Now imagine reproductions
of the same still-life used in advertising, successively, apples, cheese,
pheasant, wine — in each case, let just one word be added outside
the frame of the image: if the cheeses are Stiltons, this word could
be 'Stilton', and so on. My argument is that as the signifying matter
of the image is transposed from the activity 'fine art' to 'advertising',
so the *relationship* between the 'elements'[11] of the image changes,
according to the product which is made thematic or topical.[12] In
other words, the changes in context effect a structural reorganization
of the operative meaning (the operative semantics) of what is (in
some sense) 'the same image'.

The determinations of meaning here are contextual (pragmatic)
rather than structural (systematic, belonging to *la langue*: cf.
Pateman 1973). The products which are not advertised (not topical
or thematic) assume the structural relation of *comment on* or *support for* the product advertised, and as the topic or theme changes,
so too does the comment made or support offered. In some ways,
this process is analogous to the way in which changes in stress-
assignment alter the focal scale of semantic entailments of an
utterance (Smith & Wilson 1979, ch. 7).[13] Before we can understand the *kind* of comment which is being made on the theme
or topic of the advertisement (the product being promoted) we
have to understand the topic/comment structure, which always
exists even though the topic/comment elements may not be materially
separable (as when highlighting or the angle at which it is photographed constitutes the comment on the thematic product).

## *Beyond connotations*

The contrast between denotative (or literal) and connotative meanings plays a central part in structuralism and semiology (Barthes
1967, 1977). I have already argued that operative denotative meanings of an advertisement are not specifiable without reference to
contextual (or pragmatic) variables. It remains to say something
about connotative meaning.

It seems to me that at best, the idea of connotation is a 'dummy'
concept which identifies a domain in which the mechanisms at work
have still to be mapped out in detail. At worst, and quite often,
connotation is taken to be a straightforward semantic function or
operation in which connotations figure as properties or entailments
of texts or images, rather than as the result of structured operations
performed upon texts or images by knowledgeable readers. It is the
latter, pragmatic, view which I believe is essentially the correct one,
though *some* of the things called connotations do have a semantic
character.[14] In the rest of this section I shall focus on those con-
noted meanings which clearly have to be handled pragmatically,
and shall do so exclusively in connection with the relation between
topic and comment.

Once again I shall ask you to imagine a fragment of an advertisement rather than use a real advertisement. I do this because actual
advertisements are usually quite complex, whereas I want to make
my points as simply as possible. So imagine an advertisement for
cigarettes in which some people are shown smoking beside a natural,
rurally located waterfall. In this advertisement, the brand of cigarette
advertised forms the topic (or theme), and the waterfall is (part of)
the comment. Of such an advertisement, semiologists might say
something like either A or B:

    A   'The denoted image of the waterfall connotes a healthy
        outdoor life.'
    B   'The denoted image of people smoking by a waterfall connotes
        smoking as part of a healthy, outdoor life.'

If semiologists go on to consider the 'psychological' effects of this
advertisement, they may say things like:

    C   'By some metonymic substitution, we can come to believe
        that cigarette smoking stands for the healthy outdoor life.'
    D   'By some logic of identification, we can come to believe that

cigarette smoking *is* the healthy, outdoor life' (the problematic of totemism: see Lévi-Strauss 1964).

I do not want to consider C and D, but instead concentrate on A and B.

The first set of points I wish to make arises from the fact that, at the very least, making statement A supposes an ability to select from the possible connotations of waterfalls the operative one; this selection may be facilitated by a verbal message (which Barthes (1977) says 'anchors' the meaning), but such verbal messages are neither necessary nor sufficient to achieve disambiguation, which also has a pragmatic aspect. For what is also required is a concept of the *relevance* of the comment to the topic or theme, compatible with assumptions about the *point or purpose* with which the image is being produced.

In important work, Sperber and Wilson have sought to reduce Grice's four famous conversational maxims[15] to a single axiom of *relevance*. They argue that in the standard case, the hearer (reader, viewer, etc.) treats as axiomatic that: 'Le locuteur à fait de son mieux pour produire l'énoncé le plus pertinent possible' — the speaker has done his or her best to produce the most relevant utterance possible (Sperber & Wilson 1979, p. 89; see also Smith & Wilson 1979, ch. 8). Sperber and Wilson are thinking of 'relevance' as relevance to an ongoing discourse, and I think this can be extended to cover the bearing of a comment on an (already posited) theme or product — that the connection is not temporal but spatial in an image does not matter. 'Relevance' is a very difficult concept to analyse, and it would take me too far afield to analyse it here.[16] The points I want to make can be made informally, using the earlier-introduced idea of point or purpose.

The point of advertising cigarettes is to sell them. The main obstacle to selling cigarettes is consumers' beliefs that cigarettes ruin your health. The most *relevant* thing a cigarette advertiser can do, given the *point* of advertising, is to attempt to modify, eliminate or repress that belief. It is the consumers' ability to work this out (using knowledge of activity types, and something like Sperber and Wilson's axiom of relevance) which allows the correct (intended) connotation of the waterfall to be located — a connotation which bears *directly* on the chief obstacle to selling cigarettes.

Furthermore, and importantly, this way of analysing the figuring out of connotations allows advertisers to make, and readers to recognize, *novel* connotations which do not conceivably have a place in some pre-existing 'Dictionary of Connotations' (cf. Pateman 1973). The Dictionary Fallacy, as a particular form of the semantic fallacy which thinks that all meaning is 'in' the text or image, bedevils semiology. For example, in the propaedeutic analysis of a single advertisement for Goodyear tyres with which she begins her book, Williamson (1978, pp. 18-19) discusses the part played by a jetty as a comment (in my terms) on Goodyear tyres, and concludes: 'A system of meaning must already exist, in which jetties are seen as strong, and this system is exterior to the ad — which simply *refers* to it.' Now this is just wrong, since it implicitly denies that there can ever be new connotations (cf. Fraser 1979 on novel metaphors). What I would say in this case is that using (or even inferring) our non-semantic knowledge about jetties, advertising and Goodyear tyres, and our pragmatic axiom of relevance, we can *figure out* (infer) that in a given instance this jetty on this occasion connotes strength.[17]

The second set of points I want to make bears on the specific way in which theme and comment are related, as in B above. How is it that in B the producer of the connotation is not seen to intend it ironically or satirically? How is it that we interpret the comment as intended (in virtue of what we believe the advertiser believes we believe about waterfalls) to enhance the status of cigarettes, not diminish it in virtue of the blatant incongruity of the juxtaposition of cigarettes and waterfalls? Quite clearly, it is our knowledge of the point or purpose with which cigarette advertisements are issued which is indispensable to working out the *kind* of connotation which is appropriate, together with our sense of the relevance which the comment has to the discourse of the advertisement.[18]

Understanding that the comment is intended to enhance or support the theme or product does not, of course, commit the reader or viewer to acceptance of the relation communicated, any more than the advertisers are committed to believing in the relationship they sincerely attempt to communicate. The anonymous and non-reciprocal nature of advertising makes it generally impossible for the consumer to dialogically challenge the advertiser's relation to the claims made and connotations produced, though this is a handicap to advertisers as well as an asset. For advertisers also have few ways of defending themselves in an advertisement against a reader's disbelief in the sincerity with which the beliefs contained are held. One way they do have, however, is precisely to present the theme/comment relationship self-reflexively ('these are the sorts of ludicrous claims advertisers make about this product'), thus thematizing the *relationship* between advertisers and consumers and presenting themselves as 'honest brokers'. This is also a way of selling products (the best way to sell second-hand cars is to say: 'Who'd buy a second-hand car from someone like me?').

The third set of points I want to make concerns the elusiveness of connotations and the felt hazardousness of interpretations and critiques of advertising. I think I have an *explanation* for this felt hazardousness, and this explanation in turn illuminates some interesting features of idcology and ideological conflict. For the hazardousness is real and, *in principle*, inescapable.

Basically, connotations are hazardously attributed just because they are *pragmatic implications* of a produced text or image rather than *semantic entailments* (Smith & Wilson 1979, chs 6, 7). The difference is roughly this: a semantic entailment of a sentence (text, image, discourse, etc.) cannot be denied by someone who uses that sentence in an utterance without it being the case that they contradict themselves. So, for example, I cannot both assert that 'Reagan is President of the United States' and deny that there is someone who is a President of the United States. Nor it seems can I say of a woman that 'she is just a housewife' and deny that I am thereby expressing a low opinion of the woman and/or housewifery — it is part of the semantics of 'just' to express that kind of attitude. You could point this out to a foreigner learning English, for instance. (Of course, 'just' is ambiguous and also means something like 'precisely, wholly, exactly', but that is not a particular problem.) In contrast, pragmatic implications of an utterance are worked out by hearers on the basis not only of linguistic knowledge, but on the basis of assumptions they make about the speakers' intentions, the principles (e.g. of relevance) governing the conversation, activity type, point or purpose, and so on. Not only is there a considerable possibility of error based on mistake about speakers' intentions, about operative conversation principles, activity type definition, etc., but also it seems that the inference to pragmatic implications is probabilistic rather than a matter of strict entailment. One major consequence of this is that it is always *possible*, though not always *plausible*, for speakers to deny that they intended a pragmatic implication drawn by the hearer, and to make this denial *without self-contradiction*. In other words, some implications are cancellable.

For example, a hearer who makes the inference that a particular conversational remark has, say, racist or sexist implications, and draws attention to them, will often encounter the response: 'But I didn't intend them', and this response is neither necessarily insincere nor necessarily irrelevant. In many cases, the best the hearer can do in response to the speaker's defence is to say: 'Well, now you know that if you say things like that you are likely to be misunderstood.' One thing this example shows is that *even* in a perfectly homogeneous speech-community, in which every speaker paired sounds and meanings in exactly the same way, misunderstandings could arise between speakers on the basis of different world knowledge and employment of different inferential strategies.

In relation to advertising, the possibilities of misunderstanding, *and of its strategic exploitation* (see below), are greatly increased because of the anonymous and one-way character of advertising communication. The reader or viewer who draws a particular implication cannot usually check whether the implication was intended or whether they are 'reading into the ad. more than is there', and their position is doubly difficult because it is unclear *to whom* intentions (which are not the same as assumed point or purpose), should be attributed, if indeed to anyone (cf. Grice 1957 on traffic lights, and the discussion in Pateman 1981). It seems to me that the ideological significance of these banal facts has not been sufficiently appreciated; I shall try briefly to spell out what I take it to be.

First of all, there is little readers can do to reduce their uncertainty about the implications of an advertisement. They cannot ask the advertiser: 'What exactly do you mean?'[19] and even if they could, the advertisers could reply: 'Nothing and Everything' — in other words, deny that they intended an actual interpretation, and accept all the different interpretations offered by creative receivers — thus adopting the position of the guru who says: 'Il faut y mettre du sien' — you have to provide your own.[20] This tends to place the locus of interpretation solely in the receiver, which is just as much an error as to place it wholly in the text. It is essentially a denial of responsibility, and the passing of responsibility where it does not (in this case)[21] lie. Advertisers get consumers to do their dirty ideological work for them, and keep their own hands clean. Of course, if the consumers refused to play the game advertisers would have to change direction (cf. Parkin 1971).

Second, the anonymous and non-reciprocal character of the communication opens the doors wide to what Habermas calls 'strategic action', in contrast to 'communicative action' (1979, esp. pp. 116-23; see also Bach & Harnish 1979, pp. 97-103). If strategic action (manipulation) is defined in terms of intention to achieve an effect where the successful achievement of the effect is partly dependent on the hearer's non-recognition of the intention to achieve that effect, then advertisers are well placed to engage in strategic action (a) because they cannot be required to spell out their intentions; (b) because in the light of what was said under the first point above, it does not make much sense for readers to go looking for intentions; (c) because many of the intentions which advertisers have are undoubtedly deniable without self-contradiction in virtue of the 'open' pragmatic implications which they are getting people to draw. We can do something about (a) and (b), but (c) will always be with us, and interpretation will always be a hazardous affair, even if its uncertainty can be reduced by attention to the conditions of possibility I have written about in this essay.

## The pleasure of the advertisement[22]

A possible objection to the relevance of my emphasis on the cognitive work people do in understanding and criticizing advertisements is to say that people do not *bother* to understand or criticize them: either they consume them passively or ignore them. Actually, I think this an empirically false claim, and that most people actively enjoy advertisements. What is enjoyable about advertisements is relevant to this paper, and I shall therefore briefly discuss it.

First, many advertisements are just visually pleasurable — they are quite possibly a substitute for encounters with other art forms.[23]

Second, they are pleasurable as discourses (both verbal and visual), partly because they call upon some of our *more* sophisticated linguistic and cognitive competences: the anatomy of advertising may well be the key to the anatomy of human communication! All the figures of classical rhetoric can be found in the texts and images of advertisements (see Bonsiepe 1961 for a classification of visual metaphors in advertisements), and just understanding such non-literal messages (or, more accurately, understanding messages non-literally) gives us the pleasure of exercising our competences. Again, in their incompleteness, many advertisements provide the same kinds of intellectual pleasures as crossword puzzles.

## Conclusions

The structure of some of the competences advertisements allow us to exercise with pleasure has been the subject of this paper. Those competences cannot be studied as part of *la langue*. They are not part of it. In philosophy of language, linguistic pragmatics and cognitive psychology these competences are being actively studied. Reference to them is involved in any science of signs-in-use, that is, in any theory of communication. The development of such a theory, as part of a general theory of social action, must surely be the first priority for teachers in the emerging fields of media and communication studies. Only by thinking through the conditions of possibility of their own activity can they move from appearances to ever deeper levels of reality, which it is the object of all sciences to uncover.

## Notes

1   This essay is for the memory of Roland Barthes. I learnt about semiology in his immensely pleasurable seminars at the Ecole Pratique des Hautes Etudes, VIth section, in 1971-72. I began to feel that there were not enough constraints on my semiologically inspired connotation readings while doing such readings at the Polytechnic of Central London in 1973-4 (Pateman 1974a, b, c). In teaching and staff—student seminars at Goldsmiths College, London, in 1977-78, some of the dimensions of a rather different approach were worked out (see Pateman 1980a, a Goldsmiths seminar paper, prompted by Paul Walton). Much of the literature I cite in this paper is very recent, but Barthes knew it or knew of it: he co-edited *Communications 30* (1979), in which both a French translation of Grice (1975) and the Sperber and Wilson (1979) article of which I also make some use appeared. In the *Présentation* to that issue, he writes of 'des approches scientifiques de la conversation ...Elles relèvent de cette partie de la sémiologie, longtemps délaissée, qu'on appelle, à la suite des auteurs anglo-saxons, la pragmatique' ('scientific approaches to conversation...They stem from that long-neglected part of semiology which, to follow Anglo-Saxon usage, is called pragmatics') (Barthes & Berthet 1979, p. 4). I don't think that what I am doing in this paper is a break with the kind of work he pioneered, and from which everyone working in media and communication studies has learnt and will continue to learn.
2   I owe this way of putting things to a lecture by Giovanni Carsaniga at the University of Sussex, December 1979. He also commented in detail on the drafts of this paper.
3   Though I had read about the anticipatory character of human cognition, it was a conversation with Susan Ervin-Tripp which brought home to me the significance of the idea.
4   Though I have stressed contextual anticipation and minimal cues, it is of course true that people can figure out that something is an advertisement either out of context or in context when all the usual cues are missing, but not both together (in which case the status of a text or image becomes

*undecidable*). Schank and Abelson (1977) discuss non-script-based understanding in terms of 'plans' and 'goals', and I refer the reader to their book for further discussion.

5   This section corrects the analysis offered in Pateman 1980a, though elements of that earlier analysis can be incorporated into this new account.

6   For present purposes, I can legitimately ignore other kinds of advertisement which are designed to promote an image, activity or doctrine, rather than sell a product. Clearly, we are quite competent to understand the differences, among subtypes of the general activity type which is advertising.

7   The concept of 'genre' is inadequate just because it conflates the concept here called 'activity type' and the concept of 'formal property of the text'. My position is that activity type is specified in terms of point or purpose, independently of formal proportion, and that relevant (or *operative*; see Bach & Harnish 1979) formal properties are *only* specifiable as a function of activity type. The sets of formal properties which a text has out of context can be specified at some levels (e.g. syntactic), but these simply remind us of features of *la langue*, and do not say anything about the particular text as an instance of *la parole*.

8   The vocative reading was suggested to me by Richard Coates.

9   Time of utterance (just before Christmas) also serves to produce the reading intended, but I shall not discuss this.

10  Sloman provides a general definition, 'an analogical representation has a structure which gives information about the structure of the thing denoted, depicted or represented' (Sloman 1978, p. 165). Fregean representations do not give such structural information. Sloman's use of 'analogic' corresponds to Peirce's use of 'iconic'. For Peirce, photographs are iconic *and* indexical (because causally linked to what they represent; see Peirce 1940, pp. 98-119).

11  Because the photographic signifier is continuous, talk of 'elements' must have to do with the signifieds — in this case, the objects denoted by the image. So the structural reorganization spoken of here has to do with the *semantics* of the image.

12  In Pateman 1980a, I use Searle 1969 and call the thematic or topical content the 'referential content' of the advertisement (which I treat as a single speech-act). Since advertisements are clearly discourse acts, rather than speech-acts in Searle's sense, I abandon the use of the concept of referential content in this essay, using the less articulated ideas of 'theme' and 'topic'. In a further development of the lines of thought represented by the two studies, it might be possible to reintegrate the idea of referential content.

13  Roughly speaking, different stress-assignments produce utterances which can be heard as answers to different implicit questions, as in the following list (where italics represent heavy stress):

    *John* stole three horses (answers the question: Who stole three horses?)
    John *stole* three horses (What did John do with three horses?)
    John stole *three* horses (How many horses did John steal?)

John stole three *horses* (John stole three what?)
(cf. Smith & Wilson 1979, ch. 7.)

In Pateman 1980a I call the comment 'predication', a term I have abandoned here for reasons explained in note 11.

14  On the semantic/pragmatic distinction, see Grice 1975; Kempson 1975; Wilson 1975; Smith & Wilson 1979, chs 7, 8; Bach & Harnish 1979; Gazdar 1979; Ortony 1979 — a small selection of excellent work from a large and fast-growing literature.

15  The four maxims are: (1) Make your contribution as informative but not more so than is required (for the current purposes of the exchange); (2) Try to make your contribution one which is true; (3) Be relevant; (4) Be perspicuous (Grice 1975, pp. 45-6). These maxims are seen by Grice to derive from a general Cooperative Principle of Conversation which he states informally as: 'Make your conversational contribution such as is required, at the stage at which it occurs, by the accepted purpose or direction of the talk exchange in which you are engaged' (p. 45).

16  Smith and Wilson (1979, p. 177) offer the following informal definition of relevance (to an ongoing discourse):
    A remark P is relevant to another remark Q if P and Q together with background knowledge yield new information not derivable from either P or Q, together with background knowledge, alone.

17  One might say: there is no way in which the strength of jetties is semantically conventionalized in the way the romance of roses is conventionalized. Conventionalization shortens the inferential circuit, but does not eliminate it (cf. Bach & Harnish 1979, chs 6, 7).

18  These intentions we impute to the advertiser are what Bach and Harnish (1979), following Grice 1957 and subsequent work, call R-intentions: intentions to achieve an effect by means of recognition of the intention to produce that effect (which Habermas makes criterial for communicative action: see Habermas 1979, ch. 1 and pp. 116-23).

19  The founders of the London Women's Liberation Workshop launched it in 1969 by enhancing London Underground advertisements with campaign stickers one of which read 'What exactly are you selling?' (used particularly on advertisements for Elliott boots).

20  Lacan.

21  In both art and science, the demand for answers to 'What exactly do you mean?' questions can be thoroughly destructive of original and creative work. See, for example, Boyd 1979 for a discussion.

22  Compare Barthes 1973b.

23  I owe this point to Patricia Holland.

# 10

# Understanding advertisers[1]

KATHY MYERS

One of the problems with cultural analysis of advertising is the tendency to isolate a single preferred reading or decoding of a text or image.[2] There has been a marked reluctance to consider either the production practices and deliberate persuasive strategies which affect the design of an advert or the variety of possible interpretations which audiences may make. In particular, readings of advertisements have failed to take into account the fact that advertisements are selectively targeted, that they are encoded in such a way as to maximize their appeal for a preselected social group or target audience.

Selective targeting is a strategy for selective selling, designed to secure a predictable level of demand for an advertised product. In marketing terminology, the ability to predict the level of demand represents the difference between 'trial selling' and 'branding'. For a product to become a brand it needs to establish and maintain a position in the market over a defined period of time. Market stability ultimately depends upon repeat purchases.

Ralph Horowitz put the case for manufacturers' investment in advertising as follows: 'The role of advertising is to diminish uncertainty. Advertising sets out to secure a predetermined level of demand for a given future and to diminish fluctuations around that predetermined level.'[3] The ability to predict total revenue from advertised products is crucial if manufacturers are to accurately plan future output, product development and capital investment.

It is therefore the need to take the trial and error out of selling that motivates advertisers to create a clear picture of the audience they are selling to, and what role or function the product could play in people's lives. An agency report on consumer research emphasized the importance of 'consumer orientation' in campaign planning:

Consumer orientation is the difference between looking through the eyes of the
manufacturer and looking through the eyes of the consumer...Consumer orientation means thinking of advertising strategies in terms of what it will do to
them. Understanding the target audience, how they will use the advertising and
respond to it, are the subjects of advertising planning. (Ogilvy, Benson & Mather
1978)

It is important to make the distinction between the ability of an
audience to comprehend or decode an advertisement in terms of its
product message, and the possibility that the audience will react or
respond to it by buying the product. Agency consumer research is
geared to understanding the relationship between advertisement comprehension and purchase. The report quoted above went on to say:

[Advertisers] need understanding of the consumer's relationships with the
product − how the target consumer thinks and feels about the product and how
it is used and the way it fits in with their lives. It is wrong to begin thinking
about the brand and its attributes and how to compete with rivals without first
thinking of basic consumer requirements and habits and basic thoughts and
beliefs.

Attention to the 'needs' and 'desires' of the consumer informs every
level of marketing strategy: the design of the campaign, the kind of
media exposure given, the amount of exposure, the choice of packaging, distribution, etc. The advert which we see is only one part of
this highly coordinated marketing offensive.

The rest of this paper is divided into two sections. The first section
considers the problem of identifying advertisements in women's
magazines. The second section looks at advertisers' intentions: the
concepts of branding and selling in relation to the advertisers' image
of the consumer. Both issues have been neglected in the cultural
analysis of advertising to the detriment of theory and interpretation.

### Identifying advertisements in women's magazines

Pateman's contribution in this book (ch. 9) suggests that recognizing
an advertisement is an easy business; something which audiences
'routinely accomplish'. For Pateman it appears to be the implicit
'intention to sell' which differentiates advertisements from other
kinds of messages conveyed by the media. In fact, advertisements

differ from each other in significant ways which lead to three distinct kinds of advertising: Direct Advertising, Shared Advertising and Indirect Advertising. It would seem that in women's magazines, the intention to sell is what unites the commercial content of these publications rather than the basis for distinguishing between advertisements and other kinds of journalistic copy.

*Direct advertising.*   This refers to advertisements commissioned by manufacturing companies and produced by agencies. It is what most commentators (including Pateman) appear to mean by 'advertisements'.

*Shared advertisements.*   The expense of an advertisement may be shared by two or more interested companies, or, in the case of 'advertorials', by the magazine and manufacturer. Because of expense and problems of organization, this kind of advertising tends to be limited. An example of a shared advertisement is illustration 1, from *Cosmopolitan*. In this case, the expense of the advertisement was shared by Bellino, Bergasol and Pernod. The fashion crew flew by courtesy of Air France.

*Indirect advertising.*   All forms of advertising depend on the support which successful promotion or marketing can provide. Manufacturing companies or hired agencies and public relation services work to provide magazines with up-to-date product information. This kind of promotion aims to encourage journalistic attention in the hope that it will reap favourable 'free' advertising benefits. The scale and significance of indirect advertising is hard to detect, as it may be incorporated into a magazine article or consumer advice page at the discretion of journalists and editors. The 'Flora' press trip to an exclusive Scottish hotel illustrates the promoter's belief in the appeal of high-pressure salesmanship to supposedly influential journalists.[4] The benefits of information accrue to both advertisers and publishers. Advertisers need to expose their products or services but magazines also need up-to-date product information if they are to keep their publication topical and competitive. This is well illustrated by the 'Look Out' page of *Jackie* magazine (see illustration 2).

It is surprising that Raymond Williams's early observations on the close relationship between advertising and editorial within the context of women's magazines have been overlooked by other writers. He said: 'It is often not easy to separate advertising from editorial material. It is not only that the styles of presentation are

Summer pleasures start with a
sleek suntan, a stunning swimsuit
or bikini and a cooling drink.
Add more power to the sun, and
speed up suntanning, with Bergasol. Bergasol contains Berga-
mot oil in its formula, encouraging
your skin to tan *fast* and safely.
Celebrate your sunbathing with
Pernod. Summer is the best time
for refreshing aniseed-flavoured
Pernod, the favourite aperitif of
the French and sipped by them as
they sun themselves along the
Riviera. Why not try a Pernod à la
Française? One part Pernod, five
parts iced water. Watch clear,
neat Pernod cloud to a fresh
lemon colour.
Bare your body beautifully in
Bellino's stunning collection of
beach clothes. Show off a luscious
suntan in a bikini by Bellino,
£14.95, style H75398, also available in red, turquoise, burgundy,
dark brown or black.

Photographed by **Bill King**
in the French
Caribbean island of
Guadeloupe where we
flew courtesy of
Air France
Hair by Kerry for
Molton Brown

*Illustration 1    Advertisement from* Cosmopolitan, *May 1979*

remarkably similar. It is also that a good deal of more or less direct
advertising is normally included in certain editorial features.' (1962,
pp. 55-6) This overlap is neither a coincidence nor is it just a matter
of stylistic convention. Both advertiser and publisher may benefit
from the development of an overall 'house' style which gives predictability, consistency and coherence to the entire range of content.

To understand advertisements it is also important to know that

*Illustration 2 Page from* Jackie, *19 July 1980*

without exception all women's magazines are financially dependent upon advertising revenue. Paid advertisements account for up to a third of total page space. That publicity and product promotions are partly a consumer and partly an advertiser service is illustrated by the convention of giving front cover make-up or fashion credits to lucrative advertisers. Magazine styles have also been influenced by presentation and design innovations made within commercial advertising.

From the advertiser's point of view, women's magazines are a highly reliable way of reaching the female consumer. Readership profiles are available for each magazine on the market. The Target Group Index and National Readership Survey suggest that women make 80 per cent of domestic consumer decisions, and that one of the most cost-efficient ways of reaching this market is through the medium of women's magazines. The readership profiles also provide a detailed analysis of the female market by social group which is broken down by age, class, occupation and other variables. Magazines may sell advertising space on the strength of their ability to reach a precise social group or target audience. For example, the copy for a National Magazines advert which appeared in *Campaign* read:

ABC 1 x 3 million. Spend a month in colour with National Magazines and Cosmopolitan, Harper and Queens, Good Housekeeping, She and Company will put you in touch with 33% of all ABC 1 women. Independent, discriminating, intelligent and above all affluent. Britain's most desirable women. Spend six months with National Magazines, and the figures are even more glamorous: 51% of all ABC 1 women; 65% of all ABC 1 women under 35. No other publishing company reaches so many desirable ABC 1 women at so little cost. Be they fashion-conscious younger women, discerning housewives, or decision-making business women. Taken all in all, National Magazines are the best-written, most beautifully designed magazines now available for Britain's ABC 1 women and ABC 1 Advertisers, too.[5]

One unquantifiable benefit to advertisers is that magazines provide a 'hospitable environment' for the digestion and assimilation of advertised information. Glossy, colourful and eye-catching, women's magazines are reputed to have a 'keep' value. They may be read at leisure, used for reference, shown to friends or left about the house. Publishers and advertisers believe that these magazines provide a source of information, advice, solidarity and companionship, and that women have grown to trust the opinions voiced. It is a credibility jealously guarded by editors and highly valued by advertisers, for both groups feel that some of the journalistic credibility is carried over into the advertisements. The magazine environment as an essential ingredient of advertising success was the message of an IPC advert for their Women's Group of magazines. The copy quoted a Saatchi and Saatchi spokesman on the subject of Anchor Butter:

While our TV advertising is promoting the use of Anchor Butter in the family, we are looking to posters and women's magazines to reinforce our branding for us. We want the housewife to be absolutely certain that Anchor is the name she can rely on for real butter goodness, and we are confident that in the relaxed, intimate environment of women's magazines our message carries complete conviction.[6]

The two-way relationship between advertisers and the medium is not always untroubled. Magazine editors feel some responsibility towards readers as well as advertisers and are concerned for the integrity of their product. This may produce a conflict of loyalties between publisher, editor and advertiser. In 1980, this tension precipitated the sacking of the editor of one women's magazine. She had exercised her editorial rights and refused to carry cigarette advertising which she felt compromised the health and beauty ethos of the magazine.

Some advertisers may seek to stretch the credibility of their advertisement by plagiarizing the 'house style' of the magazine. Agency personnel I interviewed believed that this approach could make advertisements immediately accessible and appealing, especially to the younger audience. It is one way of seducing readers into paying attention to advertisements which they might otherwise selectively avoid. However, some agencies despised this approach, not because they considered it underhand, but because they felt it lacked distinction and impact, advertisements tending to 'blur' into the overall background provided by the magazine. There seemed to be a consensus of opinion among the agencies that this method could provide a useful way of 'educating' a young audience into 'product benefit'; especially when, for certain products, there are severe constraints on advertising in other media (for example, adverts for sanitary protection, vaginal deodorants). Under these circumstances teenage magazines may provide advertisers with the sole means of access to their target audience.

Use of magazine 'house style' is not limited to advertising for teenage audiences. It may be also used for the launch of a new campaign or product as part of the overall advertising offensive. For example, compare two pages in the same March 1980 issue of *Cosmopolitan*: the Irma Kurtz problem page (illustration 3) and the advertisement for Kerastase hair care products (illustration 4). The Kerastase advertisement adopted the question-and-answer format of the supposedly influential 'problem' page. Consumer research suggests that along with horoscopes, problem pages are the most avidly read section of a women's magazine. The advertisement appears to be offering impartial advice rather than directly promoting a product. The advertiser wishes to avoid being characterized by the reader as the cynical seller of wares, and adopts instead the values of journalism as expressed in the factual, well-informed, responsible and sympathetic image of Irma Kurtz, or the role of the problem page in providing answers to difficult personal problems.

# The Agony Column
### Irma Kurtz helps

Q I am twenty-five, and separated from my husband. The decision was mutual. I've settled back into living at home, and have met a boy (boy being the operative word). He's nineteen and we've been together over three months. He's very good to me, takes me wherever I want to go and we have a lovely relationship. The trouble is I'm beginning to get possessive about him. He's very mature for his age, and has started talking about holidays next year and it frightens me a lot. I just wish he wasn't so young, because we're very happy together. He hasn't invited me to his house because his mother thinks I'm too old for him which hurts me very much. Do you think I should break off the relationship before we get too involved, or should we just carry on enjoying ourselves?
A What's your problem? Is it that his mother thinks you are too old for him? Or is it that you agree with her? You say he is mature, so I suppose he knows his own mind and is capable of assuming responsibility for his own decisions. Are you? If not, then even at the age of nineteen he may be more mature than you. Come to that, twenty-five isn't exactly over the hill, you know. You've got plenty of time to find another husband if that's what you want. Meanwhile, why don't you let this relationship develop as it will? You've given me no real reasons to think that after only three months you should break it off, except perhaps to make his mother happy and, frankly, few women make their lovers' mothers happy or even try very hard. Stop looking ahead. Take each step as it presents itself or you might stumble badly.

Q I have made a terrible mistake in my life. I have been to bed with a man and he told everyone, so now I am classed as cheap. I know I made a mistake and I can't ever put it right. I do not know how I will explain this if I ever get married.
A First, your mistake was not in going to bed with a man, but in going to bed with an insecure, insensitive, pathetic lout. Such a lapse of judgement leads me to think that you must be very young. Too young to know, I dare say, that time puts most mistakes right, and that gossip blows over as soon as the next person "makes a mistake". Hold your head up high, face the fools down, put a high price on yourself: you aren't "cheap", you aren't

"damaged", you simply made a mistake. Forgive yourself. The man you marry some day need not know anything about what happened; and if he does know, I think the man you want will be man enough to forgive you this early error of judgement.

Q Although I am a man of twenty-six I just cannot help masturbating each night at the thought of sex. I have been going out with my girlfriend for the past six months and love her very much. I now feel it is time to decide about marriage, but how can I enter into it with the knowledge that I won't be able to stop my habit?
A How do you know you won't be able to stop masturbating? You don't tell me whether you have regular sex with your girlfriend now, but presumably you intend to have regular sex with your future wife. Unless satisfying a woman does not satisfy him, even a twenty-six-year-old man has a limit to his sexual potential. If by chance a woman cannot bring you sexual satisfaction, then you would be wise to put off marrying one until you have identified the problem and solved it with a therapist. However, if your sexual needs are truly greater than your wife can be expected to satisfy, you would not be the first husband who made love to his wife, and discreetly masturbated as well.

Q I've just had a baby and throughout the pregnancy had to watch my weight. I'm still slightly overweight, and cannot control my jealousy of other women—beautiful, slim, attractive—anyone who may catch my husband's eye. I've always been jealous but it has got so much worse—miserable gnawing feeling of ugliness, fatdom and massive inadequacies. I'm taking pills to counteract post-natal depression but this must be something else. Although one side of me knows he won't ever touch anyone else, even the fact that he can admire them makes me insanely jealous. I've tried reasoning with myself, and talking to my husband and still these irrational feelings continue.
A If your doctor has prescribed them, by all means continue with the pills to combat post-natal depression, but don't think they relieve you from considering the condition and thinking about it. It isn't the common cold, you know; of course, it can be cured and will be cured, but it deserves to be taken seriously. It seems to me a lot of what you are feeling

has to do with having just had a baby and having to face a whole new set of demands to which you may still be feeling inadequate. Feelings of inadequacy commonly translate themselves into jealousy. I would bet that when you get over the first stages of motherhood and begin to handle your baby with confidence and later with tender love, your jealousy will subside at least to the tolerable level of the past. Please, give yourself time. The condition will pass if you let it, and so will your weight gain, your fatigue, your fears, your uncertainty, and all the other small terrors of first motherhood.

Q My mother is infuriating me by her conversational intolerance towards homosexuality. She says it is "not natural" and "should be suppressed". Could you suggest a book to change her irrational viewpoint? I myself am not homosexual, but am increasingly worried at my failure to convince her that homosexuality is not "a sin".
A What possible difference can it make to you what your mother thinks about homosexuality? It's not what she thinks about you, is it? It's what she thinks about what you think. If you want to campaign for a liberal understanding of homosexuality, do it on a broader front. Unless your mother is in a position of influence and power over many people other than you, it doesn't matter if she clings to her prejudices. If you insist, there are many books you can give her; with your interest in the issue, perhaps you should find the books yourself and read them.

Q I've been going out with my boyfriend for two years. He's eighteen and I'm nineteen. I'm still a virgin and even though I love him I just can't bring myself to let him make love to me. I've always said that I would like to wait until I was married but seeing that that won't be for at least another three or four years it just seems such a long time to wait. He says that he can't wait that long but I don't really believe that he would go off and find another girl just for sex. I understand how frustrated he must feel and I tell him how sorry I am, but I don't know what I can do to help him.
Sometimes when I'm alone with him I really feel that I could love him, but on other occasions he will say things like he would like to see me in a black bra, black pants, black suspender belt and black stockings with seams in them. I think that the idea

*Illustration 3* Cosmopolitan, *March 1980,*
*the Irma Kurtz problem page*

The publisher's planning department has to be aware of the implications of stylistic overlap between advertisement and journalism. If advertisements are not signalled clearly, and look too much like editorial copy, readers may loose faith in the journalistic values of the magazine. Hence magazines often cover themselves by placing the word 'Advertisement' over some ads. However, the actual course of action taken will depend on the importance of the advertiser for the revenue of the magazine. Over-stringent policies which prevent advertisers from producing advertisements in the style of the magazine may result in the buyer moving elsewhere, in what is a highly competitive market.

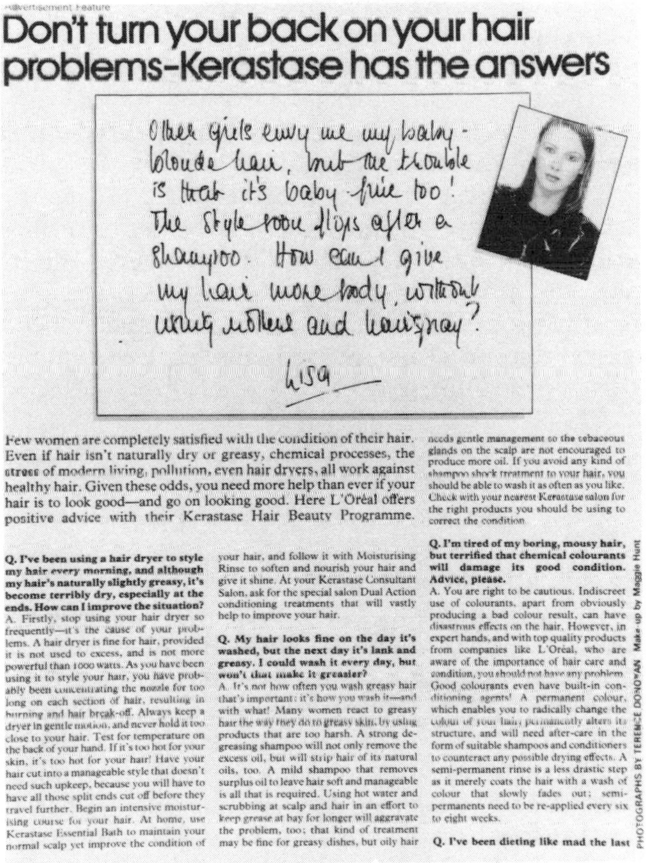

Advertisement Feature

Don't turn your back on your hair problems–Kerastase has the answers

Other girls envy me my baby-blonde hair, but the trouble is that it's baby-fine too! The style soon flops after a shampoo. How can I give my hair more body, without using mousse and hairspray?

Lisa

Few women are completely satisfied with the condition of their hair. Even if hair isn't naturally dry or greasy, chemical processes, the strees of modern living, pollution, even hair dryers, all work against healthy hair. Given these odds, you need more help than ever if your hair is to look good—and go on looking good. Here L'Oréal offers positive advice with their Kerastase Hair Beauty Programme.

**Q. I've been using a hair dryer to style my hair every morning, and although my hair's naturally slightly greasy, it's become terribly dry, especially at the ends. How can I improve the situation?**
A. Firstly, stop using your hair dryer so frequently—it's the cause of your problems. A hair dryer is fine for hair, provided it is not used to excess, and is not more powerful than 1000 watts. As you have been using it to style your hair, you have probably been concentrating the nozzle for too long on each section of hair, resulting in burning and hair break-off. Always keep a dryer in gentle motion, and never hold it too close to your hair. Test for temperature on the back of your hand. If it's too hot for your skin, it's too hot for your hair! Have your hair cut into a manageable style that doesn't need such upkeep, because you will have to have all those split ends cut off before they travel further. Begin an intensive moisturising course for your hair. At home, use Kerastase Essential Bath to maintain your normal scalp yet improve the condition of your hair, and follow it with Moisturising Rinse to soften and nourish your hair and give it shine. At your Kerastase Consultant Salon, ask for the special salon Dual Action conditioning treatments that will vastly help to improve your hair.

**Q. My hair looks fine on the day it's washed, but the next day it's lank and greasy. I could wash it every day, but won't that make it greasier?**
A. It's not how often you wash greasy hair that's important: it's how you wash it—and with what! Many women react to greasy hair the way they do to greasy skin, by using products that are too harsh. A strong degreasing shampoo will not only remove the excess oil, but will strip hair of its natural oils, too. A mild shampoo that removes surplus oil to leave hair soft and manageable is all that is required. Using hot water and scrubbing at scalp and hair in an effort to keep grease at bay for longer will aggravate the problem, too; that kind of treatment may be fine for greasy dishes, but oily hair needs gentle management so the sebaceous glands on the scalp are not encouraged to produce more oil. If you avoid any kind of shampoo shock treatment to your hair, you should be able to wash it as often as you like. Check with your nearest Kerastase salon for the right products you should be using to correct the condition.

**Q. I'm tired of my boring, mousy hair, but terrified that chemical colourants will damage its good condition. Advice, please.**
A. You are right to be cautious. Indiscreet use of colourants, apart from obviously producing a bad colour result, can have disastrous effects on the hair. However, in expert hands, and with top quality products from companies like L'Oréal, who are aware of the importance of hair care and condition, you should not have any problem. Good colourants even have built-in conditioning agents! A permanent colour, which enables you to radically change the colour of your hair, permanently alters its structure, and will need after-care in the form of suitable shampoos and conditioners to counteract any possible drying effects. A semi-permanent rinse is a less drastic step as it merely coats the hair with a wash of colour that slowly fades out; semi-permanents need to be re-applied every six to eight weeks.

**Q. I've been dieting like mad the last**

PHOTOGRAPHS BY TERENCE DONOVAN Make-up by Maggie Hunt

*Illustration 4* Cosmopolitan, *March 1980, advertisement*

Advertisers need to strike a delicate perceptual balance between making an advertisement appear 'at home' in the environment of the magazine, and designing it to stand out – maximizing 'brand impact'. The tension between environment and brand impact particularly affects the design of advertisements for products in close competition, like Martini and Cinzano aperitifs.[7] The problem may be less acute in press advertising than in television commercials because the audience can dwell on a printed image for longer, but room for confusion still exists. Because brand impact is felt to be essential for successful advertising, those advertisements which directly trade off other advertisements or editorial style tend to be in the minority. The fact that magazines also engage in this borrowing of style means that advertisers have to constantly find new ways of expressing the product message whilst keeping within the parameters of the overall stylistic conventions laid down by the magazine.

In the context of women's magazines the ability to recognize an advertisement will therefore depend on how it is signalled to the audience. Accurate recognition cannot be taken for granted, for the difference between advertisement and the varieties of journalism is often hard to define either linguistically or visually. The form which an advertisement ultimately takes will depend on a combination of advertisers' intentions, economic criteria, editorial policy and legal and voluntary restraints on practice, as well as technical developments within the medium.

### Advertisers' intentions: branding, selling and the image of the consumer

Advertisers' intentions could be described loosely as consisting of the overall marketing strategy for a specific campaign. However, within any agency there is unlikely to be a consensus of opinion on exactly how a campaign should be executed. For example, the creative team responsible for the production of artwork and copy may feel that the aesthetic form of the advertisement has been prostituted in the interests of economic or diplomatic considerations. The account director — an agency middle man — has the job of harmonizing the ideas of the creative team with the demands of the client. The relationship between client and agency is essentially that of employer and employee, and is not necessarily a smooth one. Agencies are very dependent on the diplomatic skills and organizational ability of the accounts department to ensure the smooth running of the campaign. The advertisement which emerges from these processes of imagination, financial control and human management must be a product of compromise, argument, bargaining and tight deadlines.

Attitudes expressed by agency staff on the role of advertising are often contradictory and eclectic. There is a danger in the analysis of advertising of assuming that it is in the interests of advertisers to create one 'preferred' reading of the advertisement's message. Intentionality suggests conscious manipulation and organization of texts and images, and implies that the visual, technical and linguistic strategies work together to secure one preferred reading of an advertisement to the exclusion of others.

If we take as an example the Benson and Hedges campaign (illustration 5), the advertisement can be said to work on three levels.

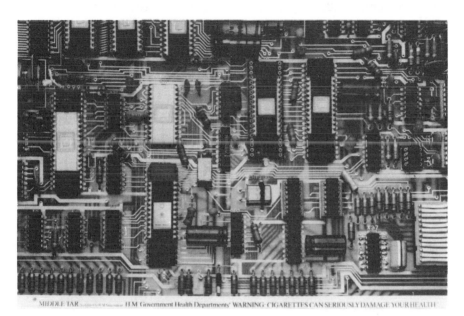

MIDDLE TAR H.M Government Health Departments' WARNING: CIGARETTES CAN SERIOUSLY DAMAGE YOUR HEALTH

*Illustration 5    Benson and Hedges advertisement*

From the advertiser's point of view it has two related functions at the level of denotation: to attract the attention of the target audience for the product and to maximize brand impact. The connotative associations work in two different ways. One is to connect the product with a visual system familiar in abstract art, so that we may read off connotations of advertising as an art form, a 'commercial' artifact which transcends its origins and acquires the prestige of art. In the other, the connotations are left open. The reader is required to do the work of making associations within and between the images present within the advertisement. Advertisers may deliberately trade on the polysemic nature of these images to hold interest and entertain the viewer. The ambiguity and complexity of the image adds richness and texture to the advertisement itself, and, in a highly competitive product field, may provide a way of securing audience attention. It may not be in the advertiser's interests to foreclose the entire range of alternative readings. It is interesting to note that a number of abstract advertisements in the same genre (e.g. Guinness,

White Horse, Number 6) were pioneered by the drink and tobacco companies whose advertising is heavily constrained by voluntary agreements with the Department of Health and Social Security, the Independent Broadcasting Authority and the Advertising Standards Authority which proscribe many associations or comments which advertisers might make for their product. As a consequence of these restrictions, advertisers have had to find an alternative way of branding which does not rely on 'country scenes', 'virility', 'social success' and similar associations.

The openness of the connotative codes may mean that we have to replace the notion of 'preferred reading' with another which admits a range of possible alternatives open to the audience. In certain cases it may also be that 'brand impact' is achieved more by single features (e.g. colour) than by the deeper and more complex levels of coding and signification within the image or text. With Benson and Hedges the intention is clearly to brand a product in a particular way. But preferential reading of the image operates only in so far as the advertisement secures the attention of a specific target audience. In other words, the determinants of the 'readings' are not present *within* the advertisement and cannot be read out of it without reference to the implicit marketing strategy of the agency concerned. It can be misleading to search for the determinations of a preferred reading solely within the form and structure of an advertisement.

Conflicts within agency strategy are reflected in the system of beliefs which validate the industry as a whole. On the one hand, members of the advertising profession see advertising mythically as consistent with the needs of a democratic egalitarian society: it helps to make the consumer aware of available market 'choices', it 'educates' the consumer into 'product benefit' and so on. But the vision of advertising as a democratic information service is distorted by the fact that it is the job of each individual agency to promote one product at the expense of competing products and, implicitly, to systematically foreclose the appeal of alternatives in the eye of the consumer. The apparent contradiction between these two aspects of commercial philosophy is rationalized in terms of the 'Darwinian' survival of the fittest product. In the Western economy, where 95 per cent of the new products introduced onto the market each year fail to maintain a market position, successful marketing and advertising is felt to be essential to give products a competitive chance.

Agencies are commissioned to promote specific products for their clients, but the cumulative effect of advertising is to promote product fields or categories. From the advertisers' point of view this effect is double-edged. On the one hand, their specific brand may benefit from the increase in public awareness of, and interest in, the product field. On the other hand, consumers may start to favour less expensive alternatives. Advertisers are aware that brand loyalty is at best idealistic, and that in terms of consumer behaviour, its probability is low. Successful marketing and promotion of a product therefore cannot depend on advertising alone. Advertising has to be seen as an integral part of a much wider marketing offensive which extends from product development through to retail distribution. It is this spectrum of product promotion which gives a commodity its total image and style. Advertisers, if not their critics, realize that they cannot rely on the linguistic or visual significations internal to the advertisement to do the selling. As one account executive put it: 'You can't sell a product if it's naff — if a need for it doesn't exist. You need the right product, the right distribution and the right sales staff. Advertising can't go it alone, it's all got to work together.' 'Good' advertising is therefore a combination of market research, intuition and so-called 'creative talent'.

One requirement of successful branding is to recognize or create the 'right' consumer for the product. As a consequence, advertisements are constructed so as to be highly selective in their form of address and appeal. Account executives tend to talk about their products fulfilling 'social needs', although they seem unclear about the aetiology of these 'needs' or the role which advertising plays in structuring them. They typically describe advertising as both 'reflecting' social needs, and as 'creating a market'. As an account executive for a men's aftershave advertisement put it, the product 'created the market, or rather, satisfied a need that was already there'.

Whatever inconsistency there may be in notions of demand, the consumer is never absent from agency strategy. The consumer profile which they build informs all levels of agency discourse. The agency concept of 'consumer experience' is supported by a complex social map which details how a product will be used, how it will fit into, shape and alter the lifestyle of the prospective consumer. An illustration of this is the concept of the female consumer.

Since most domestic purchasing decisions are made by women, agencies tend to refer to the consumer as 'she', or as the 'housewife'. Women are recognized as a social group by virtue of gender, but certain 'lifestyle' differences within this 'all housewives' group are recognized. In fact the need for a refined view of 'lifestyle' is stressed:

Beware the 'all housewives' target audience — select your prime prospect. The more accurately you pinpoint your prime prospect, the higher your conversion rate [to the product]...and when your prime prospect is defined, paint a picture of him/her using all the attitudinal data you can find. Do not settle for media jargon categories. Persil Automatic was not launched merely at 'front loading washing machine users'; its success has demonstrated a precise and continuing understanding of the attitudes and lifestyle of the women who own such a machine.[8]

However, the nebulous concept of 'lifestyle' used by agencies is not guaranteed to provide a precise understanding of consumer practice. Imported from the USA marketing industry it provided an alternative description of social difference from that of 'class'. 'Lifestyle' was felt to provide a more accurate estimation of purchasing power and actual market choices made by consumers. Advertisers' resistance to the concept of class as a structuring principle is due partly to the consensual view of society which they appear to favour, and partly to the inadequacies of the class model employed. Agencies do use the Registrar General's scale which categorizes people on the basis of occupation of head of household, but they feel that this gives a misleading picture of consumers' disposable income because women are subsumed in the general socioeconomic categories.

Lifestyle categories are said to cut across the hierarchies of occupation and status, so that social stratification is contradictory and complex. Women are stereotyped in similar ways and unified by their common interests in beauty, youth, the family, home and relationships. At the same time, however, they are segmented according to lifestyle variables: the kind of beauty look, the size of the family, the location of the house, or the woman's marital status. Typical constellations of social experience may be described euphemistically as 'sophisticated' or 'accessible' lifestyles. The effect of using 'lifestyle' categories and of separating social experiences from structured inequalities of occupation, income and ideology is to perpetuate the myth of classlessness and to promote the idea of embourgeoisement in agency thinking.

The ostensible purpose of these categories is to tailor 'aspirations' to the material circumstance of the potential consumer. Agencies are concerned that messages should be 'accessible' and not 'too far-fetched' so as to encourage audience identification with the lifestyle portrayed in the advertisement. Sometimes agencies misread the market — as for example in the case of the campaign for Boots 17 cosmetics.[9] Research proved there to be a discrepancy between the agency's vision of the consumer and the actual purchaser of the product. The campaign was targeted at young women and teenagers, but the consumer profile included women of all ages, significantly women in their late twenties. The agency considered retargeting the campaign to embrace and appeal to this wider market but then decided that it was the existing youthful, glossy, inexpensive image of 17 which was the source of its wide appeal.

Research suggested that women bought 17 cosmetics for a variety of reasons: their competitive price, large range of products and colours, packaging, ease of purchase and the trusty name of Boots. The agency responsible for the campaign felt that the advertisements were resonant enough to convey all these qualities. In response to the research findings, the agency decided to extend the media coverage of the campaign into magazines which possessed broader consumer profiles (in terms of age and lifestyle) instead of restructuring the advertising campaign.

As the 17 campaign illustrated, the same product can appeal to people for a variety of reasons. This insight was incorporated into a campaign for jewellery. The agency which handled the J. Weir jewellery account produced a press campaign focused on nine advertisements, three of which are shown in illustration 6.[10] Three thematic images were created to accompany nine alternative sets of copy. Each advertisement told a little story. The market of 'all women' was divided into three target groups. The copy writer who designed the advertisements described the groups as the 'sophisticated moderns' who read *Cosmopolitan* or *Company*: the 'middle-of-the-road mums' who read *Woman* and *Woman's Own*, and finally the 'romantics' who read *Annabel*, *True and Loving* etc. Each advertisement was tailored to maximize its appeal for the target audience; something they could 'relate to and identify with'. For the copy writer this campaign presented a familiar creative problem: the tension between rendering the advertisement 'appealing and acceptable' and at the same time 'trying to say something different' that would capture the imagination and hopefully the pocket of specific groups of the readers.

How people actually respond to campaigns is hard to determine except in hard sales terms. Most agencies receive little feedback about who buys the advertised product, or why they chose it. This is due partly to the expense of post-campaign research and partly to the problems of conducting it. Successful branding is supposed to mean the securing of the 'right' consumer for the product. In practice, however, advertising success is usually measured in terms

*Illustration 6    Three advertisements from the J. Weir campaign*

of the quantity of sales rather than the quality or characteristics of the consumer. Eventually, as products become established, incorporated into the pattern of everyday life, their significance changes. Hence, the relationship between advertising strategy and actual consumer response is rarely stable. Advertising is what René König has termed a 'restless image'. Meanings which are injected into products through advertising may be radically altered and realigned in accord with usage.

## Conclusion

Consumer orientation means thinking of advertising strategies in terms of what people do with advertising, not what it will do to them; understanding the target audience, how they will use the advertising and respond to it, are the subjects of advertising planning. (Ogilvy, Benson & Mather 1978)

Like the advertisers, cultural analysis has as yet no coherent theory of audience response to advertisements, or of how and why people consume. Existing definitions of consumption, or what is meant by relations to consumption, tend to be eclectic, ambiguous and confused. Especially within contemporary Marxist thought and cultural analysis, theories of consumption have been subordinated to theories of production. As Simon Frith has commented:

The concept [of cultural consumption] means different things according to the analytic framework involved: in the marxist economic theory it refers to a moment in the circulation of value, in recent literary and film theory it refers to a kind of pleasure, in historical sociology it refers to an institutional process. Cultural theories of consumption are left in a muddle — 'passive consumption' for example is a term used by theorists of all persuasions but as a rhetorical rather than a theoretical device. (Frith 1980)

A prerequisite for any theoretical progress is that, like consumer market research, we have to reject the notion that people consume in a passive way. And since most advertising is aimed at women, and women make the majority of domestic consumer decisions, we need a theory of consumption which will explain not only how people in general relate to advertisements, but subsequently, how this affects women's purchasing decisions. Such a theory must be concerned to reassess the significance of women's place in the home. There has been a tendency to assess women's position in the home solely as an unpaid contribution to production: for example, in housework, child care and nurturing the workforce. But the home is also the focal point for consumption. This is where most advertised goods are consumed. It is also where most advertising is directed: on television, on the radio, in magazines, by mailing, etc. Women play a crucial role within this important sphere.

The general poverty of consumption theory has not only affected our analysis of marketing but has also allowed advertising to be conceptually isolated as a social form. A theory of consumption would be enriched by incorporation into a broader theory of social communications. This would mean getting out of the ghetto of 'cultural' as opposed to 'economic' analysis and the polarities of production/consumption or encoding/decoding. The role of advertising cannot be inferred simply from a knowledge of economic interests nor deduced from structuralist or language-based theories. In future, the analysis of marketing, publicity and advertising must pay closer attention to the diversity of advertisement form and the variety of advertising strategies employed. It must also recognize the spectrum of alternative audience readings which invariably exist. Perhaps where these features are acknowledged in empirical investigation, codes and conventions of advertising practice and consumer response will emerge which can be shown to be sensitive to the whole social structure.

## Notes

1  The empirical evidence used in this paper was gathered during the period January-August 1980. Interviews were conducted in ten leading advertising agencies which have cosmetic accounts. I would like to thank Don Slater for his assistance.

2  See Williamson 1978, and Pateman's contribution in this volume for examples of this tendency.

3  R. Horowitz, 'The case for advertising', *Campaign*, 24 Aug. 1979.

4  The Flora Project for Heart Disease Prevention press trip to the Gleneagles Hotel, Perthshire, Scotland (10-12 Sept. 1980), promoted by the manufacturers of Flora margerine

5  National Women's Magazine advertisement *Campaign*, 18 Apr. 1980.

6  IPC Women's Magazine Group advertisement *Campaign*, 26 Oct. 1979.

7  T. Fawley of (TABS) has voiced the anxiety of the advertisers: 'In general product fields there is a multiplicity of brands competing for attention... unless a commercial is very well branded, how many of the target audience will be unable to differentiate between competing brands?' 'Analysis of the ITV strike', *Campaign*, 18 Jan. 1980.

8  A. Gibson, managing director of Benton and Bowles, '5 vital steps to prevent a launch disaster', *Campaign*, 18 Apr. 1980.

9  The Boots 17 cosmetic account is handled by McCormick Intermarco Farnc Ltd.

10  Agency NCK (Norman Craig and Kummel) handle the J. Weir jewellery account.

# Part IV

# Photography

# 11

## Seeing sense

VICTOR BURGIN

Although photography is a 'visual medium', it is not 'purely visual'. I am not alluding simply to the fact that we rarely see a photograph *in use* which is not accompanied by writing (though this is highly significant); even the uncaptioned 'art' photograph, framed and isolated on the gallery wall, is invaded by language in the very moment it is looked at: in memory, in association, snatches of words and images continually alternate and intermingle. It will be objected that this is indistinct and insignificant background noise to our primary act of *seeing*. If I may be excused a physiological analogy, the murmur of the circulation of the blood is even more indistinct, but no less important for that.

In a familiar cinematic convention, subjective consciousness — reflection, introspection, memory — is rendered as a disembodied 'voice-over' accompanying an otherwise silent image-track. I am not suggesting that such an interior monologue similarly accompanies our looking at photographs, nor do I wish to claim that in the process of looking at a photograph we mentally translate the image in terms of a redundant verbal description. What I 'have in mind' is better expressed in the image of transparent coloured inks which have been poured onto the surface of water in a glass container: as the inks spread and sink their boundaries and relations are in constant flux, and areas which at one moment are distinct from one another may, at the next, overlap. Analogies are of course *only* analogies, I simply wish to stress the fluidity of the phenomenon by contrast with the unavoidable rigidity of some of the schematic descriptions which will follow.

'Photography is a visual medium.' At a strictly physiological level it is quite clear what we mean by 'the visual': it is that aspect of our experience which results from light being reflected from objects into our eyes. We do not however *see* our retinal images: as is well-known, although we see the world as right-way-up, the image on our retina is inverted; we have two slightly discrepant retinal images, but see only one image; we make mental allowances for the known relative sizes of objects which override the actual relative sizes of their images on our retina; we also make allowances for perspective effects such as foreshortening, the foundation of the erroneous popular judgement that such effects in photography are 'distortions'; our eyes operate in scanning movements, the body is itself generally in motion, and such stable objects as we see are therefore *abstracted* from an ongoing phenomenal flux (Gibson 1967); moreover, attention to such objects 'out there' in the material world is constantly subverted as wilful concentration dissolves into involuntary association;…and so on. While the detail of these and many other factors as described in the literature of the psychology of perception, cognitive psychology, and related disciplines, is complex, the broad conclusion to be drawn from this work may nevertheless be simply expressed:

What we see…is not a pure and simple coding of the light patterns that are focused on the retina. Somewhere between the retina and the visual cortex the inflowing signals are modified to provide information that is already linked to a learned response…Evidently what reaches the visual cortex is evoked by the external world but is hardly a direct or simple replica of it. (Pribram 1969)

That seeing is no simple matter has of course been acknowledged in visual art for centuries. It is a fact which painting, facing the problem of representing real space in terms of only two dimensions, could not avoid (for its part, sculpture particularly emphasized the imbrication of the visual and the kinaesthetic, the extent to which seeing is a muscular and visceral activity). At times the aims of visual art became effectively *identified* with those of a science of seeing. Berenson complained of the Renaissance preoccupation with problems of perspective: 'Our art has a fatal tendency to become science, and we hardly possess a masterpiece which does not bear the marks of having been a battlefield for divided interests.' Across the modern period, at least in the West, it has been very widely assumed that an empirical science of perception can provide not only a necessary but a sufficient account of the material facts upon which visual art practices are based. Thus, in this present century, and particularly in the field of art education, the psychology of perception has become the most readily accepted art-related 'scientific' discipline, the one in which 'visual artists' most readily identify their own concerns (correspondingly, where philosophical theories have been used they have generally had a phenomenological orientation). Certainly such studies in the psychology of appearances are necessary, if only to provide a corrective to the naive idea of purely retinal vision. But if the explanation of seeing is arrested at this point it serves to support an error of even greater consequence: that ubiquitous belief in 'the visual' as a realm of experience totally separated from, indeed antithetical to, 'the verbal'.

Seeing is not an activity divorced from the rest of consciousness; any account of visual art which is adequate to the facts of our actual experience must allow for the imbrication of the visual with other aspects of thought. In a 1970 overview of extant research, M. J. Horowitz has presented a tripartite model of the dominant modes of thought in terms of 'enactive', 'image', and 'lexical' (Horowitz 1970). *Enactive* thought is muscular and visceral, is prominent in infancy and childhood, and remains a more or less marked feature of adult thinking. For example: on entering my kitchen I found that I had forgotten the purpose of my visit; no word or image came to mind, but my gesture of picking up something with a fork led me to the implement I was seeking. The enactive may be conjoined with the visual. Albert Einstein reported that, for him: 'The psychical entities which seem to serve as elements in thought are certain signs and more or less clear images... [elements] of visual and some of muscular type' (Ghiselin 1955). The enactive also merges with the verbal: Horowitz supplies the example of a person who was temporarily unable to find the phrase, 'he likes to pin people down', an expression called to mind only after the speaker's manual gesture of pinning something down. We should also note the findings of psychoanalysis concerning the type of neurotic symptom in which a repressed idea finds expression via the enactive realization of a verbal metaphor; an example from Freud's case histories is Dora's hysterical vomiting at the repressed recollection of Herr K's sexual advances, an idea which 'made her sick' (Freud 1953b).

Mental *images* are those psychic phenomena which we may assimilate to a sensory order: visual, auditory, tactile, gustatory, olfactory. For the purposes of this essay however I shall use the term 'image' to refer to visual images alone. If I wish to describe, say, an apartment I once lived in, I will base my description on

mental images of its rooms and their contents. Such a use of imagery
is a familiar part of normal everyday thought. However, not all
imaged thought is so orderly and controlled. We may find ourselves
making connections between things, on the basis of images, which
take us unawares; we may not be conscious of any wilful process
by which one image led to another — the connection seems to be
made gratuitously and instantaneously. The result of such a 'flash'
may be a disturbing idea which we put instantly out of mind, or it
may provide a witticism for which we can happily take credit; or
more commonly it will seem simply inconsequential. At times, we
may deliberately seek the psychic routes which bring these unsolicited
interruptions to rational thinking. In the 'daydream', for example,
the basic scenario and its protagonists are consciously chosen, but
one's thoughts are then abandoned to an only minimally controlled
drift on more or less autonomous currents of associations.

The sense of being in control of our mental imagery is of course
most completely absent in the *dream* itself. Dreams 'come to us' as
if from another place, and the flow of their images obeys no rational
logic. Freud's study of dreams led him to identify a particular sort of
'dream logic' radically different from the logic of rational thought:
the *dream-work*, the (il)logic of the 'primary processes' of the
unconscious. In a certain common misconception, the unconscious
is conceived of as a kind of bottomless pit to which has been consigned all that is dark and mysterious in 'human nature'. On the
contrary, unconscious processes operate 'in broad daylight'; although
they are structurally and qualitatively different from the processes
of rational thought and symbolization enshrined in linguistics and
philosophical logic, they are nevertheless an integral part of normal
everyday thought processes taken as a whole. The apparent illogi-
cality which so obviously characterizes the dream invades and
suffuses waking discourse in the form of slips of the tongue and
other involuntary acts, and in jokes. Additionally, and most important to this present discussion, the intrusion of the primary processes
into rational thought ('secondary processes') governs the mechanisms
of visual association.

Freud identifies four mechanisms in the dream-work: 'condensation'; 'displacement'; 'considerations of representability'; and
'secondary revision'. In *condensation*, a process of 'packing into a
smaller space' has taken place: 'If a dream is written out it may
perhaps fill half a page. The analysis setting out the dream-thoughts
underlying it may occupy six, eight or a dozen times as much space'
(Freud 1953a). It is this process which provides the general feature

of *over-determination*, by which, for any manifest element, there can
be a plurality of latent elements (dream-thoughts). By *displacement*,
Freud means two related things. First, that process by which individual elements in the manifest dream stand in for elements of the
dream-thoughts by virtue of an association, or chain of associations,
which links the two. Thus displacement is implicated in the work of
condensation: displacements from two or more separate latent
elements, along separate associative paths, may eventually reach a
point at which the paths meet, forming a condensation at the point
of intersection. The second, related, meaning of the term 'displacement' is that process according to which the manifest dream can
have a different 'emotional centre' from the latent thoughts. Something quite trivial may occupy centre-stage in the dream, as it were
'receive the emotional spotlight'; what has occurred here is a displacement of feelings and attention from the thing, person, or situation
which is in reality responsible for the arousal of those feelings. It is
thus possible for something as inconsequential as, say, an ice-cube
to become in a dream the object of a strong feeling.

Of *considerations of representability*, Freud writes:

let us suppose that you had undertaken the task of replacing a political leading
article in a newspaper by a series of illustrations...In so far as the article mentioned people and concrete objects you will replace them easily...but your
difficulties will begin when you come to the representation of abstract words
and of all of those parts of speech which indicate relations between thoughts.
(1961a, p. 175)

In *The interpretation of dreams* Freud describes the various ways in
which the dream deals, in visual terms, with such logical relations as
implication, disjunction, contradiction, etc. We should note a particular role of the verbal in the transition from the abstract to the
pictorial: 'bridge words' are those which, in more readily lending
themselves to visualization, provide a means of displacement from
the abstract term to its visual representation. Thus, for example,
the idea of 'reconciliation' might find visual expression through
the intermediary of the expression 'bury the hatchet', which can be
more easily transcribed in visual terms. This representational strategy
is widely to be found in advertising, which relies extensively on our
ability to read images in terms of underlying verbal texts. It may be
appreciated that such readings readily occur 'wild', that is to say,
where they were not intended.

*Secondary revision* is the act of ordering, revising, supplementing, the contents of the dream so as to make a more intelligible whole out of it. It comes into play when the dreamer is nearing a waking state and/or recounting the dream. Freud had some doubts as to whether this process should properly be considered to belong to the dream-work itself (in an article of 1922 he definitely excludes it). However, it is not important to our purposes here that this be decided; we should note that secondary revision is a process of dramatization, of narrativization.

Returning now to Horowitz's schema of types of mental representation, *lexical* thought is 'thinking in words'. It should be stressed however that this is not simply a matter of the silent mental rehearsal of a potentially actualized speech. Lev Vygotsky has identified an *inner speech* fundamentally different in its nature from externally directed communicative speech. Inner speech 'appears disconnected and incomplete, namely, omitting the subject of a sentence and all words connected with it, while preserving the predicate' (1977, p. 139). Inner speech in the adult develops out of the 'egocentric speech' (Piaget) of the small child. We should remark that Freud describes the primary processes as preceding the secondary processes in the mental development of the individual; they are pre-verbal in origin and thus prefer to handle images rather than words. Where words *are* handled they are treated as far as possible like images. Thus, when Vygotsky observes that, in inner speech: 'A single word is so saturated with sense that many words would be required to explain it in external speech' (p. 148), we may be confident that the reference is to that same centrally important aspect of the primary processes that we encounter in Freud's work as 'condensation'. Freud notes that, in dreams, words and phrases are just meaningful elements among others, accorded no more or less status than are images, and their meanings have no necessary relation to the meanings they would carry in waking speech. Thus Lyotard has spoken of 'word-things', the result of condensation:

their 'thingness' consists in their 'thickness'; the normal word belongs to a 'transparent' order of language: its meaning is immediate...the product of condensation, as the name indicates, is, on the contrary, opaque, dense, it hides its other side, its other sides. (1971, p. 244)

I prefaced my references to Horowitz's compartmentalized model of thought by stressing the fluidity of the actual processes it describes. Horowitz himself writes:

Normal streams of thought will flow simultaneously in many compartments without clear-cut division between modes of representation. Enactions blur into imagery in the form of kinaesthetic, somesthetic, and vestibular or visceral images. Image representation blends with words in the form of faint auditory images of words. Words and enactive modes merge through images of speaking. (Horowitz 1970, p. 77)

Inescapably, the *sense* of the things we see is constructed across a complex of exchanges between these various registers of representation. Differing perceptual situations will however tend to elicit differing configurations and emphases of response: just as sculpture will tend to stress the enactive and kinaesthetic suffusion of visual imagery, so photographs predominantly tend to prompt a complex of exchanges between the visual and verbal registers: as I began by observing, the greater part of photographic practice is, *de facto*, 'scripto-visual'. This fact is nowhere more apparent than in advertising, and it may help here to refer to a particular example (see illustration 1).

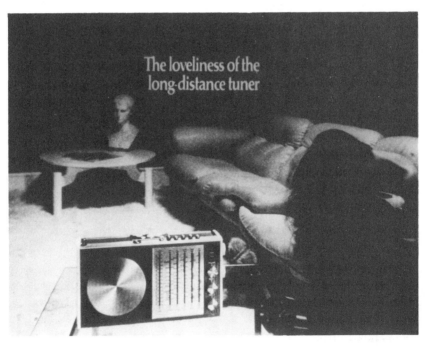

*Illustration 1    Advertisement for a radio*

The particular conjuncture into which this advertisement was launched, in Britain in the early 1960s, included a bestselling novel by Alan Sillitoe and a popularly successful film based on this novel — directed by Tony Richardson and featuring Tom Courtenay — which retained the title of the original text: *The loneliness of the long-distance runner*. The fact that Tom Courtenay was at that time a prominent emerging young 'star' of British theatre and cinema ensured that the institutional spaces of television, and newspapers and magazines, were also penetrated. During the particular months in which this advertisement appeared therefore, the expression 'the loneliness of the long distance runner' was transmitted across the apparatuses of publishing, cinema, television, and journalism, to become inscribed in what we might call the 'popular pre-conscious' — those ever-shifting contents which we may reasonably suppose can be called to mind by the majority of individuals in a given society at a particular moment in its history; that which is 'common knowledge'. Two attributes therefore are immediately entrained by this fragment of the popular pre-conscious which serves the advertisement as *pre-text*: success and contemporaneity. Additionally, the visual image across which the fragment is inscribed is clearly open to the implication of the erotic. Ambition, contemporaneity, eroticism, together with the substantial primacy of the visual in their inscription: *the daydream*.

In his 1908 essay, 'The relation of the poet to day-dreaming', Freud remarks that daydreams serve one, or both, of two impulses: 'They are either ambitious wishes, which serve to elevate the subject's personality; or they are erotic ones' (1959, p. 147). To identify these two wishes in all daydreams is not, of course, to suggest that the manifest contents of such phantasies are themselves stereotyped or unchangeable: 'On the contrary, they fit themselves into the subject's shifting impressions of life, change with every change in his situation, and receive from every fresh active impression what might be called a "date-mark". As for thinking in pictures, in his 1923 paper, 'The Ego and the Id', Freud remarks that: 'in many people this seems to be the favoured method…In some ways, too, it stands nearer to unconscious processes than does thinking in words, and it is unquestionably older than the latter both ontogenetically and phylogenetically' (1961b, p. 21). The child, prior to its acquisition of language, inhabits a mode of thought not adapted to external reality but rather aimed at creating an imaginary world in which it seeks to gratify its own wishes by hallucinatory objects. The daydream — the conscious phantasy in which the subject constructs an imaginary scenario for the fulfilment of a wish — is one form of survival of such infantile thinking into adult life.

Ambition, eroticism, contemporaneity. The theme of ambition is obviously central to advertising, as is the erotic (which is, anyhow, latent in all acts of looking). In this particular advertisement, the expression 'the loneliness of the long-distance runner' offers a phantasy identification within a syndrome of success, and with a successful figure. As a certain familiar style of promotional language might have put it: 'Tom Courtney *is* the long-distance runner', ahead of his competitors, the 'leading man' both in the fiction and in reality. This particular expression at that particular conjuncture brings the ambitious wish up to date. The conjunction of ambition and eroticism here is economically achieved through a pair of sub-stitutions — a 'v' for an 'n', and a 't' for an 'r' — which tack the manifest verbal text onto its *pre-text* in the pre-conscious. By this device, the verbal fragment faces onto both manifest and latent contents of the image.

The text says that the tuner is lovely; what it simultaneously *means* (through lexical ambiguity and reference to conventional associations surrounding women) is that the woman is lovely. Thus the word 'loveliness' acts as a relay linking the radio to the woman — a movement which facilitates the displacement of an emotional investment ('cathexis') from the one to the other. The woman is 'lovely', she is also 'lonely': the suppressed term here serving as the material absence which nevertheless anchors the meaning of the woman's posture and, beyond, the entire 'mood' of the picture. Apart from the configuration of the woman's pose, the mood is given most intensely in the way the scene has been lit; it is the sort of lighting popularly referred to as 'intimate' — a word which also takes a sexual sense. The term 'intimate' here is not reached by purely subjective association, for the association is conventionally determined to the point that we may consider this lighting effect to belong to the complex of 'considerations of representability' in respect of this term. The suppressed term 'lonely', then in conjunc-tion with the connotations of the lighting, anchors the particular sort of *narrative* implications of the moment depicted in the image, implications readily linked to the phantasy of seduction, a theme very widely encountered across advertising.

Along the axis woman/radio we encounter a double oscillation between revelation and concealment. First, the visible marks which dictate the reading 'woman' also suggest the reading 'naked' — there is not a single signifier of clothing. From the point of view offered by the shot, this additional reading cannot be confirmed, but it nevertheless inheres even in the means of concealment: the veil of hair, a time-honoured convention for signifying feminine nudity without *showing* it (see, for example, conventional pictorial representations of Eve, and the verbal text of 'Lady Godiva'). Secondly, while the woman's body is hidden, averted, the radio is completely exposed — lit and positioned to offer itself in precisely that 'full-frontal nudity' denied at the other terminal of the relay. Through the agency of this oscillation then, set in motion by the ambiguity of the woman, the cathexis of the *product* is further overdetermined.

This sketch analysis of an advertisement indicates how manifest visual and verbal elements engage with each other and with latent registers of phantasy, memory and knowledge, much as cogs engage gear-trains: transmitting, amplifying, transforming the initial input. Obviously, in the act of looking at such an advertisement we do not conduct the sort of conscious analysis I have just outlined, and this is not what I am claiming. My point is that a substantial part of its *sense* is achieved in the way I have just described, albeit we experience these effects 'in the blink of an eye'. Moreover, and most importantly, such effects are not erased, they become inscribed in memory:

Perceptions are retained for a short time, in the form of images, which allows continued emotional response and conceptual appraisal. In time, retained images undergo two kinds of transformation: reduction of sensory vividness and *translation of the images into other forms of representation (such as words)*. (Horowitz 1970, p. 78: my emphasis)

It is here that we encounter a general social effect of photographs. The social order is, in a sense, built of blocks of verbal discourse of varying degrees of formal organization. A significant social effect of a photograph is the product of its imbrication within such discursive formations. It is easily appreciated that advertising activates such formations as, for example, those which concern family life, erotic encounters, competitiveness and so on. The role of the verbal in advertising will be just as readily conceded — writing is physically integrated into nearly all advertisements. But 'art' photographs are not exempt from such determinations of meaning, determinations which are achieved even where actual writing is absent. I shall take my examples, again, from the period of the 1960s.

Throughout the 1960s in America, in the setting of the growing escalation of and protest against the war on Vietnam, blacks and women organized against their own oppression. In 1965 the Watts riots effectively marked the exhaustion of the predominantly Southern black strategy of nonviolent political struggle, and the emergence of the concept of black power. In 1967 the Black Panthers went publicly armed and uniformed in Oakland, and carried their weapons into the California State House in Sacramento. In this same year the national women's peace march in Washington marked the effective inauguration of the Women's Liberation Movement. It is surely reasonable to suppose that the knowledge of events such as these suffused the collective consciousness of Americans in the 1960s. Let us now consider two 'art' photographs of this period (see illustrations 2 and 3).

*Illustration 2    Lee Friedlander: 'Madison, Wisconsin, 1966'*

About a quarter of the way into Lee Friedlander's book *Self portrait* is a photograph captioned 'Madison, Wisconsin, 1966'. In it, the shadow of the photographer's head falls across a framed portrait photograph of a young black person. The portrait is set in an oval aperture cut in a light-coloured mount, an oval now tightly contained within the shadow of the head. Placed in this context the oval is made to serve as the schematic outline of a face, the shadows of Friedlander's ears are stuck absurdly one to each side, but the face which looks out from between the ears is black. Item 109 in the catalogue to the Museum of Modern Art exhibition *New photography USA* (Szarkowski *et al.* 1971) is an untitled photograph by Gary Winogrand taken in Central Park Zoo in 1967. It shows a young white woman close beside a young black man, each carrying a live chimpanzee which is dressed in children's clothing. In the most basic social terms, what are we to make of these images produced at that historical conjuncture?

*Illustration 3    Gary Winogrand:*
*untitled photo of couple with chimpanzees*

In everyday social life it is the face which carries the burden of identity; in these terms, to exchange one's face for that of another would be to take the other's place in society. Friedlander's photograph suggests the idea of such an exchange of identities — if I am white it invites me to imagine what it would be like if I were black. In Winogrand's picture my identity and my social position are secure. We are all familiar with expressions of irrational fear of the 'mixed marriage': from the comparatively anodyne punning of the joke about the girl who married a Pole — and had a wooden baby —

to the cliché insults of the committed racist, according to whose rhetoric the union of white and black can give issue to monkeys. In terms of these considerations therefore it should be clear that Friedlander's photograph is open to readings couched in terms of social change, to which Winogrand's image is not only closed but hostile.

A final example: the catalogue to a 1976 exhibition of Gary Winogrand's photographs contains an image in which four women, talking and gesturing amongst themselves, advance towards the camera down a city street (illustration 4). The group of women, who are of varying degrees of middle age, is the most prominent feature in the right-hand half of the image; equally prominent in the left half of the image, visually just 'touching' the women, is a group of huge plastic bags stuffed full of garbage. This photograph is also printed on the cover of the catalogue; the author of the introduction to the catalogue tells us: 'When four ageing women gossip their way past four ballooning garbage bags, it earns power for the eye that sees them.

*Illustration 4    Garry Winogrand: 'Women in street'*

If that eye laughs and gloats it condemns the women to nothing more than participation in an eternal joke...' Concluding the montage of aphorisms which is his own written contribution to the catalogue, Winogrand states: 'I like to think of photographing as a two-way act of respect. Respect for the medium, by letting it do what it does best, describe. And respect for the subject, by describing it as it is.' But what the world 'is' depends extensively upon how it is *described*: in a culture where the expression 'old bag' is in circulation to describe an ageing woman, that is precisely what she is in perpetual danger of 'being'. Neither the photographer, nor the medium, nor the subject, is basically responsible for the meaning of this photograph: the meaning is produced, in the act of *looking* at the image, by a way of *talking*.

We cannot choose what we know, and neither can we choose what part of our dormant knowledge will be awakened by the stimulus of an image, reciprocally reactivated and reinforced by it. Regardless of how much we may strain to maintain a 'disinterested' aesthetic mode of apprehension, an appreciation of the 'purely visual', when we look at an image it is instantly and irreversibly integrated and collated with the intricate psychic network of our knowledge. It is the component meanings of this network that an image must *re-present*: there is no choice in this. What flexibility there is comes in the way in which these components are assembled (and even here we may have less freedom than we like to believe). To be quite explicit: such 'racism' or 'sexism' as we may ascribe to these or other images is not 'in' the photographs themselves. Such 'isms', *in the sphere of representation*, are a complex of texts, rhetorics, codes, woven into the fabric of the popular pre-conscious. It is these which are the *pre-text* for the 'eternal joke', it is these which pre-construct the photographer's 'intuitive' response to these fragments of the flux of events in the world, producing his or her recognition that there is something 'there' to photograph. *It is neither theoretically necessary nor desirable to make psychologistic assumptions concerning the intentions of the photographer*; it is the pre-constituted field of discourse which is the substantial 'author' here: photograph and photographer alike are its products and, in the act of seeing, so is the viewer. As Roland Barthes has put it:

The 'I' which approaches the text is already a plurality of other texts,...Subjectivity is generally thought of as a plenitude with which I encumber the text, but this fake plenitude is only the wash of all the codes which make up the 'I', so that finally, my subjectivity has the generality of stereotypes. (1975, p. 10)

Such a radical displacement of 'the artist' from his or her traditional position of founding centrality in the production of meaning does, of course, run completely counter to the dominant discourse of the art institutions. This discourse itself exercises its own massive determinations on the received sense of art photographs, and it is therefore necessary to give some account of it. The discourse in dominance in art photography is, *de facto*, that of 'modernism'; there has, however, been an inconsistency in the application of a modernist programme to photography.

The first paragraph of John Szarkowski's introduction to the catalogue which contains Winogrand's Central Park Zoo picture tells us: 'New pictures derive first of all from old pictures. What an artist brings to his work that is new — special to his own life and his own eyes — is used to challenge and revise his tradition, as he knows it' (Szarkowski *et al.* 1971, p. 15). There is a vivid similarity in this passage to the style and content of Clement Greenberg's writing, indeed the criteria for evaluating photographs employed throughout Szarkowski's texts corresponds almost identically to the programme for modernist art laid down by Greenberg. The essay 'Modernist painting' is probably Greenberg's most succinct statement of his view of modernism, and may therefore serve here as a convenient check-list (Greenberg 1961). In it, he defines modernism as the tendency of an art practice towards self-reference by giving prominence to the tradition of the practice; the difference of the practice from other (visual arts) practices; the 'cardinal norms' of the practice; the material substrate or 'medium' of the practice.

   In reference to *tradition*, Greenberg states: 'Modernist art continues the past without gap or break, and wherever it may end up it will never cease being intelligible in terms of the past' — Szarkowski's endorsement of this position is quoted above. In respect of *difference*, Greenberg writes: 'Each art had to determine through its own operations and works, the effects exclusive to itself...It quickly emerged that the unique and proper area of competence of each art coincided with all that was unique in the nature of its medium.' Szarkowski says, in an interview: 'I think in photography the formalist approach is...concerned with trying to explore the intrinsic or prejudicial capacities of the medium as it is understood at that moment' (Stange 1978, p. 74). Greenberg argues for the destruction of three-dimensional space in painting — 'For flatness alone was unique and exclusive to pictorial art.' He argues for a renewed emphasis on colour, 'in the name of the purely and literally optical,...against optical experience as revised or modified by tactile associations'. Flatness, the 'purely optical', and other such things as 'norms of finish and paint texture', belong to what Greenberg calls '*cardinal norms* of the art of painting'.

Szarkowski (1966) devotes his essay to cataloguing such cardinal norms of photography, which he identifies as 'The Thing Itself', 'The Detail', 'The Frame', 'Time', and 'Vantage Point'. What is not to be found in Szarkowski's discourse is Greenberg's emphasis on the *medium* defined in terms of material substrate. Greenberg insists on the materiality of the painted surface as a thing in itself in the interests of an anti-illusionism; to make a comparable insistence in respect of photography would be to undermine its founding attribute, that of illusion. We might further note that it might very well evict the camera itself from the scene, returning photography to, literally, *photo-graphy* — drawing with light. This elision, this unresolved (albeit understandable) failure to complete the journey upon which it has embarked (modernism is *nothing* if not totally internally coherent), marks a contradiction which runs like a fault-line through Szarkowski's discourse: illusion cannot be totally abandoned, but neither can the full consequences of retaining it be accepted.

We should recall that the modernist programme for painting dictated that the art work be a totally autonomous material *object* which made no reference whatsoever to anything beyond its own boundaries: the painted surface itself, its colour, its consistency, its edge, its gesture, was to be the only 'content' of the work. Any form of representation other than self-representation, in Greenberg's words, 'becomes something to be avoided like a plague'. This impetus is in direct line of descent from the desire of Bell and Fry, early in this century, to free art from concerns 'not peculiarly its own'. Clive Bell, writing in 1913, stated: 'To appreciate a work of art we need bring with us nothing but a sense of form...every other sort of representation is irrelevant'; and he complained of those who 'treat created form as if it were imitated form, a picture as though it were a photograph' (Bell 1958, p. 29).

In the same movement in which, in the West, the issue of representation in art became a dead issue, photography became consigned to the far side, the 'wrong' side, of that divide which Cubism had opened up between the nineteenth century and the modern period. Initiatives to recover photography from this remote shore (in the history of which Stieglitz figures so prominently) were therefore unavoidably directed towards securing 'picture' status for photographs. The general programme of modernism showed the way: the *art* of photography is achieved *only* through the most scrupulous attention to those effects which are irreducibly derived from, and specific to, the very functioning of the photographic apparatus itself — representation may be the contingent vulgar flesh of photography, but its spirit is 'photographic seeing'. Szarkowski is thus able to judge that: 'Winogrand...is perhaps the most outrageously thoroughgoing formalist that I know. What he is trying to figure out is what that machine will do by putting it to the most extreme tests under the greatest possible pressure' (In Stange 1978, p. 74). However, although content in photographs may be ignored, it will not go away. The fear perhaps is that to *speak* of it would be to backslide into naturalism, that it would necessarily be to abandon the gains of the modernist discourse which has provided art photography in the modern period with its credentials and its programme. On the contrary, it would be to pursue the modernist argument with an increased rigour.

The modernist programme for a given practice is centred upon that which is irreducibly *specific* to the practice; in a sense, that which remains after eliminating the things it is *not*. The initial definition of this specificity is therefore crucial, as all subsequent modes of action and evaluation will depend on it. In an article written in 1964, Greenberg himself is in no doubt as to the locus of the specificity of photography. First, it is *not* modernist painting: 'its triumphs and monuments are historical, anecdotal, reportorial, observational before they are purely pictorial' (Greenberg 1964). But then neither is 'brute information' art — in fact: 'The purely descriptive or informative is almost as great a threat to the art in photography as the purely formal or abstract.' Greenberg concludes: 'The art in photography is literary art before it is anything else...The photograph has to tell a story if it is to work as art. And it is in choosing and accosting his story, or subject, that the artist-photographer makes the decisions crucial to his art.'

Greenberg however offers no suggestion as to how an impression of narrative can be given by a single image. Szarkowski, writing some two years later, can continue to assert: 'photography has never been successful at narrative. It has in fact seldom attempted it'. Photographs, he finds, 'give the sense of the scene, while withholding its narrative meaning' (1966). 'Narrative meaning' here is clearly equated with the sort of factual account of an event which might be sought in a court of law — obviously this cannot be derived from a single image alone. But what is this 'sense' which Szarkowski mentions but does not discuss, this 'story' which Greenberg names but cannot explain? Greenberg's equation of 'story' with 'subject' raises more questions than it answers, but they are productive questions —

questions raised around the ambivalence of his use of the term 'subject': subject of the photograph (the thing pictured); subject of the story (that which it is 'a tale of'). My purpose here has been to argue that we may only resolve this ambivalence through the introduction of a third term, the *seeing* subject (the individual who looks), and that to introduce *this* subject is, in the same movement, to introduce the social world which constructs, situates, and supports it.

To speak of the 'sense' and 'story' of a photograph is to acknowledge that the reality-effect of a photograph is such that it inescapably implicates a world of activity responsible for, and to, the fragments circumscribed by the frame: a world of causes, of 'before and after', of 'if, then...', a *narrated* world. However, the narration of the world that photography achieves is accomplished not in a linear manner but in a repetition of 'vertical' readings, in stillness, in a-temporality. Freud remarks that time does not exist in the unconscious. The dream is not the illogical narrative it may appear to be (this is the dramatic product of secondary revision), it is a *rebus* which must be examined element by element, — and from each element will unfold associative chains leading to a coherent network of unconscious thoughts, thoughts which are extensive by comparison with the dream itself, which is 'laconic'. We encounter the everyday environment of photographs as if in a waking dream, a daydream: taken collectively they seem to add up to no particular logical whole, and taken individually their literal content is quickly exhausted, but the photograph too is laconic, its meaning goes beyond its manifest elements. The significance of the photograph goes beyond its literal signification by way of the routes of the primary processes: to use a filmic analogy, we might say that the individual photograph becomes the point of origin of a series of psychic 'pans' and 'dissolves', a succession of metonymies and metaphors which transpose the scene of the photograph to the spaces of the 'other scene' of the unconscious, and also, most importantly, the scene of the popular pre-conscious: the scene of discourse, of *language*.

E. H. Gombrich (1972) has traced the lineage of the belief in the ineffable purity of the visual image. In the *Phaedo*, Plato puts into the mouth of Socrates a doctrine of two worlds: the world of murky imperfection to which our mortal senses have access, and an 'upper world' of perfection and light. Discursive speech is the tangled and inept medium to which we are condemned in the former, while in the latter all things are communicated visually as a pure and unmediated intelligibility which has no need for words. The idea that there are two quite distinct forms of communication, words and images, and that the latter is the more direct, passed via the Neo-platonists into the Christian tradition. There was now held to be a divine language of *things*, richer than the language of words; those who apprehend the difficult but divine truths enshrined in things do so in a flash, without the need of words and arguments. As Gombrich observes, such traditions 'are of more than antiquarian interest. They still affect the way we talk and think about the art of our own time.' Today, such relics are obstructing our view of photography.

# 12

# Marketing mass photography

DON SLATER

The pen is the model of media use in the consumer society: it is the cheapest media technology available; every household possesses one; some sort of literacy is a part of compulsory education; 'it' (to stretch a point) can produce an infinite range of language and expression. Yet far from producing a torrent of public discourse, this truly mass medium is mainly reduced to the filling out of official forms, shopping lists and the occasional correspondence: for most of the population the pen can only be used in passive and privatized ways, while its public use is thoroughly monopolized by a small world of media professionals.

What is true of the pen is equally true of the camera: almost two thirds of UK households possess at least one camera (93 per cent in the USA) and each year over 80 million films are sold to 27 million people. Yet this enormous productive power is effectively contained as a conventionalized, passive, privatized and harmless leisure activity. The mass of photography — snapshooting — is hardly a conscious activity at all: it is an undeliberated moment spliced into the flow of certain ritual events: watching the baby, being at a tourist site, spending Sunday with the grandparents. Where mass photography is a conscious focus of activity — as with the amateur — the focus is on the technology, which is fetishized, not on the procedures and rhetoric of representation, which are standardized. A thorough sociology of mass photography is still needed. Bourdieu (1965) is a starting point, but dated and local. However, the broad outlines of an available practice from which is somehow excluded all but the most rudimentary questioning — or instrumental use — of representation, are easy to distinguish.

In critical contrast, we must implement Raymond Williams's

(1974) crucial ground rule that any medium must be analysed not only in terms of its present use (a restriction which encourages technologism) but also in terms of its potential forms: as the practice of many community photographers and photographers in educational institutions has shown, the camera as an *active* mass tool of representation is a vehicle for documenting one's conditions (of living, working and sociality); for creating alternative representations of oneself and one's sex, class, age-group, race, etc; of gaining power (and the power of analysis and visual literacy) over one's image; of presenting arguments and demands; of stimulating action; of experiencing visual pleasure as a producer, not consumer, of images; of relating to, by objectifying, one's personal and political environment.

Yet we are still left — given camera or pen — with a passive medium, a state of the 'art' accomplished without visible constraints or enforcible laws. However, while the power of public photography — advertisements, news photos, record sleeves, etc. — preoccupies both radical theory and media hacks, the impotence of mass photography (on which that power partly depends) is almost entirely ignored. There has been no attempt at an adequate analysis which encompasses the whole complex of relations of economic forces, ideology and power within which is constructed this specific form of photographic practice and practitioner.

For what is at stake here is obviously rather more than the 'reading' of discursive texts (photos). What is at stake are the determinations and structures of *use* of a medium: mass photography is a range of material practices — practices set within developing social relations. Mass photography is integrated into the very fabric of the most intimate social relations (in particular, the family, leisure, personal remembrance and private vanity); is inscribed in institutions (from the photo press and camera clubs to high-street photographers and schools); and is bound up with the material conditions of consumption (relating to class, income, sex, advertising and retailing, the ownership of the means of distributing images). It is also the result of a complex history of competing strategies and rationalities (e.g. the business imperatives and consequent marketing aims of the photographic industry; the same concerns of complementary leisure industries; the defensive manoeuvres of professional photographers). Mass photography is not simply an encounter in discourse.

Available space — and the state of available research — precludes presenting the entire picture here. This chapter abstracts just one element from the web of forces which constructs and constricts the medium — the production and marketing imperatives of the photographic manufacturing industry. The second part of the chapter points out the implications of this analysis for one theoretical tradition — the structuralist-semiotic tradition.

## The photographer on the assembly line

In contrast to the television, film and record industries, the mono-polization of photography by professionals and the impoverishment of its wider use has not been based on restricting access to the media technology; it has actually been carried out in large part precisely through the high-pressure mass marketing of photographic equipment. It has been restricted in the course of its very proliferation, through its technical form, through its retailing, through the 'training' of consumers through advertising, the photo press and other publicity organs of the photographic manufacturing industry. The central question we must ask is: what is the relation between the proliferation of photography *in this form* and the interests of the business organizations which do the proliferating?

Any economic activity labours under the imperatives of its mode of production, operating strategically within the terms set by a level of technology, a form of economic organization and other relations of production, and a complex of other social relations (most crucially here, the structure of the family and of leisure). Moreover, as part of the very process of operating within these imperatives, economic organizations must both aim at and produce specific forms of consumption. As Marx wrote in the 1859 Introduction:

It is not only the object that production creates for consumption... [It] also gives consumption its precise nature, its character, its finish... Hunger is hunger, but the hunger that is satisfied by cooked meat eaten with a knife and fork is a different hunger from that which bolts down raw meat with the aid of hand, nail and tooth. Production thus produces not only the object but also the manner of consumption, not only objectively but also subjectively. (Marx 1973, p. 92)

The logic of this relation has, over the past century of capitalism, become somewhat more elaborate, more powerful and more conscious, both through the development of marketing and advertising as highly selfconscious functions with progressively greater directive roles in the economic calculations around production, and through the progressive concentration of capital (a crucial feature in photography). The economic imperatives of the photographic industry compel it to aim at a specific structure of photographic consumption — that is, of *media use* — which will maximize its profitability and stable growth.

Invoking the 'needs of industry' is not to advocate a simple form of economism any more than Marx did (in fact, the entire concept of 'the economic' as a hermetic entity becomes tortuous when we deal with the complex options and ideological calculations on which marketing, a crucial *economic* function, is based). Marx's statement, that production creates the consumer, is merely one moment of a dialectical argument and therefore isolated from the mediations which complete its meaning. Similarly, the premise advanced here, that the structure of photographic production and hence marketing gives us the structure of consumption and media use, does not imply that Kodak's marketing imperatives (or, technologistically, the Instamatic itself) created the snapshooter of today. However, both snapshooter and Instamatic are imbued with and inseparable from concepts of media use behind which Kodak has put its economic might for almost a century. The story of how the industry's own imperatives have been articulated with other social features — the development of the nuclear family, the structure of work and the ideology of leisure, for example — is the longer story from which the present one is abstracted. Again, *pace* Marx, production might not create the consumer concretely, without overwhelming mediation, but there is definitely an abstract specific consumer at which it is aimed, and it is this abstract relationship — of the 'manner' of production to the 'manner' of consumption — whose mechanisms must be explored.

Most generously, the capitalist press has come to our aid in this endeavour. In autumn 1979, two major reports on the marketing of photographic equipment in Britain were published, the first by the Economist Intelligence Unit (1979), from which all figures are taken unless otherwise indicated, the second by Euromarket, a service of Mintel. Both reports are designed for interested parties: investors and top management (EIU's cover price of £50 is not exactly aimed at the mass market). The information presented is organized in a form conducive to finding opportunities for profitable exploitation. Despite their obvious bias, the figures can reveal much about the aims of the capitalists involved: the structure of the market is represented as it relates to the structure they wish to bring about. The figures should therefore be taken as indications of magnitude rather than as precise measures.

We can start from a very broad picture of the size and state of the market: two thirds of British households now have at least one camera; on an individual basis, 51.3 per cent of adults own a camera. According to Euromonitor, about 15 million people own a still camera, of whom 12 million actually use it — a small figure in Western terms: for example, in 1977 average expenditure on photography per household was $37 in the UK, $114 in Germany and $73 in France. Whatever is said about the UK can be magnified for other advanced capitalist countries. Photography accounts for 0.45 per cent of all consumer spending excluding food.

EIU's estimate of overall photographic expenditure for 1979 is £400 million. 2,515,000 still cameras were sold, a growth in real volume of 4-5 per cent over the previous year. The most basic, and interesting analytical breakdown of the overall expenditure figure is as follows:

|  | *Expenditure* | *Percentage of total* |
|---|---|---|
| Equipment | £115,000,000 | 29 |
| Film | £93,000,000 | 23 |
| Developing and processing | £192,000,000 | 48 |

These proportions have remained constant throughout the decade (and possibly a lot longer): the point is that it would be exceedingly naive to retain the commonsense view that the photographic industry simply exists to sell cameras, and that all the rest of its structure follows straightforwardly from this aim, supporting it in a subordinate manner. When, at a conservative estimate, 71 per cent of expenditure goes to film and processing, the centre of power cannot be where we expect it. In fact to push the point further, 'equipment' includes not only accessories — lenses, tripods, etc. — but also cine equipment: still camera sales alone total £84,750,000, only 21 per cent of the total.

To compound the situation, the 'film' segment of our breakdown is tending to monopoly. In 1978, 90 per cent of all films sold were colour films, the vast majority of which were Kodak, with Agfa an extremely poor second. It is obvious that monopolistic film manufacturers — as well as many competing film processing firms — stand to gain from any camera sold. Moreover, Kodak is notable in that on top of selling most of the film, it also participates in much of the revenue from processing through its sale of colour paper and above all chemicals to the trade. The key phrase, then, for film manufacturer and processor alike, is 'throughput': the more films pass through cameras, the more profit all around.

But there is also a qualitative aspect which characterizes the kind of throughput that Kodak *et al.* want. It has become axiomatic in photography (as well as in hi-fi and most electronics) that, as EIU put it: 'The more specialised photography becomes, the fewer the number involved.' In terms of sale of film, and therefore of processing, this means that it is the great number of snapshooters who buy only a few films per year which accounts for the vast majority of the trade:

> Heavy film users (6+films p.a.) constitute 11 per cent of film buyers, buying 27 per cent of all films sold.
> Medium users (3-5 films p.a.) are 39 per cent of film buyers, buying 49 per cent of film.
> Light users (1-2 films p.a.) are 50 per cent of buyers, buying 24 per cent of all film.

Moreover it is at the margin that the greatest expansion is possible: convincing the light users to buy only one or two more films per year means doubling their consumption and adding 20 per cent to film revenue.

As market leader, Kodak in any case has little to gain from its competitors and need only engage in the occasional defensive operation, as for example with its vastly unprofitable incursion into Polaroid's instant film market. It is the enormous film profits to be made at the margin, through snapshooters, which defines its imperatives: to expand the photography market as a whole by selling the idea of photography to non-photographers, thus creating large numbers of new film users. Kodak shows an extraordinary historical continuity in this regard. Eastman began in 1880 as a dry plate manufacturer and processor. His development of roll film after 1885 was his technical innovation; his cameras were a *marketing* revolution. Instead of providing film backs for existing cameras, he began in 1888 to produce the cheapest, simplest cameras imaginable to act as vehicles through which he could sell as much film to as many people as possible. He had sold 100,000 of these by 1896 (Holmes 1974). Originally one bought the camera with the film already loaded; when the 100-frame film was finished, the whole camera was sent back to Kodak for processing and replacement. This end of the operation gave both the continuity and bulk of Eastman's revenues. He rated his cameras as good for 20 film cartridges each.

The development of photographic marketing therefore was and is tied to the expansion of the mass snapshooter market through the sale of cheap vehicles for film. The story of how Kodak constructed mini film monopolies through marketing 126s, 110s and other now forgotten film gauges is an old one. Monopoly was certainly a powerful motive. However another motive was equally decisive for the development of the medium as we know it. The mass marketing of cameras, on which film sales depend, means that selling of photography without the costly creation of 'photographers', which would involve teaching skills, would demand serious interest and would lose that vast part of the population which will not enter the market if the entry fee involves spending time, learning and money and frustration spent in making mistakes. Yet this is precisely the market Kodak and its ilk aim at. Thus Kodak's marketing, from 1888 on, depended on building two features into its technology, simplicity and reliability. 'You push the button and we do the rest.' Kodak's solution to this marketing problem, now forming the basis of the whole industry, was as far as possible to divorce the camera operator from the process of photography. By making the process opaque, one makes the practice transparent, if not invisible: it requires no thought to operate, therefore it can be taken for granted, and conventionally — thoughtlessly, inserted into everyday social usages.

The modern Instamatic or 110 is merely a refinement of the original Kodak idea: fixed focus and fixed speed, a choice between two (or a few more) apertures marked by pictures of sun and clouds, built-in flash becoming standard. These cameras also incorporate Kodak's greatest twentieth-century innovation, the solution to people's problem with getting film into cameras: the cartridge. The final consumer resistance was overcome. Add to this the latitude of modern films and Mr Eastman's dream has come true: utter simplicity and very near total reliability (i.e. the largest number of technically successful pictures). In fact Eastman claimed in the 1890s that the success rate for amateurs with his cameras was 80 per cent.

This camera which allows practice without process or knowledge is both liberating and constricting: it has put the technology into millions of hands, but in its most restricted (and mystified) form. Reducing process to 'point and press' means designing the technology to operate optimally under certain standard conditions, such as three people out of doors smiling at the lens from over five feet away. Trying to avoid a technologistic interpretation, one can say that some degree of versatility is possible on an Instamatic, but it requires consciously transcending the design bias and limitations which result from the imperatives of simplicity and reliability. This transcending requires some understanding of process which is kept hidden, and consciousness of the conventions, which are taken for granted. It requires that the act of taking a picture become consciously considered as an act of representation: that the viewfinder be considered not as a window to be looked through but as a 'canvas' to be worked upon. Such an attitude does not encourage exponential increases in film throughput.

Should it be felt that this argument overrates the role, power or success of Kodak, there are several further points. First, one can add to Kodak's predominance in manufacturing film and processing material, the fact that (according to Euromonitor) 62.2 per cent of all the cameras owned in the UK are Kodak. Add to this figure the Polaroid, Agfa and Boots cameras owned (all of which firms are involved in film processing *and* cameras, like Kodak), and we get to 76.5 per cent of all cameras owned. For comparison: Pentax, Nikon, Olympus and Canon together account for 7.7 per cent of cameras. Kodak, uniting film, processing and camera interests, exemplifies the logic which dominates this sector of the market and largely structures the other sectors. Second, because it is market leader and because it unites the various interests, its role, as their advertising man (quoted in EIU) put it, is to 'find its growth by stimulating the market to expand'. In 1979 Kodak's advertising accounted for 36 per cent of all advertising by photographic manufacturers. Third, on another level, Kodak is simply the exemplar but also the originator of a marketing approach which involves the whole industry: it has set the terms in which the others operate.

If Kodak (along with Polaroid, Agfa, Boots and numerous smaller names) goes for — and gets — photography as a mass, it leaves behind other areas of mass photography which are equally crucial to understanding the use of the medium: the smaller, specialist crumbs of 'amateur' and 'hobbyist' photography which Kodak leaves behind for myriad smaller operations to fight over. This market has its own logic.

Briefly, the crucial marketing problem is to achieve a high *rate* of growth (never simply stable sales) within a restricted and specialized market. A small increase is possible through bringing more people into the market (largely through upgrading amateurs). EIU actually advises the industry to form something like the Milk Marketing Board to do just this in the interests of all, but in the absence of this organization, or of a Kodak-style firm whose interests lie in performing its function of expanding the market as a whole, the growth of amateur photogrpahy cannot sustain great increase in sales. Other strategems must be employed.

First, firms must clearly differentiate their markets: their product must compete within a product category which is not interchangeable with any other. A kind of rationalization of the market is enforced on manufacturers in the scramble to retain an identifiable portion of a limited population of consumers, so as not to fall between the force-fields of available purchasing power. A striking example of this logic at work is EIU's prediction of increasingly hard times for the 35mm compact camera: its specific market is being eroded by the greater versatility of 110s and the increased simplicity of automated SLR (single lens reflex) cameras. It falls between two quite clear stools. So one of the important learning and teaching formats may go to the wall, leaving a yawning price gap between cheap 110s and expensive SLRs, forcing everyone to choose (in marketing terms) between being a snapshooter and a committed amateur. Needless to say, this would render unto SLR and 110 manufacturers captive and cleanly differentiated markets, simultaneously exploiting, rigidifying and stimulating existing schisms in media use.

However, if formats and special product groups are becoming more differentiated, within these categories the competition is simply bewildering. This relates to the second main set of stratagems employed in super-exploiting a restricted market. The paradigm case is the SLR market, the opposite pole to Kodak-style marketing. The SLR market is numerically relatively small, but in value terms is disproportionately lucrative.

*Camera sales 1979 (EIU estimate)*

| Format | Volume (000's) | % of total | Value (£mRSP) | % of total |
| --- | --- | --- | --- | --- |
| 35mmSLR | 160 | 6.4 | 20 | 23.6 |
| 35mm compact | 160 | 6.4 | 9 | 10.6 |
| 110 | 1000 | 39.8 | 25 | 29.5 |
| 126 | 180 | 7.0 | 2 | 2.6 |
| Instant | 1000 | 39.8 | 25 | 29.5 |
| Roll film | 15 | 0.6 | 4 | 4.4 |

The SLR generates a vast revenue, one quarter of the total, on an insignificant and specialized fraction of market volume — only

6 per cent. (Euromonitor puts the disparity even higher, at 36 per cent of value.) In addition, these figures only include the camera itself, whereas the biggest growth area in all photography at the moment is in SLR accessories – for example, there are 800 different lenses on the market, and a massive auto-wind sales drive. On the other hand, the already very small volume base of 6.4 per cent is further narrowed by the fact that Zenith alone (which is in a class on its own by virtue of being outrageously inexpensive but very reliable with no frills) accounts for 75,000 of the 160,000 SLRs sold in 1979, a full 47 per cent of the market.

The central stratagem employed by manufacturers to cope with the situation is the idea of permanent technical revolution. Over the past decade this has primarily taken the form of incorporating more and more electronics into cameras with a view to both increased versatility and increased automation, aiming at cameras which can do all the thinking for their human button-pushers. On the one hand, this follows Kodak logic: develop the market as a whole by simplifying operation and guaranteeing 'good results'. On the other hand its main function is quite different. In Euromonitor's words:

One need only look at the electronic equipment or electrical appliance market and observe how product development has revitalised sagging sales to realise that any new product begins a complete new cycle as far as consumer acquisition is concerned. With a new product, ownership level drops to nil – nobody has one and everybody wants one.

Through a logic complementary to product differentiation and market rationalization, the introduction of new technology is not meant to signify the entry of just another competing camera, but the replacement of all hitherto existing cameras, which are rendered redundant. The market is increased by being inaugurated anew. The sale of accessories is a version of the same game: your camera is not actually a camera at all until it has an autowinder/telephoto lens/ filter, etc. Each time the necessity of a new accessory is 'proven' to the consumer (and they do come in waves), 'ownership level drops to nil' and the small base market is recreated again, at square one.

Here at least are the economic forces which desire that snap-shooter technology ends in an ever more invisible medium, while hobbyist technology should be inseparable from the fetishism of technology. In order to grow, SLR must create gaps which did not previously exist, must create products which constitute, and are seen to constitute, totally new categories of desirability. Where the snapshooter should learn to look through the viewfinder as if it were a window, the amateur's sight should not get beyond the gleaming chrome or black body of his or her revolutionary new triumph of technology. A tremendous example of 'correct' desire is provided by the case of the Canon A1, an SLR which was voted camera of the year by the readers of *Practical Photography* two years running. As EIU comments without a glimmer of irony:

The staggering thing, however, is that this vote was made by readers who had probably had no opportunity to see or handle the camera because of the delays in delivery. Canon's publicity, which is firmly based on highlighting the innovative features of the A1... has thus made a tremendous impression.

To summarize: we have taken two major areas of photographic marketing, snapshooting and amateur photography — the former being the major structuring force in the field, the latter structuring itself through strategies appropriate to the specialized and therefore limited market dynamics which remain. We have restricted ourselves to the main outlines — mere examples really — of the richly textured field of strategies at work. We have related the marketing context and business calculations of the photographic industry to the type of consumption which these must try to produce directly or which they indirectly entail as part of their logic. This 'type of consumption' is the foundation of the use of the medium: broadly speaking, either the transparent, insertable practice without process, or the fetishized commodity without a practice.

One could add that these two areas of photographic consumption emerge in another form within the selfconscious calculations of the industry: EIU also presents a broad market profile of the consumer. It takes the form of a 'consumer ladder' which people enter on the ground floor as snapshooters and which they are then eased up, purchase by purchase, through hobbyist to, ultimately, semi-professional. The various rungs of the ladder — the types of consumer — are distinguished by the kind of equipment owned and the frequency of its use. Complementing the picture we have already drawn of the strategies and dynamics at work — the *moving* picture — the EIU 'consumer ladder', again presenting its research in the form most usable to its capitalist readership's aims, gives us a snapshot of the structure of photographic consumption to which the industry works: in its 'ideal types' of consumers and ways of consuming, it represents both the byproducts and the raw material of marketing calculation.

There are some obvious immediate extensions to be made to the analysis presented here, in particular the role and functioning of advertising (and the history of photographic advertising), the dynamics of the retail trade, and the photographic press. Though integrated into the overall marketing logic, an understanding of their specific functioning is crucial.

However, the most critical work is that of contextualizing the present level of analysis within a broader framework, of both substantively and theoretically demonstrating the ways in which the forces and strategies presented here are mediated within the totality of the photographic nexus, of returning this abstracted moment of economic calculation to its concrete history and context.

This is unfortunately not a simple matter of relating economic structures to other (political, ideological, institutional) structural instances as entities with their own specific conditions of existence, which is the current practice. The discourses underlying photography, the genres and conventions in which it takes form, the family rituals and relations which define its use and content, the values it adopts (whether the sexism, fetishism, aestheticism of camera clubs, or the nostalgia, selective amnesia, totemism of family photography), etc. − treating any of these separately, as bearing unique determinants (however unique their functioning), is an act of abstraction equal to that carried out above.

To give an example: the twentieth-century family and the structure of leisure are central to mass photography − they provide the social relations and material practices which structure most of its use. The family and the terrain of leisure are of course completely interlinked, their interweaving being crucial − historically and structurally − to the development of a consumerist capitalism wherein the dynamic space of the family and the stereotyped time of leisure have been forged into the primary, and quite efficient, unit of consumption. For this very reason, the history and dynamics of the photographic industry and that of the family at leisure have to be analysed together, as part of the same process: the social relations which constitute families (and which seem so naturally amenable to certain uses of photography) were themselves determined by the same forces which determined photographic production and marketing in the first place. The specific form of photography inserted into the family is only one instance of an evolving consumerist system colonizing the very structure which was created by the forces which created it − the overall relations of consumption necessitated by the relations of capitalist production. On one level at least this is obvious: understanding mass photography as a practice gains more from looking at the articulation of the camera with other consumption goods (for example, the bicycle in the 1890s, the car in the 1920s, the package holiday in the 1970s) than from starting from the representations it produces.

Similarly central to mass photography is the ideology of empiricism. Locally, this is the discourse of photographic truth and objective record which grounds the reading and use of photography and is instrumental to photography's appropriateness to its current social relations of consumption (for example, family album, holiday slide show, emblem of remembrance, proof of wellbeing). However, to regard empiricism as a free-floating, autonomously developing discourse fortuitously exploitable by the photographic marketing machinery is misleading: positivism as a whole is historically crucial and instrumental to capitalism, painfully constructed by it. It is not an autonomous development within ideology with which the concrete practices of photography must be brought into analytic relation as externals with separate determinants: rather, empiricism grounds the rationality of production as clearly as it emerges within specific forms of consumption. We are dealing with one history, not two. Photographic marketing and the discourse of photographic consumption are simply local achievements within industrial society's secular project.

### Semiotics and materialism

The analysis outlined above, contrary to present tendencies, does not 'decode' a single photograph, nor engage the processes of 'reading' directly. Its interest is to set the terms for explaining the *use* of a medium (i.e. terms which involve the active forces of both production and consumption of significations). It does not aim at deriving discourses through which texts are structured and read, and subjects formed, but at pointing towards the material practices and social relations within which discourses, texts and subjects operate and are forged. It also does not redefine material practices as readable discourses. This is to say, it cuts across the assumptions of the structuralist-semiotic tradition which is now the dominant discourse on processes of representation, nearly hegemonic in left cultural theory. It will be necessary to work through several aspects of this tradition in order to proceed further.

Over the past two decades, the structuralist tradition has been the most progressive and fertile strategy for engaging cultural processes. It has now become a barrier to further progress. Though it does not consciously exclude as irrelevant the political economy of media and the social relations within which they are consumed, it has ultimately consigned them to theoretical limbo. The structuralist tradition takes as assumed, as given, precisely what needs to be explained: the relations and practices within which discourses are formed and operated. It would like to specify the transactions and mutual constitution of subject and representation within the processes of signification, but to do this by appealing to discourses which are inexplicable in the terms of its theoretical apparatus. To use a vocabulary it would not recognize, the structuralist tradition aims to analyse 'ideological effect', yet takes as given precisely those discourses whose effect it would like to trace. It is still a formalist theory which refuses all substance, elaborating processes of meaning construction within an abstracted epoch. The historic and dynamic construction of discourses within a force-field of social practices is obscured and ignored in order to focus on the negotiations of meaning carried out within the ambit of the text and the moment of reading. The hallowed terrain of bourgeois criticism remains, while the groundwork of materialist theory is not begun.

A strange process has occurred to reach this state: the structuralist-semiotic tradition has always addressed itself to a very specific and limited question: 'How is meaning produced and sustained within a text?' This question points to a level of analysis whose objects are the formal and systematic properties of closed systems: it involves decoding the discourses which structure texts; the devices employed and their place within the system of signification; the formation of subjects within and between texts, etc. Though the question was broadened by moving from the productivity of texts to the more global moment of 'reading', the essential limitation of the originating premise remains: this tradition proposes a radically internal analysis of signification, an analysis which — directed entirely at uncovering the structuring of a closed system (whether text or signification as a whole) — finds all the terms necessary to analysis within its theoretical object: signification. Through its roots in structural linguistics, and a mode of analysis which stretches from the more ancient axiomatics such as logic and geometry to more modern equivalents such as ethnomethodology and Kuhnian analysis of paradigms (a tradition Terry Lovell (1980) calls 'conventionalist theories of knowledge'), semiotics has resulted in a metaphor and a procedure in which the encounter and mutual constitution of text and subject within discourse is isolated from any possible determination outside discourse, in order to abstract the formal mechanisms of this process.

If one recognizes the limits of the original question and the original process of abstraction, no danger arises. Semiotics promises ultimately to return the captured moment of reading to its determinations: this has been indefinitely postponed and then utterly forgotten. Semiotics has now taken its limited terrain to be the whole world, thereby foreclosing the possibility of ever breaking out of its limits. The process of reading, the procedures and content of discourse, are released from all the social relations which determine them and are left to formal, self-constituting emptiness.

This abstraction of reading has led to confusions over the explanatory status of semiotics: because it forgets what it has excluded it is likely to take its descriptions for explanation. This is crucially true of the category 'discourse'. Discourse is taken for a kind of 'deep structure', which in certain structuralisms was an explanatory category: that which explains the structure of the text. It is in fact a rather different animal: it is a signifying formation produced within a field of determinations, among which are those included within semiotic theory. The result is that within semiotics, discourses are in fact taken as given (formed outside the semiotic field) yet are used as if they were central explanatory concepts: they structure subjects and texts and their encounter in 'reading'.

This results in one of two sins: functionalism or tautology. Functionalism seems to be the necessary explanatory mode for theories which abstract structure from social process: it admits of thoroughly internal solutions to problems of determination. Until the mid-1970s, structuralism explained the existence of the discourse whose workings and effects it wished to determine in terms of Althusserian functionalism: capitalism produces the necessary conditions of its own existence, including its ideological means of reproduction. The history of their emergence is irrelevant; their logical necessity is crucial. Aside from the obvious circularity involved, the argument allows for a completely unspecified notion of relative autonomy, which eventually becomes full autonomy.

When these assumptions were largely discredited, their place was never filled: semiotics closed ranks against concerns outside its own terms. 'Decoding' became an end in itself, the pursuance of the specific processes of the formation of subjects within discourses becoming both beginning and end of analysis. The 'structuring discourses' and the processes of reading which were the only possible outcome of analysis could be alternatively characterized as the 'cause' and the result of the processes under analysis: everything occurs within these discourses; they are allocated no external determinations but are taken as given. Tautologically, wherever one starts one ends in the same place — the structuring discourse, the stuff of which everything is made.

The problem again is not so much what semiotics says as what it leaves out, namely whatever cannot be absorbed into the field of signification under discussion. For example, Victor Burgin (1980 and chapter 11 above) attempts to get away from the textual object/ artifact by asserting the productive role of the 'social subject' at the point of consumption of the image. However, this consumption is once again purely the abstract moment of reading, an empty encounter between subject and text whose content is given by forces not included in the terms of analysis. Moving from this abstract moment to the specific readings of specific photographs, Burgin appeals to the pre-conscious of contemporary social actors which will contain certain knowledges through which the photographs will be read: 'It is surely reasonable to suppose that the knowledge of events such as these suffused the collective consciousness of Americans in the 1960s' (see this volume, p. 236). It is a reasonable assumption. It is an explanation of nothing. Burgin purports to explain the motivation behind a particular reading while simply smuggling in an obvious content as self-evident. The crucial feature, the determinations of the structuring discourse, lie outside the terms of the theory and are simply taken as given, leaving us with a concept similar to that of 'socially available knowledge' in phenomenology. The critical question of how specific knowledges and experiences come to enter the politics of representation, come to be socially constituted, is simply assumed to be answered. What we are looking for is precisely an analysis of those institutions, technologies, power relations, specific practices and their histories which determined the 'suffusion' of the collective consciousness and allowed this reading in the first place.

'Reading', and the processes of signification, thus become a highly abstract social moment. The crime was compounded by hypostatizing the abstraction: not only was the production of discursive formations rendered self-explanatory, but the consumption of texts was construed as an equally internal matter. In the first instance, this was achieved by the assumption of 'objective readings — *the* reading of the text. The uncovering of the internal mechanisms of meaning production in the text promised logically to uncover the *actual* meanings the mechanisms were constructing. Meaning was utterly under the control of the text: the meaning was not an historical achievement but a formal one. Texts were not misread or subverted by readers; populations did not have to be trained to certain ways of reading; institutions and strategies were not involved; the objective reading of the text was simply known to be its achieved, its actual meaning.

This assumption was fractured in the mid-1970s into the 'problem of audience'. The tendency was to theorize the gap between the structured meaning of the text and the actual readings which concrete readers came to in terms of the freed play of the subject on the shifting terrain of meaning. This was the final abstraction of reading, its unhinging. It finally foreclosed the positing of any determinations outside language and discourse: instead of placing and connecting text and audience within their material conditions, their formation within the same movements of strategic historical forces, the relationship between them was bracketed for analysis, reduced to a private encounter. This courted the danger of collapsing text, subject and signification into one anarchic unanalysable morass, for — released from all possible concrete determinations — the other options were even less appealing: in order to find, let alone explain, the actual meaning established within any reading one had either to return to the worst form of empiricist sociology (ask what did individual A actually think that film X meant, then aggregate all the individuals surveyed, and extrapolate) or return to the tyranny of the text.

The fantasy we have come to — of a machinery of signification producing in a social vacuum — can be redescribed from another angle, as the history of complex negotiations between structuralism and Marxism. In rather schematic terms, structuralism and its derivations were taken up by the left as the last in a line of attempted syntheses between Marxist theory and theories of the subject, consciousness, language and ideology. As a sanctuary from the travesties of Marxist economism and base and superstructure mechanistics during the 1960s, a decade in which consciousness and ideology became structurally central in all political movement, embracing structuralism was a matter of urgent practical and political necessity. Under the banner of structuralism and then semiotics, activists and academics could deal with matters of vital urgency and still claim to be Marxist, for theoretical fusion was promised and seemed imminent. However the negotiations instead instituted a division of theoretical labour which perpetuated a division in theory between the ideological and economic instances as objects of analysis; we still retain a negotiated alliance rather than a theoretical synthesis. The relations between the semiotic and Marxist traditions reveal an artificiality and improvised nature which is only duplicated in the rickety connections drawn between their theoretical objects. Reference to the materiality of the signifier, or reliance on a language full of metaphors of materialism ('the work of the text', 'ideological production', etc.), cannot fill the gap. The division we desperately desired to overcome is not only perpetuated but dignified theoretically: the materialist analysis is not economistic now, and the analysis of signification is not reductive, but only at the cost of total separation.

The real task starts here. It is not to assert the analysis of ideology as against the economic instance, but to analyse how the economic, institutional, ideological and political forces, strategies and dynamics have constructed the social relations within which material cultural practices are carried out. The task is to establish a materialist analysis of the politics of cultural practice. In the case of mass photography this means asserting the centrality of ideological processes within the economic instance (namely 'marketing', the management of consumption and of the social relations of consumption) as much as it means finding the material determinants of signification, the social relations within which they are constructed.

We began with a concrete political problem: mass photography constructed within restrictive rationalities, within exploitative strategies, within social relations grounded in the most insidious drives of a capitalist mode of production, resulting in material practices which — posed against alternative practices — are virtually tragic. Hopefully we can finish with a political direction. Our fight for a democratized medium must certainly engage the discursive textures of our readings — we must reread, recode, converse. But unless this practice and analysis is placed solidly, integrally, within an understanding of the total material circumstances of the use of the medium, we will be indulging in an academic exercise. If our present use of photography is founded on the consumer capitalist form of the family, the site of resistance and reconstitution is within feminism and other movements within politics, in collective practices of photography, and alternative social relations such as community groups, campaigns, community arts, etc. If mass photography is privatized, our obstacle is the monopolization of the means of distribution as much as it is discourses which fetishize the home as castle and private life as sanctuary: our practice is to develop alternative distribution, construct new audiences and reclaim the 'owned' media from hoardings to satellites. If photography is trapped within leisure consumption, our battle is against the structure of work. If photography is read through notions of representation as a reflection of reality, then there is a campaign within ideology to carry out in very concrete strategic forms.

The politics of representation is waged on a broad front. If mass photography is impoverished in that sector which has hypnotized us for a decade — the textual product — the complexity of the forces which forge its use constantly turns us around to face the materiality of practice and, therefore, returns us to politics.

# Part V

# Problems of Evidence and Methodology

# 13

# Textuality, communication and media power

JOHN CORNER

An emphasis on the signifying or symbolic conventions and practices by which media meanings get made and through which the defining, semantic power of media systems variously contributes to a public imagery and consciousness has been a key contribution of cultural studies to the analysis of mass communication. This can be seen as an emphasis on textuality, though it has always importantly involved a primary concern with the social conditions, relations and settings of media processes, including the sense-making practices by which audiences 'read' media productions. In this paper I want to discuss some problems with the concepts, theories and methods of inquiry which have guided work in this area and to look at how textually-aware media research — a pragmatics of media discourse — might progress without veering into any of the forms of reductivism (economic or formalist) currently and usefully being identified (for a discussion of this issue see, for example, Hill 1979 and Morley 1980).

Through stressing the need to research the determinants and nature of the symbolic transactions constitutive of media processes (transactions not usually confronted by work on policy, organization and professional practice or by audience research using notions of behavioural change or 'need') researchers have, almost necessarily, tended to identify three phases or 'moments'. The first is the institutional and organizational conditions and practices of production, governed by media policies and by the professional and medium-related conventions of language and image use. This process has been referred to as the 'encoding' phase, the moment of 'writing'. In certain media, notably broadcasting, it can also be seen as the phase involving *transmission*, although such a notion is highly problematic in relation to the reproduction of meaning and risks confusion with the usage of 'transmission' within telecommunications engineering. Clearly, media production is a manufacturing *sequence*.

Second, there is the moment of the 'text' itself the particular symbolic construction, arrangement and perhaps performance which is the product of media skills and technical and cultural practices. This is the form and content of what is published or broadcast (a 'what' whose determinacy becomes hard to trace at certain levels of the semantic dimension and in respect of certain media forms). Some analyses refer to this phase as that of 'the message' but there seem to be considerable problems with the notions of self-containedness and an isolable *unit* of meaning suggested here. Given the very different kinds of communicational form indicated by 'media', the idea of 'text' (especially in its recent literary/philosophical guise as that awesome and generalized singularity, 'The Text') also raises some problems which I shall cover in the course of my discussion below.

The third phase is the moment of reception, consumption or 'decoding' by audiences and readerships. This involves the practices by which the reader/hearer/viewer, drawing on the particular linguistic and cultural competencies available and apparently appropriate, 'makes sense' of, and *realizes* into coherent meaning, the particular items of text and the larger textual units (the programme, the article). 'Sense-making' occurs within modifying social settings (e.g. the home, the workplace, the cinema). Although common-sensically viewed as a matter of 'taking' the meanings that are 'there' (a relatively uncomplicated act of *construing*), it is clear that 'reading' involves perceptual and cognitive activities closer to a form of 'construction' (albeit that hard-to-theorize process 're-construction') than to the passivity or merely reactive operations suggested by the term 'reception' (cf. the problems with 'transmission'). One of the most important developments in recent media research has been the attempt to investigate the extent to which audiences do, at different levels, produce variations of meaning and significance from the same media text according to the socially situated logics of meaning-production through reading (Morley 1980).

These three phases have been theorised as the 'communication circuit' (fully developed in Hall 1973), a circuit in which phases one and three are socially contingent practices which may be in a greater or lesser degree of alignment in relation to each other but which are certainly not to be thought of (following early 'communications theory') as 'sending' and 'receiving' linked by the straight conveyance of a 'message' which is the exclusive vehicle of meaning.

A lot of research in the sociology of culture has attempted to use one phase of this process as a point of entry into the exploration of another. Literary historiography, for instance, has attempted to 'read' literary texts — through theories of cultural referentiality and inscription such as those surrounding the ideas of 'structure of feeling' (Williams 1961 and later) or 'categorial structure' (Goldmann 1967, Eagleton 1975) in such a way as to map out broader features of social consciousness and its cultural and material conditions at the moment of the text's writing. Texts have been seen to consist of the 'opaque but decipherable signs' of these conditions (Eagleton 1975, p. 14). Media analysis has variously involved the use of texts to mount arguments both about production contexts and the likely influence upon audiences. It has also produced research inferring the symbolic characteristics of media products from the findings of audience surveys or from an ethnography of production routines. However, as a result of the refinement of conceptualization brought about by semiotically-informed researchers in literary and cultural theory working towards an engagement with the full complexity of *meaning-in-process* across all three moments of the above scheme, it has become increasingly difficult to think through the idea of communication in relation to a text's determinate properties at all.

The degree of referential information which texts contain concerning the conditions and subjective circumstances (including intentionality) governing their initial production, the sorts of controls and limits (closures) which they can exert on the 'readings' subsequently made of them, and, conversely, the extent to which they are 'sites' for reader constructions — all these questions have contributed to the production of a dense textual problematics. The implications of this for any research which uses texts as primary sources of research data are clear, though I suggest below that extensive abstraction in discussing textuality, together with a shortage of references to specific examples, has massively increased the uncertainties here. Nevertheless, the matter of the relationships of power exercised between phases one and three and the related matter of the method by which that significatory power (as a text-audience relation) is analysable have become increasingly open to reformulation whilst remaining central problems for research.

Clearly, the newer formulations of what constitutes 'communication' are at odds with the semiotic positivism of those claiming to

foresee a 'science of the text' which could discern the material
and ideological conditions of 'writing' and could predict cognitive
and ideological consequences exclusively from a study of textual
form (see Eagleton 1976). Such positions have nearly always been
predicated on one or other version of the marginality of the *act*
of reading before the omnipotence of textual controls. This has
been particularly true of a strand of work in film studies (see the
discussion of this in Willeman 1978), whereas in British socio-
literary criticism there has been, until recently, a striking lack of
interest in the realizational practices of reading, as these concern
both a sociology of readerships and the critic's own activities (see
Bennett 1979 for a critique of this in Marxist work).

Before I move on to discuss questions of analysis (including
power analysis) in more detail, it might now be useful to make
some further inquiries into the notion of media textuality, particularly as it relates to ideas of media language or languages.

### Media language as text

When we talk of media language, we can be using the term language
in either a literal or a metaphorical way. Assuming that we are
concerned with a range of activities and forms in publishing, television, film and visual reproduction and display etc. (though it is
worth considering what, in a given usage, 'the media' include and
exclude), we can be referring either to the ways in which a language
(say, English) is variously used across all its dimensions by those
in the media professions, or to a broader set of signifying conventions (e.g. of published or broadcast form, of genre, of studio
practice) which appear to govern the organization and structure
perhaps both of visual and verbal elements within particular items
of media material. There is also the possibility that we can indicate
by the term 'television language', 'photographic language' or, more
probably, 'film language' not some metaphoric sense of significant
ordering and rule-following at a general structural level within
specific contexts (the language of Panorama, for instance, or the
language of advertising) but, more ambitiously, a system of visual
meaning whose primary units (e.g. the forms of shot) and their
syntax (e.g. editing) achieve a level of language-equivalence. The
extent to which usage here is then metaphoric or literal is often
doubtful.

Such considerations are important because the strongest influences upon media research within cultural studies have been structuralisms of one kind or another, and one of the defining characteristics of the structuralist perspective and method is the central employment of a linguistic paradigm within a whole range of political and social inquiries. Frequently, literal and metaphoric usages of terms drawn from linguistics occur together in such a way as to erase any sense of a difference (the concept 'code' often has a governing role in 'fusions' of this sort, see Corner 1980). So media texts are formed as a combination of the variety of media uses of language, whatever levels of 'visual language' are constituted by fine art, photography, film and video, and those controlling 'languages' which are the sets of conventions by which the cultural forms and genres of media signification are organized.

One problem that follows from this is that it is extremely difficult to make a proposition about 'texts' (even when it is qualified as being about 'media texts') that holds over the range of textual types and instances possible. For example, at the level of formal charactersitics, a spoken news item on the radio will be a 'media text' of a very different kind from a scene out of a television comedy series or a newspaper gossip column. The modes of perception and cognition involved in 'reading' these distinct types of communication-form will differ too, as will their referential character and their history of development. Some of these differences will be due to properties of the medium itself. For instance, the type of capacity to articulate particular meanings which is available in the English language has no direct equivalent in the visual 'language' of film-making (see Wollen 1972 and Metz 1974 on this). It would be extremely difficult to make a wordless film sequence which was the meaning equivalent of the sentence preceding this one, though a number of suggestive indications might be attempted. If one moves to an even more particularistic level, sentences draw on a vocabulary and a range of syntactic possibilities simply beyond a purely visual articulation. How would one construct a silent TV news broadcast for example? What would be its level of informational precision?

These are highly unoriginal points, the subject of detailed theoretical and analytic treatment in the literature of both fine art and film studies, but they serve to indicate the crucial differences in kinds of meaning-unit and their modes of articulation which occur between the constituents of 'media texts'. The reliance on notions of verbal 'anchorage' and 'relay' in the development of a visual semiotics of photography and advertising is one analytic consequence of such differences (Barthes 1977).

To stay with the word/image relationship for a moment, it is also clear that the particular mode of filmic articulation, grounded in the realist ontology of the photographic image (discussed widely, but particularly in Bazin 1970, Wollen 1972, Metz 1974) with the added verisimilitude of movement, has a semantic, referential profile with powerful 'illusory' potential, most realizable when organized within the technical and cultural realisms of shooting, editing method and (in narrative forms) characterization and story-telling.

When spoken word and moving image are employed in combination, fusions can occur in which the signifying properties of the visual and linguistic elements become 'written into' one another. A crude but useful illustration of this is afforded by the story (apocryphal?) of the wartime allied propaganda film which 'showed' a German factory making sausages out of a sawdust mix; clear evidence of the desperate economic conditions. In fact (the story goes) the mix which the camera showed being put into the factory's machines did not contain any sawdust at all: 'sawdust' was a mis-informational unit articulated into the scene through the voiceover commentary. Yet the evidential strength of the visual image was such as to cause many people to claim that they had 'seen the sawdust'. This level of credibility could not so easily have been accorded to the item had it been broadcast on radio, and would have been given less easily still if the 'text' had been a newspaper account without photographs. The potential strength of such a discursive technique derives precisely from its *not* offering itself, at these moments, as discourse for reading at all, but instead presenting circumstances for 'witnessing' by the audience. Audience members are encouraged to take the (false) position of 'witnesses to reality' rather than 'readers of the text' and thence to give personal authentication, via a 'rigged' act of perception, to a textual account.

Although the element of direct lying about physical presences makes this story an untypical case, the use of related forms of 'fusion' in photo-journalism and TV news and documentary output has received close investigation in recent media research (see Brunsdon & Morley 1978, Hall 1972, Glasgow University Media Group 1976, 1980).

### Realization and response: the levels of reading

A further distinction which needs to be taken into account in any discussion of media textuality, even though it may only be possible to do this in terms of tendencies rather than separations, is that between the more textually determinate (sometimes 'literal') levels and the more implicatory/inferential, 'significant' dimensions or levels both of textual semantic potential and its reader/subject 'realizations'. Problems of terminology and of maintaining an analytic grasp which holds both differences and relations are especially pressing here. The denotation/connotation distinction, though hard to theorize with precision and harder still to maintain in analysis, still seems to me to be useful, though visual discourse immediately raises the difficulty, noted earlier, of talking about primary visual meaning.

In contrast to the difficulty of mapping the semantic determinateness of visual imagery, its capacities for differentiation and for combinatory articulation, most verbal media texts are significations based on a highly determinate readability. This interconnects with a less determinate, associative, implicatory (or, for a reader, inferrable) level of semantic organization, and it is in relation to both these dimensions of meaning that what we may (rather confusingly) call our 'reading' or our 'interpretation' (our response to *what is meant*) is organized. News texts, due both to the political importance of their direct, informational role in producing a special type of popular social knowledge and to the complementary directness of their mode of address, have attracted special attention and documentation from media analysts.

Consider this sentence from a newspaper item on the NUM executive's 1980 recommendation of a pay agreement:

But union militants are almost certain to wage a big propaganda war to get miners to reject the deal. (*Daily Star*, 13 Nov. 1980, p. 4)

Clearly, certain semantic properties of this sentence are not 'open' (or are not usefully considered as being 'open') to a range of realizations or interpretations as to *what is meant*, even though the meanings themselves may constitute a highly contestable account. Key terms in the ideological organization of the sentence (e.g. 'militants', 'big propaganda war') signify powerfully, and achieve optimum resonance, with dominant inferential frameworks for understanding 'industry today'. Yet the significations themselves have the highly determinate readability, secured by a socially objectified notation, that I suggested above (e.g. 'propaganda' operates here to mean, quite clearly, though among other things, 'illegitimate and dishonest persuasion'). Since the language is also quite explicitly evaluative — ideologically charged

— this determinateness has implications for the visibility of the statement as the expression of a 'point of view', however natural it might appear to a reader to 'see things that way'.

Keeping in mind the important question of how realizing the meaning relates to levels of response, of opposition or of acceptance, we can compare the above newspaper sentence with a broadcast news transcript from the files of the Glasgow University Media Group:

It's been a day of mixed fortune for the troubled motor industry. Thousands of Chrysler workers returned from an extended Christmas holiday and went on short time, a three-day week for most of January. But there is some hope tonight that British Leyland's latest industrial dispute won't last much longer. (BBC1 Nine O'Clock News, 6th Jan. 1975)

Here, the stance from which the statement is produced is less easy to discern, as one might expect from a news operation working under very different 'impartiality' requirements from those obtaining in the national press. Significantly, it is the 'motor industry' that is 'troubled'. The extent to which this term includes both management and workforce or the extent to which it excludes the workforce, together with the subsequent implications either of 'reading' the two groups together as the jointly 'troubled' or of seeing the 'motor industry' as the victim of workforce-caused 'trouble', are very much questions concerning ideological closure. But the closures involved are sufficiently within the processes of reader inferentiality and its social structuration (the social power of the different framings available for reading 'trouble' in this industry) to make any kind of intentionalist charge (the statement is *meant* to *mean* this or that) difficult to establish exclusively by textual analysis. How we relate to the 'hope' that the final sentence of the bulletin makes available to us is, nevertheless, consequent on these earlier acts of reading.

More difficult still, my own 'realization' of the actions described in the second sentence (a returning *followed* by a going) further involves intertextual inferences about 'trouble', 'idleness' and labour disputes in this industry. The two circumstances, extended Christmas holiday/three-day week, linked by the connective of likeness — 'and' — are realizable by me as in a 'grim joke' relation of change/no change.

This realization works crucially from the idea of the workers as *the primary agents* in both happenings. They 'returned' and then 'went' (i.e. *not* 'were put on'), and this leads to an inferrable version which, at least momentarily, elides the managerial origins of the Chrysler short-time decision to produce a one-sentence popular narrative, inferentially paraphrasable as: 'They came back from an *extended* holiday [associations of idleness] and [promptly] went on *another kind* of holidaying [reduced working week; two days 'idle']. Isn't it incredible, *though* what we've come to expect?' Moreover, the third sentence's contrastive reference to the 'hope' regarding the dispute at British Leyland seems to confirm the Chrysler events as generally readable within an 'industrial dispute/union action' framing.

Now it would be a very tricky argument to connect this reading (which I both 'produce' and find opposable) decisively to a *textual determinacy* or, even more troublesome, an idea of intentionality. This is in contrast to the very strong 'cueings' of the *Daily Star*'s remark about a 'big propaganda war', and remains so even though the text-in-performance (as delivered and inflected by the newscaster) would give additional evidence of semantic closures. An inquiry into some realizations which readers had actually performed on, with and 'from' the utterance would immediately seem to be a useful way into a sociological grasp of the significatory operations of this bulletin. Further textual investigation could be focused in relation to such 'data'.

Yet, though frequently raising this analytical difficulty at the implicatory/inferential level, broadcast bulletins are, inevitably and plottably, both *selective* in their meanings (in that they contain certain words, phrases, offered explanations and not others) and evaluative/descriptive (in that many of the words and phrases used connect determinately with particular social values and positions). Part of the strength of the *Bad news* team's findings (Glasgow University Media Group 1976, 1980) derives, I believe, from the extent to which their analyses of industrial reporting can stay close to the more semantically closed and therefore plottable levels of news discourse. The team's excellent longitudinal inquiry into the operationalization of 'balance' requirements in broadcast news fundamentally concerns the predominance or exclusion of specific terms and words and the frequency of certain patterns of phrasing within the range of contemporary 'newstalk'. See for instance, the labelling pattern and the incidence of evaluative terminology mapped out in their study of both the Glasgow dustcart drivers' strike and the engine tuners' strike at British Leyland, Cowley (1976, ch. 7). The textual determinateness available is more than adequate to clinch their case, which critically maps the constituents of actual news discourse in relation to dominant principles of broadcasting propriety; but what about the more reader-grounded levels of significance-attaching and response? These must be the levels at which any negotiation or opposition to *what is read* operates, and must also be the levels at which acceptance, perhaps without conscious resolve (e.g. through an 'understanding' that sees an item as 'speaking for itself'), is transacted and made effective.

It is only by thinking through the interacting operations of textuality and reader productivity in terms of the 'levels' or 'orders' of meaning production that any precise accounts of how media power is symbolically exercised can be offered (see Hall 1972 for a magnificently challenging 'levels' analysis of news photographs). By way of contrast one can note the problem that the term 'message' currently involves in communication theory, indicating everything from the semantic range of a particular word within an utterance to the ideological 'meta-text' of a feature film.

An analytic differentiation into levels would have to connect with differences, within the sphere of 'overall realized meaning', between realizations both of 'meaning significance' and of 'response to meaning-significance'. Within any act of reading, of course, what I have chosen to see as three levels may well be active within the same moment. Moreover, they are not normally levels realized separately (though meaning and response should in most cases be given the clearest possible differentiation). The variations, then, that can occur within and between the concurrent activities of 'understanding' a text are crucial for significatory power.

In speech and writing 'what is said or written and in what tones' is rendered by the notation (ordered words) and, in speech (through a secondary, less determinate facility), the 'voicing' of ordered words. The combinatory signs produced must provide, when read in a specific modifying context, the textual base for reader activity. It would be odd to see all the closures carried out here as, by themselves, evidence of ideological closure, even though all a text's signs are both operated and realized with active and shaping contexts of ideas, assumptions and evaluations — within ideological fields. To refer back to the sentence from the *Daily Star* item, the word 'deal' closes off and labels the 'event' which the item primarily concerns itself with, but one would want to distinguish between the closure achieved here and the closures and attempted closures (involving a more directly interpretative/significance-attaching/responsive level) operated, say, by the word 'propaganda' or the word 'militants'. This difference can be roughly paralleled in the BBC bulletin by the words 'day', for instance, and the phrase 'troubled motor industry', though in the latter case the device is more one of ideologically significant categorization than of textually authorized ideological closure.

The considerations above connect with the issue of 'variant readings'. In the *Daily Star* example, it is *possible* for a reader to take the word 'militants' to mean 'officials' (i.e. to be a synonym of it). This would be a 'variant reading' (and a misreading) generated by an insufficient knowledge of English. A more likely situation would be that readers commonly construing the meaning of 'militancy' within its postwar ideological semantic range (few would now have realizations connecting, however faintly, with older usages like 'the Church militant') would then construct the significance of this usage-in-context in different ways, the difference being produced in large part by the form of what I can only call here the 'response'.

One reading could be first, to construct upon 'militants' the connotations of illegitimate action, disruption, political extremism etc. which the term has been used to generate in a whole range of media treatments of 'problems' in modern British society and, second, to think (to operate) the meaning of 'militant' exclusively within the terms of this inflection. Another way could be, first, to actualize the usage-in-context as above and 'then' (any idea of isolated sequence here is, of course, treacherous if not plain misleading) to see the usage as an interested deployment of these meanings. In this way the reader *might* construct upon the term a significance as a unit of evaluation, an ideological device, within a definitional and explanatory set found unacceptable and, as a result, 'opposed'.

This latter procedure involves the location (indeed, the generation) of the other levels of realization within a conscious, critical meaning-frame. Even a shop steward who regularly used the word 'militant' as a positive term in arguments would not 'realize' this variant *instead of* the dominant when reading the item. The very basis for opposition would be a 'reading' which realized a primary meaning (at the level at which someone with an insecure knowledge of English would not) and realized across and through this the dominant ideological meaning being operated in the usage; the latter realization occurring either within the terms of a critical framework or, what is very similar, against the pull of an alternative, conflicting usage.

This difficult area needs sustained attention by researchers using the notion of 'multi-accentuality' (loosely, the socially governed variations of meaningfulness attaching to a sign-in use: see Voloshinov

1973; Hall 1977). The levels and exclusivity of the readings which are produced via readers working within different accentual possibilities remains, I feel, unclear within the terms of the concept as so far developed. We must remember that, in an important sense, critical or oppositional readers are critical of, or opposed to, the meanings which they have themselves realized 'from and upon' the text in question and to which they have attributed a significance, an intentionality and/or a possible consequence which are seen to warrant the opposition.

The processes by which an understanding of the spoken or written text is produced and by which its articulations regulate the production of meaning can be contrasted (here, only in the briefest manner) with the static, visual text of an advertising image or a news photograph. The level of primary meaning is at once far harder to define in the visual text. The meaning of the photograph as 'realized' by the viewer/reader appears to be constructed immediately at the level of 'significance involving response', though not that response in terms of agreement or otherwise which was one possible phase in 'reading' the news text. The idea of disagreeing with a photograph raises a number of problems, not least because the lowest level of photographic discourse seems registerable only in terms of *what the photograph is of.* However, this is not a propositional or properly discursive level at all but a registration of what the photographer pointed the camera at, which may be very different from what the photograph is 'read' as 'being about' or 'meaning'.

The discursive capacities of photography would thus appear to be exclusively a matter of connotation (see Barthes 1977, pp. 15-31 and 32-52, on the 'naturalization' of meaning produced at this level), with the analytic consequence that it is much more difficult to perform a 'close reading' of a photographic image, since there is no specific notation against whose degree of determinateness one can measure one's proximity to a meaning base. Readers become involved in a more extensive and 'open' form of productional interpretation right from the initial moment of seeing. Even the most 'closed' forms of photographic discourse work as groupings of implication and association which can remain realizable *outside* those lines of meaning-selection set up by the cues of verbal anchorage or contextual framing (see Williamson 1978 for a discussion of 'openness' in relation to the ideological operations of advertising imagery).

I have argued, then, that even the briefest and most selective consideration of the kinds of text employable within media practice serves to underline both the difficulties attending generalizations about textuality and the need to regard *reading* or *interpretation* as a combination of differently levelled activities involving different kinds of symbolic transaction. To use another term, any one act of media 'decoding' has to be seen not as a single transformation of 'message' into meaning (the reductional 'drag' of 'decoding's' technological provenance remains damaging here) but as a set of transformative productive practices.

In the final section of this paper I want to connect the consideration of textuality more fully to the idea of media power, looking particularly at one suggestive set of arguments about how texts themselves 'prefer' certain readings (meanings) over others and about the implications this has for the reader's position and possibilities.

### Media discourse and media power

From the discussion above it is clear that a theory of symbolic power must importantly involve attention to the conditions and practices within which meanings are realized: the social relations of signification. Power is related to the level of textually or contextually achieved (see below) inferential alignments between, conventionally, 'production' and 'consumption' phases. It is centrally to do with the reproduction of significance.

Eco, in a paper first published in Italian in 1965, speculates upon the possible results of field research on audience decodings:

> We could discover that the community of the users had such freedom in decoding as to make the influencing power of the organization much weaker than one could have thought. Or just the opposite. (1972, p. 101)

However, in viewing media meaning as the product of text—reader interaction, research must regard the reader's productivity as a set of practices which are just as much socially formed and structured as are the significations of texts. This is to reject completely the idea of a reader *in individualized contest with* the semantic (in most cited cases 'imaginative') hegemony of texts, an idea which has been entertained by a liberationist strand of literary criticism and which also appears to have informed some versions of what Eco, in relation to television, has memorably called 'semiotic guerrilla warfare' (p. 121). A further problem here would seem to be that confusion, mentioned above, between producing *alternative* realizations and producing *critically framed* realizations of a text.

As I have indicated earlier, the most lucid recent account and example of how it might be possible to research media meaning as *reproduction* alongside a detailed awareness of the differential productivity of readers is contained in Morley (1980). In arguing both against theories of textual openness which accord the text scarcely any determinacy of determining power whatsoever and against theories of textual closure which view the reader as subjectively regulated into reproduction and acquiescence, Morley employs an hypothesis about textual power based on the idea of 'preferred reading'. This notion was developed in the earlier work of the Centre for Contemporary Cultural Studies at the University of Birmingham and can be traced through successive refinements and redefinitions. Morley's own usage follows that pithily given in Hall *et al.* (1976, p. 53):

In relation to the messages available through television we shall suggest that they never deliver *one* meaning; they are rather the site of a plurality of meanings, in which *one* is preferred and offered to the viewers, over the others, as the most appropriate. This 'preferring' is the site of considerable ideological labour.

'Preferring' thus appears to be a textual function, working towards the aligning of the inferential structures of 'reading' with those of the moment of 'writing' in a relation of naturalized correspondence. Through such a match, the reproductive function of discourse and therefore its ideological effectivity are maximized. One fundamental problem with this idea is the notion of one reading being preferred within a plurality of possible readings. This way of putting it does not seem to fit many actual instances of media discourse.

I have earlier discussed how the realized meanings of a particular item of broadcast news can be generated within a number of difference inferential framings and responses (response constituting one level of 'what the news means') without, in the process, producing significantly variable 'realizations' at the level of what the statement is understood to say or, indeed, at the level of what attitudinal or assumptional position it is seen to be constructed from, in so far as the evaluative dimension of news is registered by audiences (Morley 1980 discusses the implications of this latter variable). It is also apparent that much of the ideological character of press and television discourse, both verbal and visual, is an integral part of the text's construction (e.g. sentence, caption, selection of shot, interview question) and therefore powerfully delimits 'what is said' in any subsequent realization.

We should not confuse a text's degree of success in determining 'taken' meanings at this level with its admittedly related degree of success in generating significances which are reproduced into accepted fact/opinion/observation/value by the reader. As noted above, 'oppositional readings' would seem only likely to occur when the text has first been realized in its particular referential and connotative/evaluative dimensions; engagement is a precondition of refusal or critique. This situation makes it hard to see where the 'plurality' suggested in 'preferred reading' theory enters. It could certainly be that 'apparent plurality' of interpretative freedom within which the reader of apparently impartial reportage is encouraged to develop an independent judgement – but, in the above quotation, it is a real rather than an apparent plurality that is argued for.

The notion of the text as a 'site of a plurality of meanings' is frequently connected with the use of the term 'polysemy', drawn from semiotics, and ambiguities in the employment of this term may relate to my problems here with textual 'plurality'. In some usages polysemy appears to mean nothing more than the capacity of *meaning-units* or *textual components* to 'mean' a number of different things according to textual location and to contextual settings. In others it suggests a theory about the concurrent existence of a plurality of potentially realizable meanings 'within' the same text. Whilst it is clear that words and images are extensively determined in semantic character by their textual and pragmatic positioning and are thus, in themselves, 'open' in varying degrees (e.g. the word 'pencil' less than the word 'freedom'), it is not so clear just how the particular articulations (texts) they constitute *in usage* can preserve the range of such possibility – the text's very production is an exercise in delimitation.

Of course, the range of *unit* (word or image) possibilities out of which the text is an organization of chosen and worked closures (as we have seen, closures at different levels) *can* to some extent be 'reconstituted' by a reader criticizing and rejecting textual forms, but this returns us precisely to the problems of accounting for such activity in terms of the different orders of practice constitutive of reading. To register absences through an interrogatory reading is not to avail oneself of a *textual* plenitude.

The most apparent examples of preferring within a plurality seem to be those media practices in which one strip of text more or less directly closes the openness of another or others. The verbal 'anchorage' and connotative orienting of a still image by a caption or by copy would be one such example, as would related voice-over film techniques in television. Another example, one which has received detailed analysis, is the preferring work done by current affairs programme presenters as they underline, amplify, rework or efface the significations produced elsewhere in the programme. Here, the 'preferred reading' is developed from the presenter's own reading of the other items or offered viewpoints — an untypically literal case.

Despite the problems arising from current formulations, however, the concept of 'preferred reading' and the way of thinking about reader activity which it involves seem to me to remain among the most suggestive and usable ideas in 'media language' research concerned with power as ideological reproduction. The most likely developments in this area will come through a more detailed socio linguistics of the practices involved in 'reading' the varieties of media text (see the types of language analysis proposed in Fowler *et al.* 1979 and Kress & Hodge 1979), coupled with a wider range of empirical work on audiences — in particular, as part of correlational studies attempting to work across all the 'moments' of symbolic production. This latter course of investigation is particularly necessary where research involves visually dominant or narrative forms. The related, general need, developing the tendency of recent inquiries, will be to shift attention away from the production of some general 'textual theory' designed to complement a general theory of ideology and to move instead through a phase of more form-specific and sociologically documented analyses of situated instances.

# 14

# Some constructs for analysing news

PAUL L. JALBERT

## Introduction[1]

The main concern of this paper is to show, by 'deconstructing'[2] news media presentations, how ideological work is involved in them. Ideology is seen to be a routine feature of the social production of news stories which is congruent with political and economic interests, organized and unorganized. The mass media are seen to occupy a significant place as organizers of ideological production.[3]

Media discourses embody certain devices which enable us to see just what ideology-as-presented involves. These devices and procedures include (1) membership categories and their selection options,[4] (2) the exploitation of the reifying character of synecdochic and metonymic constructions,[5] (3) *de re/de dicto* transformations,[6] (4) the juxtaposition of transparent descriptions for opaquely true descriptions,[7] and (5) the analysably distinct orders of presupposition.[8]

## Membership categorization

In social interaction, we routinely use categories to refer to people, places and things. It is not difficult to see that we may categorize these in various ways so that the selections we make in one setting may not be appropriate in another, as, for example, if a child were to call his grandmother 'Edith'.

In the selection of names or 'categorization devices', we affect the meaning of our utterances. Sacks defines the term 'categorization device' as:

that *collection of membership categories*, containing at least a category, that may be applied to some population, containing at least a Member, so as to provide, by the use of the rules of application, for the pairing of at least a population Member and categorization device member. A *device* is then a *collection* plus rules of application. (1972, p. 32)

The selection of one category may create a bond between the person, place or thing categorized and other members of that category. To select the appropriate category requires that we learn to recognize the import of such selections. Just as we select categories so that we will be understood, we also select categories to describe events and circumstances which display our understandings of them. Although Sack's observations were based on conversational interactions, they have clear relevance to media studies because it is fair to expect that organizations and their representatives also select categories in strategic, although unreflective ways. The analytic points can be illustrated by the following *Newsweek* excerpt, which is about the tumult caused by the Katangan rebels who entered the Shaba Province of Zaïre in May 1978.

### Massacre in Zaire

Zaïre's President Mobutu Sese Seko stared through the window of a mining-company guesthouse in the shattered city of Kolwezi. The battlehardened President, a former army sergeant, put his hands to his face and moaned. '*Mon Dieu*, they have smashed their heads in.' Inside the guesthouse, 35 European men, women and children lay dead. They had been herded into a room and executed by Katangan invaders before the attackers themselves were driven out of town by the French Foreign Legion.

The ghastly massacre in Kolwezi came hours before a gallant rescue effort. By last week, it appeared that more than 100 white hostages had been butchered by Katangan rebels — but that nearly 3,000 more had been saved by the French legionnaires and Belgian paratroopers who flew in, with American help, to prevent a slaughter that might have been even worse....Armed with Soviet weapons and apparently trained by Cuban advisers, the Katangans drove Zaïre's troops out of Kolwezi and kept them out...[9]

The text reads as if it were an eye-witness account of the events depicted, which may enhance the credibility of the report. It seems that the reporter is in the presence of President Mobutu (although this is not made explicit) because he reports that Mobutu puts 'his hands to his face' and quotes him directly. This impression carries through right into the report of the incidents: 'They had been herded into a room and executed...' The word 'herded' is used without qualification, implying that the people were treated as subhuman, as cattle, and later the word 'butchered' maintains the metaphor, although we have no *direct* evidence of these events. The report makes a significant juxtaposition between Mobutu, who is described as a sympathetic observer ('he moaned') and as being identified with the Zaïrian masses ('a former army sergeant'), and the 'ghastly massacre' caused by these 'attackers'.

The Katangan people are referred to as 'invaders' and 'rebels'. The category 'rebels' creates an affiliation between its members and the territory on which they are fighting. The category 'invaders' strongly implies that its members are not affiliated with but imposing force on the territory. Who are the Katangan people and where do they come from? Further, the reporter reifies the Katangan rebels by referring to them merely as 'Katangans'. By contrast, other forces are referred to in full as organised forces, for example, the 'French *Foreign Legion*', 'French *legionnaires*', the 'Belgian *paratroopers*' and 'Zaïre's *troops*'. The reference to 'Soviet weapons', suggests that there is a political and military tie with the Soviet Union; whereas we are told that there was some 'American help', which leaves us wondering what kind of help the Americans provided in the face of such a 'slaughter that might have been even worse'. The contrast is made between the specific character of the word 'weapons' (which carries with it aggressive connotations) and the open-endedness of the word 'help' (which implies a kind of humanitarian commitment). However, the 'help' the Americans rendered could have itself consisted of weapons.

One final observation about this article is that the Katangese account is excluded from it. The upshot is that the Katangan people are indicted on the basis of a supposedly factual account of the situation. It is clear that in reading this story the reader might arrive at some mistaken conclusions. It is the manner in which the news is presented that plays the crucial role in the way that information will be understood by the reader. The selection of categories and the ordering of these selections is paramount; for, whether explicitly or implicitly, they carry with them content and meaning which create a message congruent with the beliefs of the author.

*Time* magazine published an article on the same events. Here is an excerpt:

### The Shaba Tigers Return

...An estimated 5,000 Katangese guerrillas of the Congolese National Liberation Front (F.I.N.C.), which has been seeking autonomy for Shaba since Zaïre gained its independence from Belgium in 1960, launched a deadly strike on the region from their bases in Marxist-run Angola...The rebels carried out cold-blooded executions, slaughtering at least 100 whites and 300 blacks, before they were driven from the city...[10]

This report has a little more continuity, since the Katangese people are referred to as 'guerrillas' and 'rebels'. These categories, however, are juxtaposed with 'their bases in Marxist-run Angola'. The impression is given that Marxists condone 'cold-blooded executions' and the 'slaughtering' of people. There is also a subtle implication that a country espousing Marxism could not have a government, but could only be 'Marxist-run'. We learn, however, that these Katangese people are members of the FINC, which grants them some political legitimacy, and seems to give them some purpose, in contrast with the *Newsweek* article, which gave us the impression that these people were 'invaders' who performed acts of violence for no justifiable reason.

Even though the *Time* article attributes the invaders some purpose, consider another excerpt a little later in the same article:

They insisted that no 'Cubanos' had come with them. Nonetheless, guerillas declared that their goal was not simply the liberation of Shaba from Kinshasa's rule but the ouster of Mobutu and the creation of a more radical government in Zaïre.[11]

The word 'Nonetheless' implies that the Katangese people do not really have their *own* goals, that the goals they express are really Cuban goals, which implies further that the Katangese people are not capable of articulating such goals on their own.

These media presentations have allowed us to show how the selection of categorization devices can point to ideological relations predicated on power relationships, in these instances, of an international character. However, some of the strength of a given report can be attributed to a particular sort of categorization device. One such device is *category boundedness*. Sacks suggests the following 'viewer's maxim':

If a member sees a category-bound activity being done, then, if one can see it being done by a member of a category to which the activity is bound, then: See it that way. The viewer's maxim is another relevance rule in that it proposes that for an observer of a category-bound activity the category to which the activity is bound has a special relevance for formulating an identification of its doer. (Sacks 1974, p. 225)

Sacks developed this notion within his discussions of category-bound activities, where members of a category are recognized as performers of certain activities (e.g., voters elect, police officers arrest), although they are not intended to be considered sterotypical. Sacks constructed a second viewer's maxim:

If one sees a pair of actions which can be related via the operation of a norm that provides for the second given the first, where the doers can be seen as members of the categories the norm provides as proper for that pair of actions, then: (a) see that the doers are such-members and (b) see the second as done in conformity with the norm. (p. 225)

A logical extension of such a notion would be to consider the *ascribed* attributes of members of one category to be bound to another category whose attributes can be understood to be identical to those of the first. This has importance in our discussion of ideological production in news accounts, if and when the contestability of certain juxtapositions of categories becomes clouded because those very same juxtapositions are treated as mundane. Consider the following example.

For years now the Palestinian people have been referred to as 'terrorists'. At first, there was a distinction made between the Palestine Liberation Organization (PLO) and Palestinian people. But since it became clear that the majority of Palestinian people support the PLO and recognize it as their sole representative, the category 'terrorist' has been routinely applied to the category 'Palestinian'. The repeated reference to Palestinians as 'terrorists' by the media has created this category-boundedness between the members and the category. To show how effective is the juxtaposition of 'Palestinian'/ 'terrorist', *Time* magazine conducted a poll in 1980 asking the United States public how they would best describe Palestinians. These are the results:

30% of the U.S. public think Palestinians are best described as 'terrorists', 17% regard them as 'displaced persons who will eventually settle in another country', and 19% think of them as 'refugees seeking a homeland.'[12]

Although it may be noteworthy that the highest response reported in the article was that of those who described Palestinians as 'terrorists', it is significant that no positive references to Palestinians were reported. When we observe that only 66 per cent of the responses were reported, which include the descriptions of Palestinians as 'refugees' and 'displaced persons', a doubt is raised. The critical reader is left to wonder what sentiments could have been expressed in the remaining 34 per cent. One could give the pollster the benefit of the doubt and think that the remaining percentage comprised several other responses, none of which were significant to report, or one could conjecture that the entire 34 per cent gave descriptions of Palestinians as wronged people whose cause is just. Because of the omission, the poll's descriptive preference may be conceived of as a spontaneous and natural preference on the part of 30 per cent of the United States public, which has all along merely been 'reflected' in the categorical selections used by the media. On the other hand, the ambiguity allows for the possibility that the descriptive preference is a function of those very same categorical selections to which recipients of media presentations are routinely exposed. Naturally enough, this latter possibility is not seriously entertained in discussions of opinion formation. Consequently, government policies may be affected by such reporting and, it could then be argued, are 'truly' in the 'national interest' because they reflect the people's freely formed moral position.

Here production of these ideologically powerful images and messages is difficult to characterize as purposive. This is because not all ideological productions are selfconsciously organized. However, on occasion we can show how aspects of media productions are formulated explicitly to effect a specific ideological slant. The Press Office of the Third Reich frequently practised this sort of category selection. Claus Mueller cites several of these selections in the form of 'directives' about appropriate vocabulary in news reports and editorials:

| *Date* | *Directive* |
|---|---|
| September 1, 1939 | The word 'war' has to be avoided in all news coverage and editorials. Germany is repulsing a Polish attack. |
| June 9, 1941 | Be reminded once again that the U.S.A. Jew, (sic) *Baruch*, cannot be attacked. He is a 'protected Jew'. |
| October 16, 1941 | There should be no more reference to Soviet Russian soldiers. At most they can be called Soviet army members (*Soviet-armisten*) or simply Bolsheviks, beasts, and animals. (Mueller 1978, pp. 30-2) |

Whilst it might not surprise us to discover that such tactics were practised by the Press Office of the Third Reich, it puts the following in a new light:

Bombing is 'protective reaction', precision bombing is 'surgical strikes', concentration camps are 'pacification centers' or 'refugee camps'...Bombs dropped outside your target area are 'incontinent ordnance', and those dropped on one of your own villages are excused as 'friendly fire'; a bombed house becomes automatically a 'military structure' and a lowly sampan sunk on the waterfront a 'waterborne logistic craft'. (Bolinger 1973, p. 545)[13]

These terms were systematically used by the Nixon administration in press releases during the Vietnam War. The resemblance between the 'euphemisms' selected by the Nixon administration and the 'directives' of the Third Reich Press Office is apparent enough.

The specific categories chosen make a difference to the meaning conveyed. This is true not only because different categories have different implications, but also because those categories orient us to contexts which also affect the meaning of what is heard and read, whether the purpose is to sell newspapers, secure high TV ratings or promote a particular interpretation of events.

### Synecdochic and metonymic reification

Two powerful literary devices which demonstrate the kind of impact that can be created simply by selecting words which do more than describe are *synecdoche* and *metonymy*. *Synecdoche* involves the substitution of one term for another within a prearranged hierarchy. 'It is a form of metaphor which in mentioning a part signifies the whole or the whole signifies the part' (Holman 1972, p. 522). Such mentioning of parts to indicate the whole could entail an anatomical classification, as when manual labour is referred to as 'hands'. Clearly, the expression 'All *hands* on deck' should not be taken literally. Indeed, the non-literal character of the device is precisely what creates the image intended. Other synecdoches create a relationship between the category and what the category can represent in that context. For example, the expression 'Get that *smell* out of here' could apply to a variety of circumstances.

*Metonymy*:

involves a replacement of a term where the relationship from the first to the second is felt to be more functional: cause/effect, actor/action, container/contained, and the like. None...can be taken literally and each reflects a substitution of one term for another because of some preexisting relationship. (Fraser 1979, p. 175)

Some examples of these non-literal devices are: 'He hit the *bottle*, where we understand that utterance to mean 'he is drinking,' the bottle representing the action of drinking; 'the crown' can stand for 'the king'; and 'sweat' can represent 'hard labour'. Let us now look at some examples of the use of these devices in the media.

A *synecdoche* occurs in the following:

...and the White House announced that 18 Air Force C-141 transports,... were assisting the French and Belgian operations.[14]

The White House, the President's home, can be seen as the 'container' for the President; and the President as the 'contained'. To select the term 'White House' serves to remove the President from personal responsibility for the action, while maintaining the power assignable to the announcement. The effectiveness of this strategy depends on the reification of power. People can be held responsible for actions, buildings cannot.

A kind of implicit generalization through reification is common in news reports. Here is another example:

There are no lingering illusions in Washington, Paris or Brussels about the quality of Mobutu's regime.[15]

The choice of the names of their capital cities to refer to powerful statesmen detaches those persons in power from the ascription of knowledge made by the reporter. The very next sentence creates a contrast which counter-balances the admission that the 'quality of Mobutu's regime' is less than laudable:

But the Zaïrian leader is a staunch anti-communist and a proven friend of the West, while the Cuban-backed insurgents apparently have Marxist goals.[16]

Here the category 'West' glosses those countries which are understood to be 'anti-communist'. The word 'But' detracts, through contrast, from a negative ascription to the 'quality' of Mobutu's regime and also sets up grounds for justifying support for this less-than-laudable leadership. To present further grounds for this particular reading, consider this caption to a photograph showing demonstrators in Kinshasa expressing an anti-Soviet-Cuban sentiment, noting once more the use of the capital city to represent those who are in power:

Since Washington agrees with the sentiment, it will hold its nose and continue support.[17]

The expression 'hold its nose' creates another non-literal relationship, indicating that Mobutu's regime is even nauseous, and that no matter how distasteful it could be, it is still preferable to the implicit alternative: 'communism'. It is understandable, therefore, that no reference to this regime as being 'Fascist' is ever made. To do so would create a bond of a different order between Mobutu's regime and the United States government, about which one could conclude that it too is 'Fascist', or an ally of Fascism.

These devices not only serve to reify the people in power, but they also serve to mystify power relationships. The political declarations in the above excerpts may not be subtle, but the ideological relations are both subtle and hard to recognize because of the way in which the 'facts' are presented.

Metonymies are equally important devices whose impact relies primarily on the strength of the relationship between the reference forms. An example of metonymy in television news reports may be found in the title of a news special that the ABC Network produced nightly in November 1979 after the American embassy in Tehran was seized by Iranian students and American hostages were taken. The title was 'The Iran Crisis: America Held Hostage'. The claim that the ABC Network is making here is not a literal one: *America* is not being held hostage. It is via the *reification* of the hostages in this hyperbolic way that the network can make the statement that *all* Americans are being held hostage. This reifying mechanism creates a context which can be exploited by the government to legitimate any attempt to free the hostages, justifying it as in the 'national interest'. The word 'hostage' implies that the persons being held are innocent victims and that there is some cause for concern about this unjust imprisonment. Other newscasts suggest that the American embassy in Iran was the base for espionage against the Iranian revolution. However, the news special title appears to absolve any liability or responsibility for these activities. Consequently, any action directed against the 'holders' of the 'hostages' could be seen as righteous.

## De Re/De Dicto
*modalities and transparent/opaque transformations*

Although we routinely categorize people, places and things, we often do so ambiguously. One of the ways in which the ambiguities can be understood is as *mutually exclusive* versions, where only one version of the proposition can be true. Consider the following proposition:

1 The house Joe claimed that Peter lived in was old.

Here, the 'house…Peter lived in' can be understood either to be (a) the *actual* 'house…Peter lived in' or (b) the house Joe *claimed* 'Peter lived in'. The distinctions between these two interpretations of the ambiguity can be made clear by discussing *de re* and *de dicto* modalities. *De re* means 'about the thing' and *de dicto* means 'about what is said' (about the thing). Consequently, in the above proposition, rendition (a) is the *de re* version because the focus is on the 'thing' in the actual world; whereas, rendition (b) is the *de dicto* version because the focus is on the claim expressed about the 'thing'. Only one version can be true, thereby characterizing them as *mutually exclusive* versions.

Not all renditions are mutually exclusive in terms of truth-value. Some elements of some propositions are interchangeable, so that truth-values can be assigned to both. Consider this syllogism:

2 a Jupiter weighs 150 pounds.
  b Jupiter is my dog.
  c My dog weighs 150 pounds.

Since 'Jupiter' and 'my dog' refer to the same animal, what is true of one term must also be true of the other; hence the truth-value is interchangeably assignable.

Discussions of the assignability of truth-value are not restricted to notions of mutual exclusivity and interchangeability. Two other notions are helpful, namely: *opacity of reference* and *transparency of reference*. While still attending to truth-value, these notions can help us understand ambiguities of a different order. We will also couple these notions with the *de re* and *de dicto* modalities we discussed above. What makes a report *opaquely true* is that the predicate is assignable to the subject's knowledge as well as to the reporter's knowledge. What makes a report *transparently true* is that the predicate is strictly assignable only to the reporter's knowledge. Consider the following proposition:

3 Oedipus wanted to marry his mother.

To say this of Oedipus early in the play ($T_1$) would only be *transparently true* — that is, this *de dicto* characterization of Oedipus wanting to marry his mother is available *only* to the reporter and not to Oedipus. Oedipus wanted to marry *Jocasta*, who, unknown to him, was his mother. Thus the report is not *opaquely* true at $(T_1)$. Moreover, after the marriage has taken place $(T_2)$ and Oedipus discovers that Jocasta is also his mother, the characterization of Oedipus in (3) is *still* only *transparently true* because Oedipus *never* wanted to marry *his mother*.

However, consider this report:

4    Oedipus married his mother.

This is a *de re* report, which is *transparently true* since the predicate, 'married his mother', is assignable to the reporter's knowledge. This report is also *opaquely true* if the reader has no reason to believe that Oedipus did not know what he was doing. In other words, the reporter's knowledge that Jocasta was Oedipus' mother is assigned to Oedipus, such that Oedipus knew that Jocasta was his mother when he married her. The *transparently true* report (4) becomes an *opaquely true* one by virtue of a knowledge ascription. The issue here is: if we are given a *de re* report which is *transparently true*, i.e. (4), without any other information qualifying it, the first option of the reader or hearer is to treat the report as also *opaquely true*.

These theoretical constructs and their transformations can be applied to news reports, where the *de re*, *transparently true* versions are read to be also *opaquely true* versions. Let us apply this framework to the following extract from a *Time* magazine report on the Zaïre conflict.

But there was killing aplenty. The rebels apparently went hunting for French and Moroccans, the two nations that did the most to stop their invasion of Shaba Province last year. If they found them, they killed them — along with anyone else unfortunate enough not to have papers...

The commander of the invading force, which calls itself the Congolese National Liberation Front, is Gen. Nathaniel M'Bumba....'We want to drive President Mobutu out of power', he said...Reports quickly reached Kinshasa that four Belgians, including a married couple, also were murdered. In Brussels, Prime Minister Léo Tindemans announced that 'tens' of other Europeans had been killed. Foreign Minister Henri Simonet added to the crisis atmosphere by stating that the invaders were conducting a *chasse aux européens* — a 'manhunt of Europeans.'[18]

Consider the following mapping of the different sequentially ordered versions accounting for the presence of Katangan rebels in the Shaba Province of Zaïre in May 1978.

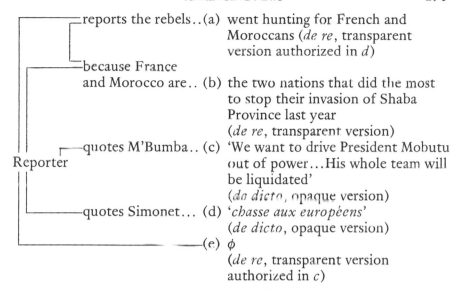

reports the rebels.. (a) went hunting for French and Moroccans (*de re*, transparent version authorized in *d*)

because France and Morocco are.. (b) the two nations that did the most to stop their invasion of Shaba Province last year (*de re*, transparent version)

Reporter

quotes M'Bumba.. (c) 'We want to drive President Mobutu out of power...His whole team will be liquidated' (*de dicto*, opaque version)

quotes Simonet... (d) '*chasse aux européens*' (*de dicto*, opaque version)

(e) $\phi$ (*de re*, transparent version authorized in *c*)

What we observe in (d) is an *opaque* version in a *de dicto* modality that is treated by the reporter in (a) as a *transparent* version in a *de re* modality. What this means is that although version (d) is understood by the reader to be the motives of the Katangan rebels as ascribed by Foreign Minister Simonet (the *de dicto* opaque version), the reporter's version (a), which is the *de re* transparent version, is in complete agreement with version (d) and is treated as the actual motives of the Katangan rebels. This transformation of versions (from *de dicto* to *de re*) effects their interchangeability and creates an identity between the ascribed motives of the Katangan rebels and their actual motives. Moreover, this putatively transparent version (a) is predicated on another putatively transparent version (b).

However, what is most interesting about this transformation is illustrated in the remaining part of the mapping. In this display, the reader is supplied with the rebel leader's account (c), which is a *de dicto* opaque version, without any contrasting version (e) provided in a newly introduced *de re* transparent counterpart. What the reader is tacitly asked to do is to search for what was previously supplied to fill the nul set ($\phi$). The naive reader is then left with the account regarding the motives of the Katangan rebels (which coincides with Foreign Minister Simonet's account) as the factual account of the nature of the conflict. M'Bumba's own account of the rebels' motives is contextualizable in the light of the Foreign Minister's account, thus suggesting that M'Bumba and his rebels are racists whose purpose for going into Shaba Province was to hunt down whites and friends of whites. Consequently, the reason for M'Bumba's desire to oust Mobutu and his regime (including its European backing), is left to the reader's grasp of the implications established by the sequence of the report, or consigned to the reader's independent knowledge (if any) of the conflict.

A practical rule for use by readers to locate 'what is the truth or the putative truth of the matter?' may be formulated technically in terms of the observability of an accord between the transparent/ *de re* components of the account and the opaque/*de dicto* components.[19] Concretely, the reporter is performing an analysis on the truth of the matter and providing the reader with a version, which, if not critically read, can lead him only to see what is presented as the real world, and not to see what could actually constitute the real world. The importance of this for the study of ideology in news productions is clear. The effectiveness of ideology is predicated on non-critical readings of reports, especially on treating transparent versions as opaquely true.

Jayyusi has given a real insight into transparent and opaque transformations. In presenting her discussion, she demonstrates the importance of understanding these routinely encountered ambiguities in news descriptions. Ever since reporting on the 1979 Iranian Revolution began, much of it has revolved around the issue of 'modernization' and the Iranian people's opposition to it. Jayyusi's point is that if a reader/hearer is not versed in the intricacies of the contexts within which the reports operate, there remains uncertainty about just how the Iranians themselves understood the reasons for their revolution:

In the recent reporting on the Iranian Revolution of 1979, many of the descriptions were couched in terms of the Iranian people's opposition to 'modernization'. Now, if the reader or hearer does not know what context such descriptions are operating within, she may remain unsure whether the Iranians indeed saw themselves opposing some *other* development or set of practices which the reporter identifies as 'modernization'...what remains ambiguous is also whether indeed these practices can be taken to be what *we* (or the reporter) would mean by 'modernization', and whether indeed the reporter really believes that these practices being opposed are what most people would mean by 'modernization', or simply wishes the reader to believe that. (Jayyusi 1979, pp. 268-9)

However, when the reader does understand the account transparently, the upshot will be 'that the Iranians are opposed to "westernization" or to "foreign influence"' (p. 269). These considerations make it increasingly clear that in order to secure a better understanding of events and issues reported by news media, people must learn to become critical readers and listeners.

## Presuppositions in media discourse

When people communicate with each other, their discourse is informed by the beliefs and values they have acquired as members of a culture. These are mostly tacit and unobtrusive; but, when assertions are made about events and issues, they may be activated and become an important part of the meaning conveyed. Accounts can be seen routinely to express beliefs and values in an implicit way.

The observability of these commitments is predicated on the *presupposition-analysis* performed by the reader/hearer. This analysis is necessary where the beliefs and values are not explicitly stated. J. L. Austin's discussion of 'illocutionary actions' is helpful in establishing a stronger link between language-use and presupposition. According to Austin, illocutionary actions are acts performed in the course of using language, e.g. 'I acknowledge your assistance', where the illocutionary force is in the explicit act of acknowledgement. But, as Coulter argues: 'there are many cases where the identification of an illocutionary action in conversation itself depends upon the hearer's performing the relevant presupposition-analysis' (1979b, p. 167). Although Coulter's discussion is oriented to conversation analysis, it is also relevant to other forms of linguistic discourse, including news reporting. What Coulter points out is that analyses of presupposition are routinely performed by readers and hearers, enabling them to grasp the illocutionary force of the statement. This is necessary because not all illocutionary acts are marked by an *'explicit performative formula*...such as "I promise..." or "I warned you that..."' (p. 168).

To concentrate on presupposition-analyses performed by readers and hearers of news reports, let us examine one domain which is rich in presupposition, the use of *contrastive categories*, where the illocutionary force very clearly becomes available at the level of presupposition. Contrastive categorization is used in this example:

The Israelis put their own losses at fifteen soldiers killed, while the Palestine Liberation Organization had apparently lost about 150 men...[20]

The contrastive categories here are 'killed' and 'lost'. The predicate 'killed' carries with it strong elements of agency and responsibility, while the predicate 'lost' does not. The PLO is attributed the responsibility for the deaths of the Israeli soldiers, while responsibility for the 'lost' 150 men is attributed to no one. We know that these groups were fighting against each other and that presumably the '150 men' did not shoot themselves nor did they get 'lost' in Southern Lebanon. How else then could the PLO have 'lost about 150 men'? The effect of the contrast creates an uneven display of the facts of the matter, implying that the Israeli soldiers can be seen as victims of killings, while the PLO can be seen as only having 'lost about 150 men'.

Let us look at another example:

After the PLO raid, in which 31 Israelis and an American woman were *massacred* outside Tel Aviv, it was almost a foregone conclusion that the Israelis would strike back...

...Israeli Defense Minister Ezer Weizman confirmed that the raid had occurred... and admitted that 'civilians may have been *unavoidably killed*.' (italics added)[21]

The contrastive categories displayed here are 'massacred' and 'unavoidably killed'. Both categories enable responsibility to be attributed to one or the other group. It is interesting to note that the same event is reported in two different ways. On the one hand, the '31 Israelis and an American woman' we know to have been the civilians who occupied the bus at the time of the attack are depicted as having been 'massacred'. Although the article does not explicitly attribute this 'massacre' to the PLO, the juxtaposition of the two categories implies that the PLO did indeed perpetrate the 'massacre'. No authorization statement is assigned to this report, leaving the truth of the matter up to the discretion of the reader.[22] On the other hand, Weizman's statement about the civilians as having been 'unavoidably killed' displays a version of the events that can be understood as presupposing minimal culpability on the part of the Israeli troops.

The contrasts in these reports create images which express certain tacit beliefs. It could be argued that the report has presented the 'facts' of the matter in a manner which can elicit or reinforce specific understandings concerning what the PLO represents and what the Israeli army represents. The duality of such reports can be disambiguated by employing the reasoning procedure: 'Where the context of the expression cannot resolve some ambiguity, choose whichever hearing [/reading] makes better sense in terms of your beliefs, and/or the beliefs assignable to the user of the expression.'[23]

I have tried to demonstrate how we are able to explain what makes media presentations ideological by employing a number of analytical constructs. Sociopolitical judgements and values which express the interests of certain groups are implied in most news reports. Only if they were explicit would they be characterizable as propaganda. Because it is implicit, the ideological element is often only discernible through the asymmetry between the perspectives of the journalist and the viewer or reader. This can be illustrated when *de dicto* and *de re* accounts are discrepant, where there is a component of de-authorization of the *de dicto* account, in either direct or indirect speech. Here is an example:

Along with his usual anti-American diatribe, there was this remarkable comment today from the Ayatollah Khomeini. He said, *and there's no way of knowing where he got the numbers*, the public opinion polls show 55% of the American people oppos[ing] military action against Iran... (italics added) [24]

The reporter is discrediting Khomeini's remarks on a poll by interjecting a comment which undermines the account before it is even made. Thus the *de dicto* account is de-authorized by a *de re* account.

This kind of discrepancy is selectively introduced by reporters to suggest desired interpretations. Consider this example later in the same report:

Once again this crowd demonstrates and knows it is getting heard and seen in America. Once again *they reaffirm the remarks of one observer*, that Iran has America by the networks... (italics added)

There is an interjection of an unidentified source, 'one observer'. It could be argued that such dubious anonymity works to de-authorize the account. But it is clear that instead of treating it as de-authorization, the reporter is using it as a means to gloss the account while maintaining at least a minimal measure of authority.

When we are able to unmask these and other devices which can be identified as supporting the interests of a particular social class or grouping, we will have succeeded in explaining the relational character of ideology-as-presented. Laclau states that the correct method is:

to accept that ideological 'elements' taken in isolation have no necessary class connotation, and that this connotation is only the result of the articulation of those elements in a concrete ideological discourse. This means that the precondition for analysing the class nature of an ideology is to conduct the inquiry through that which constitutes the distinctive unity of an ideological discourse. (1979, p. 99)

In the light of the analysis offered here, perhaps the most likely of all the forms of linguistic discourse to show this 'distinctive unity of an ideological discourse' is news in the mass media.

## Notes

1   I want to thank the following people, without whose help I would not have been able to accomplish this work: Jeff Coulter, Lena Jayyusi, Mary Anne Deveau and the members of the Interaction Research Group Forum.

2   The term 'deconstructing' is borrowed from Jacques Derrida. Its selection over the term 'decoding', which presupposes that a prior 'encoding' procedure has taken place, eliminates the problems associated with coding. This enables us to 'dissect' the news reports as presented revealing their elements and components; thus allowing us to treat them systematically without being constrained by questions of 'prior codification'. See Derrida (1976).

3   There are many studies which have addressed the problems related with the concept of 'ideology' and the mass media, while also attending to the power relationships involved on the corporate and governmental levels. *Inter alia*, see the work of Stuart Hall, James Halloran, Richard Hoggart, Graham Murdock and Philip Elliot, in Cohen & Young 1973; Glasgow University Media Group 1976; Miliband 1969; and more recently Leggett *et al.* 1978.

4   Sacks 1974; Sacks & Schegloff 1979.

5   Fraser 1979.

6   Jayyusi 1979, ch. 6, 'Ways of describing'.

7   Jayyusi 1979; Quine 1960.

8   Coulter 1979a, b.

9   *Newsweek*, 29 May 1978, p. 34, cols 1-2.

10   *Time*, 29 May 1978, p. 28, col. 1.

11   Ibid., p. 29, col. 2.

12   *Time*, 14 Apr. 1980, p. 42, col. 3.

13   Bolinger is here drawing on Henry Steele Commager 'The defeat of America', *New York Review of Books*, 5 Oct. 1972, pp. 7-13.

14   *Time*, 29 May 1978, p. 28, col. 2.

15   *Time*, 29 May 1978, p. 30, col. 1.

16   Ibid.

17   Ibid., photo caption.

18   *Time*, 29 May 1978, p. 36, col. 1 and p. 39, cols 2-3.

19   This assumes that the *de dicto* modality can indeed be mapped onto the opaque version, which in turn presupposes that those quoted verbatim meant what they said.

20   *Newsweek*, 27 Mar. 1978, p. 27, col. 1.

21   Ibid., p. 28, col. 1; p. 31, cols 2-3.

22   Interestingly, some Israeli press reports (e.g. *Yediot Aharonot*) attributed the deaths of the Israeli civilians to the precipitate action of Israeli troops

who lobbed grenades into the bus and machine-gunned it from various directions. This set the bus on fire, killing all inside. Without taking sides here, it is worth noting that these reports were not used in the US media even as contrastive materials.

23 D. G. Williams, 'Some reflections on the methodology of conversational analyses' (unpublished MA Dissertation, University of Manchester 1975), as quoted in Coulter 1979b.

24 WCVB-TV, Channel 5, Boston, 21 Dec. 1979, 11.30 pm, ABC Special on the Iranian crisis.

# References

Altheide, D. 1976: *Creating reality*. Beverley Hills/London: Sage.

Althusser, L. 1971: Ideology and ideological state apparatuses. In Althusser, L., *Lenin and philosophy and other essays*. London: New Left Books.

Anderson, D. 1978: Some organizational features in the local production of a plausible text. *Philosophy of Social Science* 8, 113-35.

Anderson, D. & Sharrock, W. 1979: Biasing the news: technical issues in 'media studies'. *Sociology* 13, 367-85.

Annan Report 1977. *Report of the Committee on the Future of Broadcasting*, Cmnd 6753. London: HMSO.

Armstrong, R. P. 1959: Content analysis in folkloristics. In de Sola Pool, I., editor, *Trends in content analysis*. No. 1. Urbana: University of Illinois Press.

Bach, K. & Harnish, R. 1979: *Linguistic communication and speech acts*. Cambridge Mass.: MIT.

Barrett, M., Corrigan, P., Kuhn, A. & Wolff, J., editors, 1979: *Ideology and cultural production*. London: Croom Helm.

Barthes, R. 1967: *Elements of semiology*, translated by A. Lavers & C. Smith. London: Jonathan Cape.

Barthes, R. 1973a: *Mythologies*, selected and translated by A. Lavers. St Albans: Paladin.

Barthes, R. 1973b: *Le plaisir du texte*. Paris: Seuil. (English translation by R. Miller, 1976, *The pleasure of the text*. London: Jonathan Cape.)

Barthes, R. 1975: *S/Z*, translated by R. Miller. London: Jonathan Cape.

Barthes, R. 1977: *Image—Music—Text*, selected and translated by S. Heath. London: Fontana.

Barthes, R. & Berthet, F. 1979: Présentation. *Communications* (Paris) 30, 3—5.

Baylen, J. O. 1972: 'The new journalism' in late Victorian Britain. *Australian Journal of Politics and History* 18.

Bazin, A. 1970: *What is cinema?* Berkeley: University of California Press.

BBC 1928: *Broadcast English I. Words of doubtful usage*. London: BBC.

BBC 1971a: *BBC pronouncing dictionary of British names*. London: BBC.

BBC 1971b: *Principles and practices in news and current affairs*. London: BBC.

BBC 1972: *Fifty years of broadcasting* (Record). London: BBC.

BBC 1974: *BBC pronunciation policy and practice*. London: BBC.

BBC 1976: *The task of broadcasting news*. London: BBC.

Beharrell, P. & Philo, G., editors, 1977: *Trade unions and the media*. London: Macmillan.

Bell, C. 1958: *Art*. New York: Capricorn.

Belson, W. 1978: *Television violence and the adolescent boy*. Farnborough: Saxon House.

Bennett, T. 1979: *Formalism and marxism*. London: Methuen.

Bernstein, B. 1971: *Class, codes and control*, vol. 1. London: Routledge & Kegan Paul.

Bhaskar, R. 1979: *The possibility of naturalism*. Brighton: Harvester Press.

Black, P. 1972: *The biggest aspidistra in the world*. London: BBC

Bloch, M., editor, 1975: *Political language and oratory in traditional society*. & Kuper, A., editors, *Councils in action*. Cambridge Papers in Social Anthropology, No. 6.

Block, M., editor, 1975: *Political language and oratory in traditional society*. London: Academic Press.

Blumler, J. & Katz, E., editors, 1974: *Uses and gratification studies: theories and methods*. London: Sage.

Bok, S. 1978: *Lying: moral choice in public and private life*. New York: Pantheon.

Bolinger, D. 1973: Truth is a linguistic question. *Language* 49, no. 3, 539-50.

Bonsiepe, G. 1961: Persuasive communication: towards a visual rhetoric. *Uppercase* 5, 19-33.

Boreham, P. & Dow, G., editors, 1980: *Work and inequality*. Melbourne: Macmillan.

Bourdieu, P. 1965: *Un art moyen: essai sur les usages sociaux de la photographie*. Paris: Minuit.

Bourdieu, P. 1972: *Cultural reproduction and social reproduction*. London: Tavistock.

Bourdieu, P. & Passeron, J. C. 1977: *Reproduction in education, society and culture*, (translated by R. Nice). London: Sage.

Bowyer-Bell, J. 1978: *A time of terror*. New York: Basic Books.

Boyce, G., Curran, J. & Wingate, P. editors, 1978: *Newspaper history*. London: Constable.

Boyd, R. 1979: Metaphor and theory change. What is a 'metaphor' a metaphor for? In Ortony 1979.

Briggs, A. 1961: *The history of broadcasting in the United Kingdom*, vol. 1, *The birth of broadcasting*. Oxford: OUP.

Briggs, A. 1965: *The history of broadcasting in the United Kingdom*, vol. 2, *The golden age of wireless*. Oxford: OUP.

Brown, R. & Gilman, A. 1972: The pronouns of power and solidarity. In Laver, J. & Hutchinson, S., editors, *Communication in face to face interaction*. Harmondsworth: Penguin.

Brunsdon, C. & Morley, D. 1978: *Everyday television: Nationwide*. London: British Film Institute.

Burchfield, R., Donaghue, D. & Timothy, A. 1979: *The quality of spoken English on BBC radio*. London: BBC.

Burgin, V. 1980: Photography, phantasy, function. *Screen* 21, no. 1, 43-80.

Burns, T. 1977: *The BBC: public image and private world*. London: Macmillan.

Carey, J. & Kreiling, A. 1974: Cultural studies and uses and gratifications. In Blumler & Katz 1974.

Cassirer, E. 1946: *The myth of the state*. New Haven: Yale University Press.

Chapman, S. F. 1979: Advertising and psychotropic drugs; the place of myth in ideological reproduction. *Social Science and Medicine* 13, 751-64.

Chibnall, S. 1977: *Law-and-order news*. London: Tavistock.

Clarke, A., Taylor, I. & Wren-Lewis, J. 1981: Inequality of access to political television: the case of the general election of 1979. Paper presented to the Annual Conference of the British Sociological Association, University College of Wales, Aberystwyth, 6-9 April.

Clegg, S. 1978: Towards a re-conceptualisation of organisations as a total power phenomenon: an essay in social theory. Paper presented to the 1978 conference of the Sociological Association of Australia and New Zealand, University of Queensland, St Lucia.

Cobler, S. 1978: *Law, order and politics in West Germany*. Harmondsworth: Penguin.

Cohen, P. & Robbins, D. 1978: *Knuckle sandwich*. Harmondsworth: Penguin.

Cohen, S. & Young, J., editors, 1973: *The manufacture of news*. London: Constable.

Cooper, D. 1974: *Presupposition*. The Hague: Mouton.

Corner, J. 1980: Codes and cultural analysis. In *Media, Culture and Society* 2, 73–86.

Coulter, J. 1979a: *The social construction of mind*. Totowa, N.J.: Rowman & Littlefield.

Coulter, J. 1979b: Beliefs and practical understanding. In Psathas 1979.

Coulthard, M. 1977: *An introduction to discourse analysis*. London: Longman.

Coward, R. & Ellis, J. 1977: *Language and materialism*. London: Routledge & Kegan Paul.

Critcher, C. 1975: Structures, cultures and biographies. *Working Papers in Cultural Studies* 7/8, 167-73.

Curran, Sir Charles 1979: *A seamless robe: broadcasting philosophy and practice*. London: Bodley Head.

Davis, H. H. 1979: *Beyond class images: explorations in the structure of social consciousness*. London: Croom Helm.

Davis, H. & Walton, P. 1976: Bad news: TV and the new linguistics. *Theory and Society* 3, no. 3.

Davis, H. & Walton, P. 1977a: News ideology: neutrality and naturalism. *Papers in Linguistics* vol. 10 (3-4), 313-39.

Davis, H. & Walton, P. 1977b: Bad news for trade unionists. In Beharrell & Philo 1977.

Davis, H. & Walton, P. 1983: Sources of variation in news vocabulary: a comparative analysis. *International Journal of the Sociology of language* 40.

Davis, H. & Walton, P. 1982: Sources of variation in news vocabulary: a comparative analysis. *International Journal of the Sociology of language* 34.

Derrida, J. 1976: *Of grammatology*, translated by G. C. Spivak. Baltimore: Johns Hopkins University Press.

Dittmar, N. 1976: *Sociolinguistics. A critical survey*. London: Edward Arnold.

Dobb, M. 1973: *Theories of value and distribution since Adam Smith: ideology and economic theory*. Cambridge: CUP.

Dorfman, A. & Mattelart, A. 1975: *How to read Donald Duck*. New York: International General.

Duncan, H. D. 1972: *Symbols in society*. London: OUP.

Dunoon, D. 1980: *Survey of Sydney school children's cigarette brand preferences*. Monograph of the Movement Opposed to the Promotion of Unhealthy Products (MOP UP), Kensington, NSW, Aus.

Eagleton, T. 1975: *Myths of power: a marxist study of the Brontës*. London: Macmillan.

Eagleton, T. 1976: *Criticism and ideology*. London: New Left Books.

Eagly, R. V., editor, 1968: *Events, ideology and economic theory*. Cambridge: CUP.

Eco, U. 1972: Towards a semiotic enquiry into the television message. *Working Papers in Cultural Studies* 3, 103-21.

Economist Intelligence Unit 1979: Special Report No 70, *The UK market for amateur photography*. London: Economist.

Egger, G. J. & Champion, R. A. 1978: Adolescent drug and alcohol use in NSW 1971-1977. Report of the Health Commission of NSW, Aus.

Egger, G., Moniem, A. & Munro, R. 1978: *North Coast Healthy Lifestyle Program* research report no 1. Sydney: Health Commission of NSW.

Eliade, M. 1957: *Myths, dreams and mysteries*. New York: Harper Torch Books.

Elliott, P. 1972: *The making of a television series*. London: Constable.

Elliott, P. 1977: Reporting Northern Ireland: a study of news in Britain, Ulster and the Irish Republic. In *Ethnicity and the media*. Paris: UNESCO.

Emmett, B. 1972: The television and radio audience in Britain. In McQuail, 1972.

Epstein, E. J. 1973: *News from nowhere: television and news*. New York: Random House.

Fillmore, C. J. & Langendcon, P. T., editors, 1971: *Studies in linguistic semantics*. New York: Macmillan.

Fishman, J. 1974: The sociology of language. In Sebeok, T., editor, *Current Trends in Linguistics* 12, 3 (The Hague).

Fishman, M. 1978: Crime waves as ideology. *Social Problems* 25, 531-43.

Foucault, M. 1979: Governmentality. *Ideology and Consciousness* 6, 5-21.

Fowler, R. *et al.*, 1979: *Language and control*. London: Routledge & Kegan Paul.

Frank, R. S. 1973: *Message dimensions of television news*. Lexington, Mass.: Lexington Books.

Fraser, B. 1979: The interpretation of novel metaphors. In Ortony 1979.

Freud, S. 1953a: The interpretation of dreams. *Standard edition of the complete psychological works of Sigmund Freud, vol. IV*. London: Hogarth Press.

Freud, S. 1953b: Fragment of an analysis of a case of hysteria. *Standard edition of the complete psychological works of Sigmund Freud*, vol. VII. London: Hogarth Press.

Freud, S. 1959: Creative writers and day-dreaming. *Standard edition of the complete psychological works of Sigmund Freud*, vol. IX. London: Hogarth Press.

Freud, S. 1961a: Introductory lectures on psychoanalysis. *Standard edition of the complete psychological works of Sigmund Freud*, vol. XV. London: Hogarth Press.

Freud, S. 1961b: The Ego and the Id. *Standard edition of the complete psychological works of Sigmund Freud*, vol. XIX. London: Hogarth Press.

Friedlander, L. 1979: *Self portrait*. New City, NY: Haywire Press.

Frith, S. 1980: Music for pleasure. *Screen Education* 34, Spring.

Gans, H. J. 1979: *Deciding what's news*. New York: Pantheon Books.

Garfinkel, H. 1967: *Studies in ethnomethodology*. Englewood Cliffs, NJ: Prentice-Hall.

Gazdar, G. 1979: *Pragmatics*. New York: Academic Press.

Gellis, R. & Faulkner, R. 1978: Time and television news: task temporalization in the assembly of unscheduled events. *Sociological Quarterly* 19, 89-102.

Gerbner, G. 1964: Ideological perspectives and political tendencies in news reporting. *Journalism Quarterly* 41, 4, 495-508.

Ghiselin, B. 1955: *The creative process*. New York: Mentor.

Gibson, J. J. 1967: Constancy and invariance in perception. In Kepes, G., editor, *The nature and art of motion*. London: Studio Vista.

Giglioli, P., editor, 1972: *Language and social context*. Harmondsworth: Penguin.

Gimson, A. 1970: *An introduction to the pronunciation of English*. London: Edward Arnold.

Gimson, A. 1977: *English pronouncing dictionary*. London: Edward Arnold.

Glasgow University Media Group 1976: *Bad news*. London: Routledge & Kegan Paul.

Glasgow University Media Group 1980: *More bad news*. London: Routledge & Kegan Paul.

Goffman, E. 1971: *Encounters*. Harmondsworth: Penguin.

Goffman, E. 1978: *Gender advertisements*. London: Macmillan.

Golding, P. & Elliott, P. 1980: *Making the news*. London: Longman.

Golding, P. & Middleton, S. 1982: *Images of welfare*. Oxford: Martin Robertson.

Golding, P. & Murdock, G. 1978: Theories of communication and theories of society. *Communication Research* 5, 339-56.

Goldmann, L. 1967: The sociology of literature: status and problems of method. *International Social Science Journal* XIX, 4.

Goldway, D. 1967: Appearance and reality in Marx's Capital. *Science and Society* 31, 428-47.

Gombrich, E. H. 1972: *Symbolic images*. Oxford: Phaidon.

Goody, J., editor, 1968: *Literacy in traditional societies*. Cambridge: CUP.

Gray, N. J. & Hill, D. J. 1977: Patterns of tobacco smoking in Australia. *Med. J. Aust.* 2, 327-8.

Greenberg, C. 1961: Modernist painting. In *Arts Year Book*, vol. 4.

Greimas, A. J. 1972: Comparative mythology. In Maranda 1972.

Greenberg, C. 1964: Four photographers. *New York Review of Books* 23 Jan.

Grice, H. 1957: Meaning. Originally in *Philosophical Review* and much reprinted, e.g. in Strawson, P., editor, *Philosophical logic*. Oxford: University Press (1967).

Grice, H. 1975: Logic and Conversation. In Cole, P. & Morgan, J., editors, *Syntax and semantics*, vol. 3, *Speech acts*. New York: Academic Press.

Habermas, J. 1979: *Communication and the evolution of society.* London: Heinemann.

Hall, S. 1972: The determinations of news photographs. *Working Papers in Cultural Studies* 3, 53-87.

Hall, S. 1973: Encoding and decoding in the television discourse. Stencilled occasional paper, Centre for Contemporary Cultural Studies, University of Birmingham.

Hall, S. 1977. Culture, the media and the ideological effect. In Curran, J., Gurevitch, M. & Woollacott, J., editors, *Mass communication and society.* London: Edward Arnold.

Hall, S., Connell, I., & Curti, L. 1976: The 'unity' of current affairs television. *Working Papers in Cultural Studies* 9, 51-93.

Hall, S., Critcher, C., Jefferson, T., Clarke, J. & Roberts, B. 1978: *Policing the crisis.* London: Macmillan.

Hall, S. & Jefferson, T., editors, 1976: *Resistance through rituals.* London: Hutchinson.

Halliday, M. A. K. 1971: Language structure and language function. In Lyons, J., editor, *New horizons in linguistics.* Harmondsworth: Penguin.

Halliday, M. A. K. 1979: *Language as social semiotic.* London: Edward Arnold.

Halloran, J., Elliott, P. & Murdock, G. 1970: *Demonstrations and communication.* Harmondsworth: Penguin.

Halmos, P., editor, 1969: *The sociology of mass media communication.* Keele: University of Keele.

Hamilton, A. 1975: Snugglepot and Cuddlepie: happy families in Australian society. *Mankind* 10, 84-92.

Hartmann, P. 1976: Industrial relations in the news media. *Industrial Relations Journal* 6, 4-18.

Hartmann, P. 1979: News and public perceptions of industrial relations. *Media, culture and society* 1, 255-70.

Hartmann, P. *et al.* 1970. *Race as news: a study of the handling of race in the British national press from 1963 to 1970.* Paris: UNESCO.

Hartmann, P. & Husband, C. 1974: *Racism and the mass media.* London: Davis-Poynter.

Harvey, S. 1978: *May '68 and film culture.* London: British Film Institute.

Henderson, J. L. 1964: Ancient myths and modern man. In Jung, C. J., editor, *Man and his symbols.* New York: Dell Publishing.

Hill, J. 1979: Ideology, economy and the British cinema. In Barrett *et al.* 1979.

Hoggart, R. 1957: *The uses of literacy.* London: Chatto & Windus (Penguin, 1969).

Holman, C. H. 1972: *A handbook to literature.* New York: Odyssey Press.

Holmes, E. 1974: *An age of cameras.* Fountain Press.

Horowitz, M. J. 1970: *Image formation and cognition.* New York: Meredith.

Independent Broadcasting Authority 1978: *The need for news: audience attitudes towards nine news topics.* London: IBA.

Jalbert, P. L. 1978: Ideology and language: a discussion of their relationship. Unpublished MA thesis: University of Boston.

Janowitz, M. 1975: Professional models in journalism: the gatekeeper and the advocate. *Journalism Quarterly* 52, 618-26.

Jayyusi, L. 1979: Categorization and the moral order: studies in practical reasoning. Unpublished PhD thesis: University of Manchester.

Johnstone, J. W. *et al.* 1976: *The news people: a sociological portrait of American journalists and their work.* Urbana: University of Illinois Press.

Jones, D. 1969: *An outline of English pronunciation.* Cambridge: Heffers.

Katz, J. 1972: *Semantic theory.* New York: Harper & Row.

Kempson, R. 1975: *Presupposition and the delimitation of semantics.* Cambridge: University Press.

Keynes, J. M. 1936: *The general theory of employment, interest and money.* London: Macmillan.

Kohler, K. 1970: Deutsche Hochlautung. *Muttersprache* 80, 238-47.

König, R. 1973: *The restless image. A sociology of fashion.* London: George Allen & Unwin.

Kress, G. R. & Hodge, R. 1979: *Language as ideology.* London: Routledge & Kegan Paul.

Kress, G. R. & Trew, A. A. 1978: Ideological transformation of discourse: or how the *Sunday Times* got its message across. *Sociological Review* 26, no. 4, 755-76 and *Journal of Pragmatics* 2, 311-29.

Labov, W. 1969: The logic of nonstandard English. In Giglioli 1972.

Labov, W. & Fanshel, D. 1977: *Therapeutic discourse.* New York.

Laclau, E. 1979: *Politics and ideology in marxist theory.* London: New Left Books.

Lakoff, R. 1976: *Language and woman's place.* New York: Harper & Row.

Lang, K. & Lang, G. 1953: The unique perspective of television and its effects: a pilot study. *American Sociological Review* 18, 3-12.

Langholz Leymore, V. 1975: *Hidden myth: structure and symbolism in advertising.* London: Heinemann.

Lazarsfeld, P. 1972: *Qualitative analysis.* Boston, Mass.: Allyn & Bacon.

Leggett, J. C., de James, D. V., Somma, J. & Menendez, T. 1978: *Allende, his exit and our 'Times'.* New Brunswick: Cooperative.

Leitner, G. 1979: BBC English und der BBC. Geschichte und soziolinguistische Interpretation des Sprachgebrauchs in einem Massenmedium. *Linguistische Berichte. Papiere 60.* Braunschweig: Vieweg Verlag.

Leitner, G. 1980: 'BBC English' and 'Deutsche Rundfunksprache': a comparative and historical analysis of the language of radio. *International Journal of the Sociology of Language* 26, 75-100.

Leitner, G. 1982: The consolidation of 'educated southern English' as a model in the early 20th century. *International Review of Applied Linguistics in Language Teaching* 20, 91-107.

Lerman, C. L. 1981: A sociolinguistic study of political discourse: the Nixon White House conversations. Unpublished PhD dissertation: University of Cambridge.

Levinson, S. 1978: Activity types and language. *Pragmatics* 3,

Lévi-Strauss, C. 1964: *Totemism*, Harmondsworth: Penguin.

Lévi-Strauss, C. 1968: *Structural anthropology*. Harmondsworth: Penguin.

Lévi-Strauss, C. 1969: *The raw and the cooked*. New York: Harper & Row.

Lewicki, A., Masłowski, W., Sambor, J. & Woronczak, J. 1971: *Słownictwo współczesnej publicystyki polskiej: Listy frekwencyjne*. Warsaw.

Lovell, T. 1980: *Pictures of reality: aesthetics, politics and pleasure*. London: British Film Institute.

Lyotard, J.-F. 1971: *Discours, figure*. Paris: Klincksieck.

McKeganey, N. & Smith, B. 1980: Reading and writing as collaborative production. *Sociology* 14, 615-21.

McLuhan, M. 1959: Myth and mass media. *Daedalus* 88, 329-48.

McQuail, D. 1969: *Towards a sociology of mass communications*. London: Collier-Macmillan.

McQuail, D., editor, 1972: *Sociology of mass communications*. Harmondsworth: Penguin.

McQuail, D. 1977: *Analysis of newspaper content*. Royal Commission on the Press, Research Series No. 4. London: HMSO.

Mann, M. 1973: *Consciousness and action among the western working class*. London: Macmillan.

Mant, A. & Darroch, D. B. 1975: Media images and medical images. *Social Science and Medicine* 9, 613-18.

Maranda, P., editor, 1972: *Mythology*. Harmondsworth: Penguin.

Marx, K. 1959: *Capital*, vol. III. Moscow: Progress Publishers.

Marx, K. 1973: *Grundrisse*. Harmondsworth: Penguin.

Mattelart, A. & Siegelaub, S., editors, 1979: *Communication and class struggle*, vol. 1. New York: International General.

Meek, R. 1967: *Economics and ideology and other essays*. London: Chapman & Hall.

Merton, R. & Kendall, P. 1946: The focused interview. *American Journal of Sociology*, L1, 541-57.

Metz, C. 1974: *Film language*. New York: Oxford University Press.

Miliband, R. 1969: *The state in capitalist society*. London: Weidenfeld & Nicolson.

Mills, C. Wright 1939: *Power, politics and people*. London/New York: OUP.

Mistrik, J. 1968: *Slovnik tlače*. Bratislava.

Morley, D. 1974: Reconceptualising the media audience. Stencilled occasional paper, Centre for Contemporary Cultural Studies, University of Birmingham.

Morley, D. 1976: Industrial conflict and the mass media. *Sociological Review* 24, 245-68.

Morley, D. 1980: *The 'Nationwide' audience.* London: British Film Institute.

Mueller, C. 1978: *The politics of communication.* New York: OUP.

Munby, J. 1978: *Communicative syllabus design.* Cambridge: CUP.

Murdock, G. 1976: Youth in contemporary Britain: misleading imagery and misapplied action. In Marsland, D., and Day, M., editors, *Youth Service; youth work and the future.* NYB occasional paper, 12 March 1976, pp. 15-17.

Murdock, G. 1980: Misrepresenting media sociology. *Sociology* 14, 457-68.

Neale, S. 1977: Propaganda. *Screen* 18, 3, 9-40.

Nichols, T. & Armstrong, P. 1976: *Workers divided.* London: Fontana.

Ogilvy, Benson & Mather 1978: *A consumer's view of how advertising works.* London: Ogilvy, Benson & Mather Planning and Research Unit.

Ortony, A., editor, 1979: *Metaphor and thought.* Cambridge: CUP.

Orwell, G. 1949: *1984.* London: Secker & Warburg.

Parkin, F. 1971: *Class inequality and political order.* London: MacGibbon & Kee (also Paladin, 1972).

Pateman, T. 1973: review of R. Barthes, *Mythologies. The Human Context* 5 (reprinted in Pateman 1980c).

Pateman, T. 1974a: Ideological criticism of television technical manuals. *Screen Education* 12, 37-45.

Pateman, T. 1974b: The painted face of capitalism. *Women and Film* 5/6, 97-9.

Pateman, T. 1974c: *Television and the February 1974 General Election.* London: British Film Institute.

Pateman, T. 1980a: How to do things with images. *Theory and Society* 10, 20-30 (reprinted as Appendix 5 to Pateman 1980b).

Pateman, T. 1980b: *Language, truth and politics* (second edition). Lewes: Jean Stroud.

Pateman, T. 1981: On communicating with computer programs. *Language and Communication* 1, 3-12.

Petöfi, J. S. & Franck, D., editors, 1973: *Präsuppositionen in Philosophie und Linguistik.* Frankfurt: Athenäum.

Philo, G., Hewitt, P., Beharrell, P. & Davis, H. 1982. *Really bad news.* London: Writers & Readers Cooperative.

Peirce, C. 1940: *The philosophy of Peirce, selected writings,* edited by J. Buchler. London: Routledge & Kegan Paul.

Piepe, T., Emerson, M. & Lannon, J. 1978: *Mass media and cultural relationships.* Farnborough Saxon House.

Polakova, G. P. & Solganik, G. A. 1971: *Chastotnie slovary yasyka gazeta.* Moscow.

Polanyi, K. 1971: The economy as an instituted process *and* Aristotle discovers the economy. In Dalton, G., editor, *Primitive, archaic and modern economics: essays of Karl Polanyi.* Boston, Mass.: Beacon Press.

Powers, R. 1977: *The newscasters: the news business as show business.* New York: St Martin's Press.

Prather, J. & Fidell, L. S. 1975: Sex differences in the content and style of medical advertisements. *Soc. Sci. Med.* 9, 23-26.

Pratt, M. 1977: *Towards a speech act theory of literary discourse*. Bloomington: Indiana University Press.

Pribram, K. H. 1969: The neurophysiology of remembering. *Scientific American*, January.

Psathas, G., editor, 1979: *Everyday language: studies in ethnomethodology*. New York: Irvington Publishers.

Quine, W. V. 1960: *Word and object*. Cambridge, Mass.: MIT.

Quirk, R. 1980: Speaking into the air. Unpublished MS for the Leeds Castle Symposium on 'The Foundations of Broadcasting Policy', 17 May 1980.

Raffel, S. 1979: *Matters of fact*. London: Routledge & Kegan Paul.

Ricoeur, P. 1976: *Interpretation theory*. Fort Worth, Tx.: Texas Christian University Press.

Robinson, J. 1964: *Economic philosophy*. Harmondsworth: Penguin.

Ronchey, A. 1978: Terror in Italy. *Dissent*, Spring.

Rosaldo, M. 1973: I have nothing to hide. *Language and Society* 2, 193-223.

Rosen, H. 1972: *Language and class*. Bristol: Falling Wall Press.

Rosenblum, B. 1978: *Photographers at work: a sociology of photographic styles*. New York: Holmes & Meier.

Rosengren, I. 1972: *Ein Frequenzwörterbuch der deutschen Zeitungssprache. Die Welt, Süddeutsche Zeitung*. Lund.

Rositi, F. 1976: *The television news programme: fragmentation and recomposition of our image of society*. Radiotelevisione Italiana.

Ross, Sir D., editor, 1971: *The works of Aristotle*, vol. XI, *Rhetorica*. Oxford: Clarendon.

Rossbacher, P. 1966: The Soviet journalistic style. *Gazette* 2/3, 201-11.

Sacks, H. 1972: An initial investigation of the useability of conversational data for doing sociology. In Sudnow, D., editor, *Studies in social interaction*. New York: Free Press.

Sacks, H. 1974: On the analysability of stories by children. In Turner 1974.

Sacks, H. 1975: Everyone has to lie. In Sanches & Blount 1975.

Sacks, H. & Schegloff, E. A. 1979: Two preferences in the organisation of reference to persons in conversation and their interaction. In Psathas 1979.

Safire, W. 1975: *Before the fall*. New York.

Sanches, M. & Blount, B. G., editors, 1975: *Sociocultural dimensions of language use*. New York/London: Academic Press.

Saussure, F. de 1959: *Course in general linguistics*, translated by W. Baskin. New York: McGraw Hill.

Schank, R. & Abelson, H. 1977: *Scripts, plans, goals and understanding*. New Jersey: Lawrence Erlbaum Associates.

Schlesinger, P. 1978: *Putting 'reality' together: BBC news*. London: Constable.

Schudson, M. 1978: *Discovering the news*. New York: Basic Books.

Schumann, H.-G. 1975: Ideologische Probleme der Nachrichtensprache. In Strassner, E., editor, *Nachrichten*. Munich: Wilhelm Fink Verlag.

Schütte, W. 1971: *Regionalität und Föderalismus im Rundfunk (1923-45).* Frankfurt/Main: Josef Knecht.

Schutz, A. 1964: *Selected papers*, vol. 2. The Hague: Nijhoff.

Searle, J. 1969: *Speech acts.* London: Cambridge University Press.

Sheehan, T. 1978: Behind the ski mask. *New York Review of Books* 16 Aug.

Sigelman, L. 1979: Reporting the news: an organizational analysis. *American Journal of Sociology* 79, 132-51.

Sinclair, J. 1978: *The teacher's accents of English* (with accompanying tape). Wuppertal: Centre of British Teachers in Europe.

Slobin, D. I. 1974: *Psycholinguistics.* Glenview: Scott Foresman.

Sloman, A. 1978: *The computer revolution in philosophy.* Hassocks: Harvester.

Smith, A. 1974: *British broadcasting.* London: David & Charles.

Smith, D. 1978: 'K is mentally ill': the anatomy of a factual account. *Sociology* 12, 23-53.

Smith, N. & Wilson, D. 1979: *Modern linguistics.* Harmondsworth: Penguin Books.

Smith, R. R. 1979: Mythic elements in television news. *Journal of Communication* 29, 51-7.

Spender, D. 1980: *Man made language.* London: Routledge & Kegan Paul.

Sperber, D. & Wilson, D. 1979: L'interprétation des énoncés. *Communications* 30, 80-94.

Stange, M. 1978: Szarkowski at the Modern. In *Photography: current perspectives.* Rochester, NY: Light Impressions.

Stich, A. 1973: Persuasive style: its relation to technical and artistic styles. *Journal of Literary Semantics* 2, 65-77.

Sumner, C. 1979: *Reading ideologies.* London: Academic Press.

Syme, R. 1939: *Roman revolution*, London: OUP.

Szarkowski, J. 1966: *The photographer's eye.* New York: Museum of Modern Art.

Szarkowski, J. *et al.* 1971: *New photography USA.* Università di Parma/New York: Museum of Modern Art.

Szasz, T. 1961: *The myth of mental illness.* New York: Hoeber/Harper.

Therborn, G. 1976: *Science, class and society.* London: New Left Books.

Thompson, E. L. 1978: Smoking education programmes: 1960-76. *American Journal of Public Health* 68, 250.

Tracey, M. 1977: *The production of political television.* London: Routledge & Kegan Paul.

Tribe, K. 1978: *Land, labour and economic discourse.* London: Routledge & Kegan Paul.

Tuchman, G. 1972: Objectivity as strategic ritual: an examination of newsmen's notions of objectivity. *American Journal of Sociology* 77, 660-79.

Tuchman, G. 1978: *Making news.* New York: Free Press.

Tunstall, J. 1970: *The Westminster lobby correspondents.* London: Routledge & Kegan Paul.

Tunstall, J. 1971: *Journalists at work.* London: Constable.

Turner, R., editor, 1974: *Ethnomethodology*. Harmondsworth: Penguin.

Tyler, S. 1971: *Cognitive anthropology*. New York: Holt Rinehart & Winston.

Tyler, S. 1978: *The said and the unsaid*. New York/London: Academic Press.

US Government Printing Office 1974a: *Presidential statements on the Watergate break-in and its investigation*. Washington DC.

US Government Printing Office 1974b: *Transcripts of eight recorded presidential conversations*. Washington DC.

Voloshinov, V. N. 1973: *Marxism and the philosophy of language*. New York: Seminar Press.

Vygotsky, L. 1977: *Thought and language*. Cambridge, Mass.: MIT.

Wenham, B. 1981: Talking heads. *Listener* 29 Oct. 490-2.

Willemen, P. 1978: Notes on subjectivity. *Screen* 19, no. 1, 41-69.

Williams, R 1961: *The long revolution*, London: Chatto and Windus (Penguin, 1965).

Williams, R. 1962: *Communications*. Harmondsworth: Penguin.

Williams, R. 1974: *Television: technology and cultural form*. London: Fontana.

Williams, R. 1976: *Keywords*. London: Fontana/Croom Helm.

Williamson, J. 1978: *Decoding Advertisements*. London: Marian Boyars.

Willis, P. 1978: *Profane culture*. London: Routledge & Kegan Paul.

Wilson, D. 1975: *Presupposition and non-truth — conditional semantics*. New York: Academic Press.

Winogrand, Gary 1976: Catalogue. Grossmont College Gallery. El Cajon, California.

Wisman, J. 1979: Legitimation, ideology-critique and economics. *Social Research* 46, 291-320.

Wittgenstein, L. 1974: *Tractatus logico-philosophicus*. London: Routledge & Kegan Paul.

Wollen, P. 1972: *Signs and meanings in the cinema*, 2nd edn. London: Secker & Warburg.

Wood, S. & Elliott, R. 1977: A critical evaluation of Fox's radicalization of industrial relations theory. *Sociology* 11, no. 1, 105-25.

Woods, R. 1977: Discourse analysis: the work of Michel Pecheux. *Ideology & Consciousness* 2.

Woolfson, C. 1976: The semiotics of working class speech. *Working Papers in Cultural Studies* 9, 163-97.

Wright, C. B. 1935: *Middle class culture in Elizabethan England*. University of North Carolina Press.

Wyld, H. 1936: *A history of modern colloquial English*. Oxford: Blackwell.

# Contributors

Victor Burgin is Senior Lecturer in the School of Communication, Polytechnic of Central London. Previous publications include *Two essays on art photography and semiotics* (London: Robert Self, 1976) and *Thinking Photography* (London: Macmillan, 1981).

Simon Chapman taught sociology and health education in the Department of Preventive and Social Medicine at the University of Sydney. He has published work on tobacco advertising and voluntary codes of advertising. He is presently Director of Anti-Smoking and Health Education for the government of New South Wales, Australia.

John Corner spent twleve years in naval communications and a brief spell as a features reporter before studying at the universities of Oxford and Cambridge. He taught Communication Studies at Sunderland Polytechnic and is now Lecturer in the Centre for Communication Studies at the University of Liverpool.

Howard Davis is lecturer in the Faculty of Social Sciences, University of Kent. He was Research Fellow with the Glasgow University Media Group 1974-76 and co-author of *Bad news* and *More bad news* (both Routledge & Kegan Paul, 1976, 1980). His PhD thesis was published as *Beyond class images* (London: Croom Helm, 1979).

Garry Egger spent some time as a consultant in marketing and market research before moving to health research. He is currently Research Director of the North Coast Healthy Lifestyle Program, Lismore, NSW, Australia.

Mike Emmison has degrees in Sociology from the universities of Bradford and York. He is currently a tutor and a doctoral candidate in Sociology at the University of Queensland, Australia. His present research is concerned with lay perceptions of economic practices and media presentation of economic discourse.

Paul L. Jalbert is doing research in the Department of Sociology, Boston University.

Gunther Kress is Dean of the School of Communication and Cultural Studies, Hartley College of Advanced Education, South Australia. He is co-author of *Language as ideology* (London: Routledge & Kegan Paul, 1979).

Gerhard Leitner is Professor of English, Free University of Berlin. He is editor of a special issue of the *International Journal of the Sociology of Language* on 'Language and mass media' (1983).

Claire Lindegren Lerman has spent much of her life observing institutional voices in the academic and political worlds of the United States and Britain. She has recently gained her PhD in discourse analysis from the University of Cambridge.

David Morley has worked for a number of years with the media group of the Centre for Contemporary Cultural Studies at the University of Birmingham. He is currently Lecturer in Communications at Lanchester Polytechnic.

Kathy Myers studied for her first degree at the University of Cambridge and is currently doing research at Goldsmiths' College, University of London, into visual aspects of culture and the identification of women.

Trevor Pateman is Lecturer in the Department of Education, University of Sussex. Previous publications include *Language, truth and politics* (2nd edn Lewes: Jean Stroud, 1980).

Walvery Pisarek has contributed to numerous international journals and conferences. He is a member of the Press Research Centre, Cracow, Poland.

Don Slater works at the Half Moon Photography Workshop as joint coordinator of *Camerawork*. He taught for three years at the Central School of Art and Design and has been doing research on the ideology and organization of the advertising industry.

Paul Walton is Reader in Communications, Goldsmiths' College, University of London. He has published books on sociology, criminology and economics and is co-author with the members of the Glasgow Media Group of *Bad news* and *More bad news*. His latest book is *Space-light: a holography and laser spectacular* (London: Routledge & Kegan Paul, 1982).

# Index

ABC (Australia) 150
ABC (USA) 290
Abelson, H. 189, 191, 202-3n.
activity type 189-90, 203n.
advertising 4, 166-223, 230, 247, 256
    agencies 214-21
    anti-smoking 184-6
    butter 210
    cosmetics 218-19
    identifying 188-9, 206-14
    in women's magazines 204-14
    pharmaceuticals 186n.
    production of 205-14
    tobacco 166-86, 196-8
    types of 207
    see also Benson & Hedges; Boots 17;
        Guinness
Advisory Committee on Spoken English
    60-1, 63-4, 68, 72n., 73n.
Age, The 128, 130, 132-6
agenda-setting 9
Agfa 249
Althusser, L. 190, 259
Anderson, D. 4
Annan Report 56, 59-60, 68, 73n.
ARD 15, 41, 49n.
Armstrong, P. 110
Armstrong, R. P. 171
audience
    for radio 65-71
    problem of 261
    research 117, 266
    sections of 105-7, 110
    target 205-6, 218-19, 223n.
Austin, J. L. 295
Australian Broadcasting Tribunal 124
Australian, The 151, 153

BBC 50, 74
    Chrysler story 273-4
    Moro story 16-39
    radio 56-7
    Thatcher interviews 95, 97
Bach, K. 200, 203n., 204n.
balance 8-10, 15, 54
Bazon, A. 271
Barthes, R. 44, 168, 170, 173, 188, 196,
    202, 239, 270, 277
Bell, C. 241
Bennett, T. 269
Benson & Hedges 191, 215-16
Bernstein, B. 108-9
bias 8, 43, 73n.
Bloch, M. 81
Bolinger, D. 288
Bonsiepe, G. 201
Boots 17 218-19, 223n.
Bourdieu, P. 245
Boyd, R. 204n.
Broadcasting Act (1980) 60
Brunsdon, C. 106, 108, 111, 271
Burgin, V. 260

cameras 249-53
    sales 249, 253
Carter, J. 96-7
Cassirer, E. 170-1
categorization devices 282-8
Champion, R. 184
Chapman, S. 169, 186n.
Chicago Tribune 40-1
Chomsky, N. 192
Clegg, S. 154

closure 8-9, 15, 273, 279-80
  ideological 273, 276
  moral 14, 47-8
  see also consensus
Cobler, S. 48
code 3, 51, 104, 105-17, 239, 270
  connotative 216
  decoding 113-16, 172-3, 205, 222, 257, 259, 267, 278
  encoding, 10, 44, 107, 222, 266
  non-complementarity of 105-7
  restricted 43
  switching 54
commodity fetishism 143-5, 255; see also fetishism
communications 1-4
  interpersonal 65-8
  non-reciprocal 200
  theory of 104, 189, 202, 222, 268
connotation 196, 198-9, 215, 272, 276
  dictionary of 198
consensus 8-10, 48; see also closure
content analysis 3, 140
conversation analysis 283, 295
Corner, J. 270
Coulter, J. 295

Daily Express 40
Daily Mirror 40, 42
Daily News 41
Daily Star 272, 274-6
Daily Telegraph 40
decoding see code
de-construction 282, 298n.
denotation 215, 271; see also connotation
de re/de dicto reports 290-4, 297
Derrida, J. 298n.
Dictionary Fallacy 195, 198
discourse 75, 106, 235, 243, 259
  analysis 3
  dominant 75-103
  economic 139-55
  media, and power 278-81
  photography and 256-7
  subject of 78
distancing 42, 81-8
  markers of 85-7
Dorfman, A. 168
Duncan, H. 170

Eagleton, T. 268-9
Eco, U. 105, 278
Economist 145, 147, 149
Economist Intelligence Unit 248-50
economy 139-55

Egger, G. 184
Eliade, M. 167
Elliott, P. 10, 298n.
encoding see code
ethnomethodology 4, 258
exclusion, techniques of 15, 40-3
  boundaries 47

fetishism 245, 254, 256
Financial Times 40-1
Foucault, M. 140
Fowler, R. 281
Fraser, B. 198, 288
Freud, S. 3, 228-31, 233, 243
Friedlander, L. 236-8
Frith, S. 221-2

Gazdar, G. 204n.
Ghiselin, B. 228
Gibson, J. 227
Glasgow University Media Group 1, 5n., 10, 15, 42, 45, 51, 54, 74n., 155n., 271, 273-4, 298n.
Goffman, E. 168, 170, 172
Golding, P. 10
Goldmann, L. 268
Goldway, D. 144-5, 150
Gombrich, E. 243-4
Gray, N. 184, 186n.
Greenberg, C. 240-2
Greene, H. 59, 65-6
Grice, H. 197, 200, 202n., 204n.
Guardian 40-1
Guinness 191, 215

Habermas, J. 142, 200, 204n.
Hall, S. 105, 109, 170, 267, 271, 275, 277, 298n.
Halliday, M. 138
Hamilton, A. 168
Harnish, R. 200, 203n., 204n.
headlines 14-15
Heath, E. 80, 98
Henderson, J. 182
Hill, D. 184, 186n.
Hill, J. 106-7, 266
Hodge, R. 281
Hoggart, R. 2, 298n.
Holman, C. 288
Holmes, E. 250
Horowitz, M. J. 228, 231-2, 235
Horowitz, R. 205, 223n.

icon 43, 140, 191, 194
  in advertising 195

iconic
    representations, and analogic 203n.
    shots 45-6
ideological
    effect 143, 258, 294
    form 104-5
    reduction 42
    structure, and linguistic structure 122
ideology 3, 47, 68, 120-38, 151, 168, 173,
    282, 297
illocutionary 191, 295
index 43, 45
Institutional Voice 75-103
    characteristics of 77
    media IV 99-102
intentionality 43, 190, 274, 277, 287
    of advertisers 200, 214-21
*International Herald Tribune* 96, 98
ITN 9, 49n., 53

James, L. 61, 70, 72n., 74n.
Jayyusi, L. 294

Katz, J. 192
Kempson, R. 204n.
Keynes, J. M. 147-9
Kodak 248-53
König, R. 221
Kress, G. 51, 54, 122, 281

labelling 15, 274
Labov, W. 108
Lacan, J. 204n.
Laclau, E. 297
Lakoff, R. 108
Langholz Leymore, V. 171-2
language
    domain 55
    *langue* 102, 201
    media 269-71
    of radio 50-74
Leitner, G. 51, 54, 103n.
Levinson, S. 189
Lévi-Strauss, C. 168, 171, 197
lexeme, boundaries of 43
Liddell, A. 68, 73n.
linguistics 189; *see also* sociolinguistics
*Los Angeles Times* 40-1
Lovell, T. 258
Lyotard, J-F. 231

Mann, M. 110
Maranda, P. 167
marketing 205-6, 214-21
Marx, K. 143-4, 247-8

Marxism 221-2
    and structuralism 261-2
Mattelart, A. 104, 168
McKeganey, N. 4
McLuhan, M. 167
meaning
    contextual 136
    intention and 239
    interpersonal 134-6
    systems 109
metaphor 76, 87, 103n., 146, 150, 156-7,
    163, 198, 201, 243, 258, 262, 284
methodology 128, 266-99
metonym 193, 243, 282
metonymic
    reification 288-90
    substitution 196
Metz, C. 270-1
Mills, C. Wright 111
*Miami Herald* 40
Mintel 248
modernism 240-2
Morley, D. 106, 108, 110-11, 266-7, 271,
    279
Moro, A. 12-42
Mueller, C. 287
multi-accentuality 276
Murdock, G. 4, 298n.
myth/myths 167, 169, 171
    hero 182-3

narrative 45, 231, 234, 242-3, 271
Nationwide 106, 111, 113
NBC
    and hostage crisis 96
    Moro news story 16-39
news
    reading 68-9
    reporting 8-49, 52-3, 120-37, 272-8,
    282-98
*News, The* 122, 131-4
*New Statesman* 145, 147-8
*Newsweek* 282-3, 295-6
*New York Times* 40-1, 145
Nichols, T. 110
Nixon, R. 75-93

orthoepism 64, 69
Ortony, A. 204n.

Parkin, F. 109-10, 113, 116, 200
passive (voice) 86, 126-7, 137
Pateman, T. 206-7
Peirce, C. 43, 203n.
phonology 63, 71

photography 226-63, 277
   expenditure on 248-9
Piaget, J. 231
Plato 84
Polanyi, K. 141-2
polysemic 44, 107, 215, 280
pragmatics 3, 194, 199
   of media discourse 266
   of photographic image 195
Pratt, M. 192
presupposition 124, 295-6
Pribram, K. 227
pronunciation 52-3; see also received
   pronunciation
propaganda 47
proposition
   analysis 112
   radical 44
Punch 151-2

Quirk, R. 53-4, 71, 72n.

RAI 12
readings 246, 257-8, 260, 267-9
   levels of 271-8
   preferred 74n., 113, 205, 214, 216,
      279-80
received pronunciation 60-4, 66-7; see also
   pronunciation
Red Brigades 12-49
   descriptions of 40-3
reification 288
Reith, J. 58-9, 61, 70
relevance, axiom of 197-8
rhetoric 78, 201, 239
Robbins, D. 105
Rosen, H. 108-9

Sacks, H. 282-3, 285-6
Safire, W. 82
Saussure, F. de 102, 172, 188, 193
Schank, R. 189, 191, 203
Schumann, H-G. 51
Searle, J. 196, 203n.
semantics 192, 194, 199
semiotics 3-4, 173, 188-9, 191, 196, 198,
   257-63
Sharrock, W. 4
shot 43-6, 269
Sloman, A. 203n.
sociolinguistics 3-4, 281

speech community 50, 84
Spender, D. 108
Sperber, D. 197, 202n.
Smith, B. 4
Smith, N. 188, 195, 197, 199
Smith, P. 64
Smith R. 167
Stich, A. 157
structuralism 188, 191, 196, 257, 270;
   see also Marxism
style 67-9, 138n., 157
stylistics 157, 208, 268
Sunday Times 40
symbol 43, 45-6
Syme, R. 78, 83
synecdoche 282, 288
syntactic analysis 192-4
Szarkowski, J. 237, 240, 242

text 267-9
   formal organization of 188
   media language as 269-71
   —image relationships 9, 46, 271, 281
Thatcher, M. 80-1, 95-8
Therborn, G. 142
Thompson, E. L. 183
Time 145, 150, 284-5
Times, The 40-1, 145-7, 150
topic transformation 76-81
Trew, A. 51, 54, 122, 138n.

viewer's maxim 285-6
visual experience 226-8
visuals 43-7
Voloshinov, V. N. 112, 154, 276-7
Vygotsky, L. 231

Washington Post 40
Weilburger Tageblatt 41
Weir, J. 219-21, 223n.
Welt, Die 40-1
Willemen, P. 269
Williams, R. 2, 145, 207, 245-6, 268
Williamson, J. 171, 188, 198, 223, 277
Wilson, D. 188, 195, 197, 199, 202n., 204n.
Winograd, G. 237-40, 242
Wisman, J. 142-3, 149
Wittgenstein, L. 44
Wollen, P. 270-1
word frequency 158-63

ZDF 15, 41, 49n.